110653055

RSPB
Nature
Reserves

With best wishes

Frank Hamilton

Christmas 1983

RSPB
Nature
Reserves

Published by the Royal Society for the Protection of
Birds,
The Lodge, Sandy, Bedfordshire SG19 2DL.

Photoset in Palatino by Bedford Typesetters Ltd,
Kempston, Bedford.
Illustrations originated by Saxon Photolitho Ltd,
Norwich.
Printed and bound by W S Cowell Ltd, Ipswich.

Illustrations

Line drawings are by John Busby and R A Hume.

p 19	*S C Porter (RSPB)*
p 20	*S Warner (RSPB)*
p 23	*David and Katie Urry*
p 35	*C J Smale (Aquila)*
pp 38-39	*John Reaney*
pp 42-43	*John Reaney*
p 47	*Michael W Richards (RSPB)*
p 51	*M C Wilkes (Aquila)*
p 55	*Michael W Richards (RSPB)*
p 58	*Frank V Blackburn*
p 62	*Roger Wilmshurst*
p 63	*Roger Wilmshurst*
p 66	*Bob Scott*
p 67	*Frank V Blackburn*
p 70	*R H Fisher*
p 71	*Maurice Walker (Nature Photographers Ltd)*
pp 74-75	*John Reaney*
p 78	*Frank V Blackburn*
p 79	*G E Hyde, Heather Angel, G E Hyde, L Beames (Ardea) and Stephen Dalton (NHPA)*
p 82	*T Andrewartha (Nature Photographers Ltd)*
pp 86-87	*John Reaney*
p 90	*Michael W Richards (RSPB)*
p 91	*John Robinson*
pp 94-95	*John Reaney*
p 105	*Martin Robinson*
pp 108 & 109	*John Busby*

**Publication of this book has been made
possible by a generous grant from Mobil
North Sea Limited.**

Contents

The authors

All the authors are members of the staff of the
Royal Society for the Protection of Birds.

Colin J Bibby, Senior Research Biologist
Reedswamps

John Crudass, Chief Reserves Officer
How the RSPB acquires reserves and *Managing reserves the RSPB way*

John Day, Deputy Chief Reserves Officer
Lowland flood meadows, Lowland heath and *Upland oakwoods*

Michael J Everett, Species Protection Officer
Seabird cliffs

John Hunt, Reserves Manager (Scotland)
Highland birchwood

Eric Meek, Orkney Officer
Orkney moorland

Tony Prater, Regional Officer for South-east England
Estuaries

Bob Scott, Reserves Manager (England)
Lagoons and open water

Gareth J Thomas, Senior Research Biologist
Terns on RSPB reserves

Stewart Taylor, Warden, Loch Garten
Native pinewoods

Michael J Walter, Warden, Church Wood, Blean
Lowland deciduous woods

Graham Williams, Reserves Manager (Wales)
Moorland in Scotland and Wales

Editor: Nicholas Hammond
Designer: Patsy Hinchliffe
Line drawings by John Busby and R A Hume

The Gazetteer of RSPB reserves was compiled by Peter E Newbery, Assistant Reserves
Manager, from entries written by wardens and other staff listed below.

Dave Allen	Peter Gotham	David Mower	Jeremy Sorensen
Rob Berry	Bob Gomes	Russell Nisbet	Dick Squires
Mike Blackburn	Andrew Grieve	Alan Parker	Les Street
Graham Burton	Ray Hawley	John Partridge	Stewart Taylor
Roger Butterfield	John Humphrey	Robert Petley-Jones	Reg Thorpe
Cliff Carson	John Hunt	Bryan Pickess	Bobby Tulloch
Trevor Charlton	Douglas Ireland	Tony Pickup	Richard Wakely
John Chester	Russell Leavett	Bernard Planterose	Michael Walter
Stephen Denny	Joe Magee	Ivan Proctor	Maurice Waterhouse
Jim Dunbar	Peter Makepeace	Kevin Roberts	Geoff Welch
Nick Dymond	Eric Meek	Martin Robinson	Colin Wells
Alan Ferguson	Peter Moore	Norman Sills	John Wilson

The total area of nature reserves owned or managed by the Royal Society for the Protection of Birds is now well over 100,000 acres. The bulk of this has been acquired over the last ten years and has only been possible because of the generosity of the Society's members and of grant-making bodies including the Countryside Commission, National Heritage Memorial Fund, Nature Conservancy Council and World Wildlife Fund. That, once acquired, the reserves are almost always positively improved from the point of view of birds and other wildlife is thanks to the skill and dedication of a variety of people — wardens, reserve managers, research biologists and volunteers.

The reputation of the Society for imaginative and effective reserve management is worldwide and staff have been invited to many countries to advise on the creation and organisation of nature reserves. There has also been a stream of overseas visitors to our reserves to look for ideas that might be applied in their own countries.

In the early days of acquiring reserves the Society was often seeking to protect specific rare birds. Today, however, the emphasis is the conservation of habitats and, therefore, this book deals in some detail with the threats to specific habitats and the role of reserves in combating these. These chapters are followed by a Gazetteer aimed at giving an impression of each reserve to the intending visitor.

We hope that this book will enhance the readers' understanding of reserves and their enjoyment of visiting them and we are most grateful for the generous grant from Mobil North Sea Limited that makes the publication possible.

How the RSPB acquires reserves

by John Crudass

"For to my mind bird protection nowadays is far more a matter of preserving bird haunts than of making laws to protect birds which may easily, like the Kentish plover, be exterminated by progress in the form of bungalows, though officially protected by law."

Thus wrote E C Arnold in the 1930s, and despite an enormous increase in support for conservation of our fauna and flora and advances in planning and protection laws, the threat holds good today and is greater than ever and shows scant sign of abatement. While Arnold's words are unlikely to have been the direct cause of the Society embracing the policy of having reserves, the philosophy has for many years been a main theme of its policy. Indeed, to many people, the ownership and management of reserves is the main outward manifestation of the Society's work in the conservation field. Of course, great efforts are made by other means to prevent the desecration of the countryside and the destruction of important and disappearing habitats which in turn seriously affect the wildlife, but the voracious demand for land for development or its use for purposes unsympathetic and even antipathetic to wildlife coupled with economic factors so often results in defeat or, at best, temporary postponement of the threat.

Whilst the Society subscribed to the view that reserves should be part of its overall policy for the protection of birds as long ago as the 1930s, shortage of resources meant that there was little immediate positive progress. A small membership and very limited financial support from other sources allowed little possibility for land purchase and less for wardening and management, both prerequisites for proper control and development of reserves. Indeed, there is some evidence that some of today's habitat management and manipulation was not necessarily considered to be a good thing, a view which prevails in certain circles to this day.

In its earlier days ownership of land was a practice in which the Society indulged in no more than a peripheral way and then usually because of a gift or bequest of some kind. The emphasis was on the protection of particular species which was effected not by creating reserves, but by the appointment of 'Watchers' who were local worthies interested and experienced in wildlife who were paid a small sum, usually for work during the breeding season. The first Watcher was appointed in 1901 and his responsibility was to protect pintail on Loch Leven. By 1920 no less than twenty-nine Watchers were employed during the breeding season covering thirteen acres. Collectively for the year's work they were paid £405. By 1937 the number of Watchers, now voluntary as well as paid, had risen to 68. At a time when the threats to land were light the employment of Watchers was a reasonably efficient method of protecting species if not habitats.

However, a few reserves had been acquired during this time. Cheyne Court on Romney Marsh was purchased in 1930 but disposed of a few years later because its ornithological interest was considered to have been badly affected by the drainage of surrounding land. In 1930 East Wood at Stalybridge came as a bequest and, about the same time, 250 acres at Dungeness were given. These two reserves still remain in the Society's ownership but in the meanwhile Dungeness has increased by gift and purchase to 1,193 acres and is still growing.

Black-tailed godwit

What policy would have been followed had not the war intervened is a matter of conjecture. The necessity for maximising food production during and after the war resulted in reclamation to agriculture of land previously considered unsuitable and uneconomic.

More recently, largely because of grant aid, an initially relatively innocuous policy has widened and accelerated to include land which would once have been considered entirely beyond redemption. The most serious effect has probably been on wetlands, but amongst other habitats ancient woodlands, moorland and saltings have also been savaged. As well as the availability of grant aid, advances in technology and the development and use of new machinery have been important contributory factors. One outcome has been that land unsuitable, or at best only marginally so, for any purpose and producing little if any income can now be improved and thus its capital value enormously increased. This type of land, which includes reedbeds that can be drained and brought back to arable use, water meadows where the periodic flooding can be avoided by speeding the flow of rivers and the land improved for grazing or arable use, heather moorland which can be turned into grazing land or planted with conifers and heaths which can also be used for economic forestry, invariably constitutes the richest sites for wildlife of the sort conservation bodies wish to acquire as reserves. That these improvements can be carried out so easily means that the value of a reedbed or other type of habitat is no longer what it is, but what it might become. No more than in any other walk of life will a landowner dispose of a capital asset at a figure less than its maximum and conservation bodies have had to accept this hard fact of life and rid themselves of the foolish idea that choice sites could be preserved on the cheap. There is the additional fact that these days the classical method of assessing land values by associating it with annual income no longer applies. Much agricultural land changes hands at values so high and the return on capital so low as to be laughable to those in the investment business.

Despite this high, and increasing, demand for land with its affect on value, the Society must meet the problem squarely and acquire more reserves as quickly as it can. To do so obviously means that more and more, and a greater proportion, of its resources must go to purchase and management. In 1970 the sum of £125,000 was allocated for the purchase of reserves and it proved to be sufficient. Twelve years later over one and a half million pounds was spent for this purpose in one financial year. Increasing land prices are clearly shown by the costs of land in the Ouse Washes: in the late 1960s we could buy one acre for a little more than £25, whereas today the cost has risen to £1,000 and more. Although there has recently been a slowing of the increase and even, in one or two cases, a drop in value, history suggests that the long-term trend in land values will be upward.

That large sums of money are now involved and will become larger as the years go by dictates more than ever the absolute necessity for ensuring value for money and acquiring the best possible sites.

There are a number of reasons for having reserves, the most obvious being the preservation of desirable habitats and thus protection, and with management, the improvement of the wildlife they normally support. As has been said, in recent years habitat has been disappearing at a rapidly increasing rate and unless some examples of the most threatened types are acquired and preserved they might well disappear. The reclamation of moorland in Orkney, where the Society owns nearly 10,000 acres, is a case in point. Such is the pace of conversion from heather moorland of low economic value, useful only for limited sheep grazing, shooting and peat digging, to better quality grassland that it has been said that by the end of the century the only area remaining as it is now will be that owned by the Society. Open waters, valuable on their fringes for breeding waterbirds and for wintering wildfowl are in demand for such recreational purposes as yachting, water ski-ing, fishing, etc. Whilst if the water is extensive enough integrated use may be possible, in many cases it is not.

Osprey

Sadly, in the past conservationists, particularly birdwatchers, have felt entitled to enjoy the privilege of exercising their hobby over such areas at little or no expense while many other users of the countryside, such as fishermen and yachtsmen, have long been prepared to pay considerable sums for the pleasures of their activities. Woodland birds, which comprise the majority of our breeding species, are threatened because ancient woodlands are continually being clear-felled for such purposes as the realisation of valuable timber assets, conversion to agriculture or reafforestation usually with quick-growing, exotic conifers that will never have the same value for wildlife as the hardwoods they replace. Incidentally, it is interesting that so many people should be surprised that when buying woodlands for reserves, in addition to the land itself the trees themselves have to be purchased.

These are a few examples of the threats facing valuable wildlife habitats. That some others may not at present appear to be under threat is no reason for complacency many of those habitats which have suffered severely in recent years were not thirty or forty years ago even thought to be remotely threatened. The necessity for purchasing cliffs such as Bempton and Westray is sometimes questioned since there appears to be no threat but that is not so. Quarrying is a distinct possibility and there is one stretch of cliffs with a good population of breeding seabirds which the Society would like to buy, but which the owner refuses to sell, because he hopes and indeed expects one day to be allowed to mine the chalk.

Besides the communities of birds in the various habitats, some individual species have benefited from reserve protection. Little terns, which have the unfortunate predilection for nesting on beaches attractive to holiday-makers, have benefited enormously as have roseate terns of which most of those breeding in this country are now on reserves. In the case of the little tern, Britain's rarest breeding seabird, the erection of simple fences on the beaches at Minsmere and Titchwell, with explanatory notices asking for the co-operation of the public, has in very few years resulted in increases in the breeding population from single figures to over sixty pairs. The marsh harrier and bittern, both birds of the reedbed, a few years ago were down to very low numbers, but because most of the remnant population were on reserves, they have taken advantage of protection and management and are now spreading out to recolonise old and find new nesting places. The increase is slow and it cannot be claimed that either species is yet safe, but the protection which reserves afford has clearly been of value to both.

Many of the Society's best known reserves were set up specifically for the benefit of species which had become rare and endangered, such as Balranald for the red-necked phalarope, or had returned to breed after an absence from this country of very many years, such as Minsmere and Havergate for the avocet. As it happens in all these cases the habitats were rich in bird life and thus fortuitously the acquisition criteria of endangered habitats and bird communities, adopted in the 1970s, are more than adequately fulfilled.

Successful management can influence adjoining farmers and landowners and finally reserves can be used for research and, where visiting is possible, for encouraging and quickening the interest of the public in wildlife and thus in conservation. Finally, as has already been said, they are the outward manifestation of the Society's work and a measure of success which plays a big part in attracting members.

Thus, if it is accepted that reserves are a good thing, because they are expensive both to buy and manage, a critical process of selection is essential in order to be sure of getting the best examples of the various habitats. Because, in the early seventies, it was felt that the method of deciding which sites should be acquired did not adequately meet the threats then being posed and thus ensure the preservation of rich sites, the alternative of the habitat/bird community was developed. The reasoning was that if examples of the existing habitats were preserved, because each supports a characteristic community of birds, all species from the common to the rare would enjoy some measure of protection. The best description of a

Golden eagle

habitat is "an area in which wildlife naturally lives," but it is normally used to indicate the kind of locality, such as, for instance flood meadows, mixed lowland broad-leaf, or heathland. Since each habitat supports a different community of organisms which interact with each other, in preparing a programme of reserves acquisition the first thing to be done is to identify the various habitats and the bird communities which exist in them. That the emphasis has changed from the all-embracing term 'wildlife' to the more specific 'birds' arises because within the terms of the Charter, under which the Society operates, the primary responsibility is for birds and their place in nature.

Consideration and assessment has identified twenty defined ornithological habitat types throughout the United Kingdom each with a bird community distinctive in having a combination of species differing from that supported by any of the others. These are set out with short descriptions at the end of this chapter. Only areas sufficient in themselves to form viable reserve units are included in our plan. Others, whilst having a definable community but not being of sufficient interest or importance to warrant separate acquisition, are considered for inclusion under the main habitat type. The most obvious habitat of this sort is scrub, which can occur in many habitat types. A bird community is defined as an association of species characteristically to be found in a habitat type either as a breeding or wintering species or on passage'. A species can be either 'typical' in that it occurs continuously throughout the range of the habitat and is present in all the suitable geographical regions or 'local' which, whilst characteristic of the habitat, is more restricted in its range. To illustrate the point, the sedge warbler is 'typical' of the fringes of wetland habitats throughout the country but the marsh harrier is more restricted in its range and listed as 'local'. In a few instances a species is listed as 'typical', even though it is not present in all suitable areas (*eg* reed warblers in southern Scottish reed swamps) because it is so characteristic a species of the habitat elsewhere that it cannot be described as 'local'.

As well as the common, rare and occasional breeding species, four other categories are taken into account because their importance imposes a particular responsibility. These are: species whose breeding or wintering population forms 10% or more of the north-west European, European, or World populations (*eg* Leach's and storm petrels, pintail, common scoter); scarce breeding species with up to 1,000 pairs in the United Kingdom (*eg* golden eagle, little tern, gadwall, garganey, black-tailed godwit, little ringed plover); some species particularly under threat (*eg* bittern, Slavonian grebe, nightjar, stone curlew, red-backed shrike, etc) and species such as the hen harrier which, whilst coming within one or other of the above categories, winters outside its normal breeding range in the United Kingdom. There is also the matter of potential breeding species. This point is a fascinating subject which involves forecasting which species might next jump across from the Continent and start regular breeding in this country. Savi's and Cetti's warblers have already made the journey, but what might be next? There is quite a selection of possibilities including purple heron, spoonbill, little bittern, whooper swan, black tern, golden oriole, bee-eater, black woodpecker, great reed warbler and others. Some have bred occasionally but all are possible on a regular basis.

Tenure is a matter of great importance since the length of time land is likely to be held has a bearing both on the amount of work which can be done and the money which can properly be spent. If land is leased for a relatively few years, obviously it is not in the interests of the Society to spend considerable sums of money on management if reversion to the owner is not far distant. Habitat management and manipulation, wardening, the provision of visitor facilities and wardens' houses all add up to a high level of expenditure that can only be justified if a reserve is to be held for a long term. For this reason the Society prefers freehold purchase and considers any other form of tenure far less acceptable.

If purchase is not possible leasing will be considered provided that the term, other than in

Nightjar

very exceptional circumstances, is for not less than 21 years and the conditions include management rights. If a landowner is only prepared to grant a lease, the chances are that he has some good reason for holding on to his property and quite often this can be disadvantageous to the proper running of the reserve. Conditions will be imposed in the lease to protect the owner's interests and in many cases give him the opportunity to exercise the rights retained. Examples are shooting, mineral extraction, which would almost certainly ruin the site, and any 'making good' would merely replace the topsoil but not the habitat. On reserves leased or held on management agreements it is imperative that the Society should be able to carry out proper management without interference from the landlord. Of course the Society's management can work to the disadvantage of the landowner; in the case of one important reserve the owner once complained that the Society had developed his property to such a level of ornithological importance that he could do nothing more than renew the lease at the end of the term when his own preference would have been to take the land back.

In selecting land for reserves four main criteria are taken into account.

(a) The site must include one, or more, of the listed habitat types.

(b) The habitat or habitats must have a typical community of birds or, if not, the potential for the development of such a community or communities.

(c) There must be the capability for habitat control and management permitting the maintenance and improvement of the associated bird community.

(d) It should have been declared a Site of Special Scientific Interest by the Nature Conservancy Council or, if not, the site must satisfy the criteria under which the NCC declare such sites.

The aim is eventually to have a representative selection of the various habitat types throughout the country. Because of the regional variation in bird communities, this will mean having examples of the same type of habitat in different parts of the United Kingdom. For instance, the ownership of a reedbed in Scotland lacking reed warblers, marsh harriers and only rarely having bearded tits when all these species occur in similar habitat in East Anglia would not satisfy this aim. In many cases a reserve has more than one habitat. Minsmere for instance has five: sand dunes, brackish water/mud, reed swamp, heath and mixed lowland broad-leaf wood. Such a variety makes for a rich and varied wildlife and it is not surprising that Minsmere has such a wealth of breeding, visiting and wintering birds.

In some cases, although the habitat exists there is no typical bird community, but the potential is there. At Elmley, for instance, rough grazing which had been drained but not enormously improved, had very few birds and was heavily grazed and shot. In the past it had been a rich and attractive area for birds and had the potential to be managed back to that state. The Oxford University Chest, the owners, leased the land and allowed us to block the old, but still existing, creek systems, thus causing flooding over considerable areas. The varying but generally shallow depths were most attractive to breeding and wintering wildfowl and waders and passage birds. This is a necessarily brief outline of a very long story. The recreation of habitats is possibly the most exciting field of management and one which conservation bodies may have to explore more in the future if they wish to continue expanding reserve holdings. This practice is not restricted only to wetlands: planting broad-leaf woodland is another possibility albeit a very long-term process. Habitat on reserves can also be diversified and perhaps the most striking example has been at Dungeness where a great area of shingle supported few breeding and passage, and virtually no wintering birds. After discussions with the Nature Conservancy Council and the Kent Trust for Nature Conservation to ensure that no important natural history interest was being destroyed, an arrangement was made with a gravel company for the excavation of about 70 acres of shingle. Not only were considerable royalties received but the pit left

Grey heron

behind, with its water, islands and sand spits, now has a thriving colony of common and Sandwich terns as well as breeding and wintering wildfowl and passage birds in considerable numbers.

The absence of scientific grading does not, in itself, rule out a site as a reserve. The Nature Conservancy Council was unable to schedule all the desirable sites and in the particular case of woodland only a minority were designated. Indeed, acquisition by the Society has in more than one case actually resulted in designation and management of sites will almost certainly make others suitable for SSSI status in the future. Even if it does not, provided the wildlife interest is, or can be, of a sufficiently high standard, a site can qualify for purchase or lease.

It may come as a surprise that size is not one of the criteria. In fact there is no set size for a reserve but, where a site has a year-round interest, it should be large enough to justify a full-time warden. The practice is to judge each case on its merits and decide accordingly. For instance a wood of, say, 100 acres in one part of the country might justify full-time management, whilst a similar sized site elsewhere may not.

Amongst other things the level of wildlife interest, the amount of management and the number of visitors are taken into account and might swing the balance for or against full-time staffing. It is not Society policy to have small sites which do not justify a warden for at least part of the year. Reserves that do not justify wardening are very often subject to vandalism, difficult to manage and eventually turn out to be no good advertisement for the owning body.

Managing reserves the RSPB way

by John Crudass

Having acquired a reserve, the next step is to decide how to look after it. A reserve can no more be left to its own devices than can a farm, or a garden, or in fact any other property: unless it is managed, it will deteriorate and lose its value. There is a school of thought which considers that to manage a habitat is to interfere with nature and the natural course of events and is wrong. Nature, it is argued, should take its course with the inevitable result that it will gradually change into something totally different whether or not it is good, or bad, for the flora and fauna. This is not the RSPB view. Habitats are purchased because of their intrinsic interest and the practice is to manage them to retain, and improve, this particular interest.

There are three aspects to management. First, and most simply, at least in terms of necessity and justification, is the management usually required in the ownership of land — fencing, ditching, repairs to buildings, tracks and footpaths — what would normally be referred to as 'estate management'. On ninety reserves, some with farm buildings, many with wardens' houses, reception centres, hides, fencing, gates and stiles, this is a formidable task. Much of the work is done by wardens; only for major tasks are outside contractors called in.

The second aspect in management lies in the land use. A number of the Society's reserves are farmed or have some farming practices on them. The suggestion that farming and reserve management are inimical is far wide of the mark as can be seen from what goes on at many reserves. That these two types of land use can go hand in hand results from reasonable compromise on the use of pesticides and herbicides, grazing levels of cattle and sheep and the retention of hedges to mention just three aspects of farming. It cannot be denied, however, that agricultural tenancies under which, in law, the farmer holds the land under an agricultural tenancy with rights of succession, and is permitted to carry out, for instance, drainage, without the owner being able to do much about it, is not conducive to good conservation management. In practice the Society prefers that any agricultural use of land on its reserves remains under its own direct control. This is easy enough when grazing is involved but not other agricultural uses.

Fishing can be arranged to avoid affecting wildlife adversely as can a number of other activities including shooting. Shooting is a legal activity in the ethics of which, the Society, within the terms of its Charter, cannot involve itself. The same applies to fishing and hunting. However, so far as the reserves are concerned, whether or not shooting is allowed is entirely a matter for the Society, no more or less than is the case with any other landowner. In practice, the Society prefers not to have its reserves shot, but in a few exceptional cases it is not possible to obtain the shooting rights. For instance when, shortly after the war, the Society asked the owner of Minsmere for a lease under which the area would become a reserve he was enthusiastic, but a condition was that he and his friends would continue shooting. This presented a dilemma — could the Society hold Minsmere as a reserve and at the same time allow shooting to go on? Was this not a negation of the word 'protection'? On the one hand wildfowl would be shot on a limited number of days each year, on the other the breeding birds would benefit from the management of the various habitats. More important, if Minsmere did not become a reserve there would have been a

Nightingale

possibility of it being drained and brought back to arable use. Before the last war Minsmere was arable land: its demise as such and subsequent development as a major wetland reserve came about because the sea sluices were opened and the area deliberately flooded as a barrier against possible invasion. To reverse the process would not have been difficult. After much thought and discussion it was decided that the balance of advantage very much lay with taking a lease and accepting shooting on a limited basis.

Who can now deny that the wealth of birds using Minsmere have benefited even though some unfortunate wildfowl were shot? It has become one of the country's, indeed the world's, most famous reserves. Our patience was finally rewarded and shooting ceased when, in 1975, we were able to buy the freehold and with it the shooting rights. The same circumstances apply to Arne, Loch Garten and a number of other sites and continues to apply. The decision to allow shooting must clearly show that the balance of advantages lies with conservation and some clear advantage can be proved. This has been shown in the case of Minsmere, and other reserves, but it can also be part of a *quid pro quo*, as at Gayton Sands, where wildfowlers are leased the shooting rights over a small area of the reserve in exchange for freeing a more important area elsewhere on the Dee and so avoiding disturbance to important wader roosts. There is no doubt that the birds have benefited from such arrangements, although it remains the aim to have all reserves as sanctuary areas free of shooting. As in many aspects of conservation, compromise is a necessary ingredient.

To return to management, the third aspect is the control of the habitat. Reserves are acquired because they have, or can be made to have, communities of birds which would normally be expected in the particular habitats. However, a habitat, left to its own devices, will develop into something quite different from the original and almost certainly less interesting. For instance, in a reedbed litter from dead vegetation gradually builds up, causing drying out, in the process willows and alder come in forming a 'carr' habitat, followed eventually by birch and other species of tree. The result is an entirely different habitat with a completely different community for birds. This is a necessarily brief exposition of what happens over a long period in one particular habitat, but any unmanaged habitat will change similarly. The purist will say there should be no interference with natural succession and that management results in artificiality. That may be so, but the RSPB takes the view that maintaining the original variety of habitats and thus the species is an entirely proper course to follow and the methods used to carry out this management are discussed in other parts of the book. Suffice to say, at this stage, that the Society has pioneered a number of types of habitat management and its advice is sought and followed by bodies around the world.

Accepting that management is necessary and desirable, how is its type and extent decided, planned and controlled? Briefly, when a site is being considered for acquisition, an assessment of its existing value for wildlife is made, using a variety of sources such as the Nature Conservancy Council's scientific designation, the Nature Conservation Review, the British Trust for Ornithology's Site Register, information from the Society's own regional staff, local bird clubs, County Naturalists' Trusts and individual RSPB members. This is not usually in fine detail but suffices to decide if the site is worth acquiring. At the same time it is often possible to assess what broad management would benefit the site. For instance, bringing back water to a dried-out wetland site, the improvement of a reedbed by raising the water level, creating more edge by opening up channels and pools, clearing glades and rides in woodland to provide more edge, reinstatement of a coppicing regime and the better control of grazing on flood meadows are obvious and from experience can easily be assessed. Thus it is not difficult to see what is there and what major improvements might be made. It is not so easy to be certain that carrying out such improvements will not damage some other important wildlife interest. Therefore, when a warden is appointed, one of his

Bittern

first tasks is to ensure that he becomes aware of the total natural history interest of the site before any major management is carried out. At the same time he is setting about preparing the Reserve Management Plan, a document that details not only the aims of management for the various compartments, the method of carrying out the work and the time scale, but also the full story of the site including details of location and access, tenure and rights, official status, public and private rights and expansion potential, the history of the site and the scientific interest including climate, geology (soils, topography and drainage), habitats, flora and fauna.

Next come the objects of management which in a typical case would include the prime objective, because of the Society's Charter, of maintaining and improving the ornithological interest but would also require non-ornithological interests to be properly managed and preserved and, usually, the encouragement of visiting to promote a better understanding of conservation. Finally comes the management programme which includes conservation work, research and survey, estate management and provision of visitor facilities.

Under conservation management, the practice is to divide the site into a number of separate compartments each of which is easily recognisable by some sort of boundary, be it a water course, interface between two habitats, track or field boundary. Each compartment is then examined, fully described and a management programme decided. With this as his 'bible' a warden is able to carry on his management without continual reference back to headquarters. In his Annual Report he details the work he has done in the past year and his proposals for work during the ensuing year, together with estimated costs. In its turn, headquarters staff can then approve his work programme, collate financial requirements from all the reserves and allocate resources to the extent they are available.

In the first instance the Management Plan is drawn up by the warden himself and he can call in assistance from any expert. His proposals are then discussed in detail with headquarters staff, who advise and amend as necessary and when completed become the document to which he works. It is not inflexible, being examined from time to time and in the light of experience management proposals can be changed. The great advantage of having a Reserve Management Plan is that if wardens change, there is complete continuity in the management of the reserve.

It is obvious from what has been said that reserves need to be staffed, but how is the level of staffing decided and how are wardens selected and appointed?

The first and most obvious factor to be taken into account is the level of the bird interest. A reserve with breeding, passage and wintering birds calls for year-round wardening. The size of the reserve, amount of management and the level of visiting are key factors in deciding whether one or more wardens are necessary. Minsmere has a wide range of breeding birds in its reedbeds, scrape, woodland and heath, is famous for its passage birds in spring and autumn and has a good wintering population of wildfowl. Because its varied habitats call for almost continual management and its birds attract many thousands of visitors, a number of staff, both permanent and temporary, are needed. Leighton Moss is similarly manned, but another reserve of smaller size with less varied habitats and fewer visitors, might be managed by one warden helped by volunteers. Other reserves have only a seasonal interest: the cliffs at Bempton, St Bees, Westray and Rathlin Island have to be wardened only when their colonies of seabirds are present during the breeding season. Similarly, but in reverse, the interest in tidal mudflats is in their large flocks of passage and wintering waders and wintering wildfowl and have little of interest during the remainder of the year. These differing requirements can be filled, respectively, by permanent and temporary staff but because the former, often with wives and families, look for a much more settled existence the seasonal reserves are more often than not in the hands of temporaries or trainee permanent assistants.

Black tern

At the time of writing the Society employs 45 full-time wardens and to join their ranks requires a deal of patience and dedication. Between 30 and 40 temporary staff are employed on short-term contracts each summer and a much smaller number during the winter. It is from these that the permanent staff is recruited. Temporary wardens come from different walks of life — students with time to kill before going to, or after coming down from, university; out of work birdwatchers looking for any form of employment to fill in time and bring in a little money. While some can be described as well-educated, others might not be but they are no less intelligent and well qualified for the work. Some come from the country, others from inner cities. Generally they fall into two groups, those who are merely filling in time before going on to do something else and those whose aim in life it is to become a warden of a nature reserve.

Dedication is vital, because the aspirant, temporary warden must face low pay, remote and lonely reserves, often less than comfortable living conditions, long hours of work and the knowledge that vacancies for permanent posts are few and far between. Quite often he will have slogged away for four or five years before having the chance of a permanent post, but in that time will have moved from place to place gaining experience of different management and visitor problems, and really learning the trade the hard way. Typically, his first contract might be on a wardened reserve with the benefit of advice and help from an experienced man. Next might be a stint at a reserve, wardened only during the breeding season and with no one on whom he could fall back on for help except in emergency. A season might follow on a remote site, possibly an island, completely cut off from immediate help and support and then another on a reserve such as Loch Garten with voluntary staff to organise and many thousands of visitors to deal with. It all goes towards giving the experience and developing the self-confidence needed by a warden who must be a person capable of managing a reserve without, other than in the last resort, having to call in help from headquarters.

And at the end of the day what does he look forward to? To a large extent a warden becomes the monarch of all he surveys, enjoying a life in the country, with a working day, week, month and year he has largely planned himself. He has the opportunity to use his initiative and to exercise responsibility with, at the end of it all, the satisfaction of seeing his reserve develop and improve in the image that he, with the help of headquarters staff, has planned. It is not surprising the waiting lists are always much longer than the posts available.

Whilst permanent and contract staff are at a level sufficient to carry out essential work, without the help given by volunteers they would be hard pressed to satisfy all the demands they have to meet. This is particularly the case during the breeding and visiting seasons when the pressures are very heavy. All-night watches on those birds whose eggs are in particular demand, the issue of permits and the control of visitors, not to mention their cars, help to the less knowledgeable and straightforward physical work are some of the tasks which volunteers, over the years, have carried out. Volunteers fall into two groups — those who live on reserves for a week or two (but occasionally longer), provided with accommodation usually in a hut or caravan but otherwise paying their own way and those who come in occasionally, either as individuals or members of local RSPB members' groups or other conservation groups. Whatever the circumstances the debt they are owed is considerable.

Reserves attract visitors and access is encouraged provided there is no danger of harming the habitat and its wildlife. In deciding on the pattern of visiting there are three factors to take into account. Where can the visitors go, how many can be admitted and how often can the reserve be open?

In practice it is usually easy to decide on a route, the key factors being the whereabouts of

Dartford warbler

the birds and how to get the visitors to them. In the past visitors were taken into the reserve, as at Minsmere, but recently the practice has been to allow them to look in from the outside by siting facilities on the boundary. This has been done at Titchwell and has the advantages of avoiding habitat damage and disturbance, reducing the time staff spend in controlling visitors and avoiding the necessity of denying access at any time. The occasional criticism that visiting harms the birds is only rarely justified. At Minsmere, the most visited reserve, of the whole area of 1,600 acres only a very small part on either side of the footpath is affected — the proof of this lies in the continued high number of birds which can be seen.

Many of those who visit reserves have no great knowledge of birds and are looking for entertainment and help. This is done by providing close-up views of the birds with staff and displays to aid in identification. The aim and expectation is to awaken or, where it already exists, strengthen an interest in the countryside and its wildlife which will manifest itself in supporting conservation work.

Because demand is heaviest during school and summer bank holidays, it is between Easter and mid-September that visiting is allowed in those reserves where the facilities are within the site. During the remainder of the year there is surprisingly little demand, even though some reserves have a wealth of wintering birds. It is during the autumn and winter that heavy management work is normally done but during the visiting season reserves and wardening staff both need to be free of visitors for part of the time to rest and carry out essential work. There are some reserves to which visiting cannot, for the sake of the birds, be allowed. A case in point is Coquet off the Northumbrian Coast which has a very large breeding population of common, arctic, Sandwich and roseate terns as well as eider ducks on a very small, flat area where even a single visitor would cause the birds to leave their nests and let in the waiting, predatory gulls. To allow visiting on such a sanctuary would be a clear dereliction of duty.

We have discussed the reasons and necessity for reserves, how they are obtained and managed, and the use to which they are put, but what of the future?

Recently there has been more emphasis on enlarging reserves by either buying contiguous or nearby land and entering into lease or agreement with owners who are not willing to sell. The advantage in this is that extra land is protected without increasing the staff and thus the annual expenditure which, more than capital, is a burden on resources because it is a commitment for so long as the Society exists. The acquisition of land is a firm commitment which will go on in the future — crystal ball gazing does not suggest a lessening of the importance of reserves. However, the emphasis may change. As more and more of the best sites are gathered in or protected by other means such as are possible under the new Wildlife and Countryside Act, there is the exciting probability of buying poor quality land and re-creating habitats which will continue, in their natural existence, to disappear.

Opposite: Avocet, one of the first species to benefit from the development of reserve management techniques.

Ditch clearance

Seabird cliffs

by Michael J Everett

Twenty years ago the RSPB negotiated a management agreement over Handa in Sutherland, an island with spectacular cliffs of Old Torridonian Sandstone and huge numbers of breeding seabirds. It seems surprising to us now that this was only the second RSPB major sea-cliff reserve, the other being the renowned gannet island of Grassholm off the Pembrokeshire coast. What seems even more remarkable now is that in the early 1960s nobody seriously believed that the acquisition of more major seabird reserves was a priority issue. After all, it was argued, other habitats were more immediately threatened and, in any case, seabird colonies were often remote and, it seemed, perfectly safe. A few were reserves and others enjoyed some sort of semi-protected status. Even in the mid-1960s I remember our Orkney representative, the late Eddie Balfour, being asked about seabird reserve acquisitions in Orkney and replying that he thought such things were of low priority — a view shared by many in those days, and one which was not at all far-fetched in the climate of the times. How very differently we see things now. . . .

During the last fifteen years or so the study of seabirds has intensified to such an extent that they are now possibly the 'top group' among birds, enjoying a following that may be greater than that enjoyed by waders, wildfowl and even birds of prey. Our knowledge of their numbers, distribution, biology, ecology and conservation is growing all the time. Two significant events since the 1960s have been the formation of the very active Seabird Group, of which the RSPB is a joint-sponsor, and *Operation Seafarer*, in which our seabirds were mapped and counted for the very first time. *Seafarer* may have had its shortcomings, as shown by more sophisticated recent studies on certain species and areas, but its pioneering work crystallised in our minds what had previously been little more than a vague notion — that our huge seabird colonies are among our richest assets in natural history terms and are of prime international importance. This realisation alone was in itself ample justification for the acceleration of seabird reserve acquisition which was so much a feature of the 1970s.

Looking at the position now we can see that the Society has a superb selection of important sites established as reserves, either by direct ownership or a leasing arrangement. They represent a major contribution to the network of reserves established by the voluntary conservation movement (which in a seabird context includes both the National Trust and the National Trust for Scotland) and, in the form of National Nature Reserves, by the Nature Conservancy Council. If we add sites in Ireland, we can fairly conclude that the British and Irish have managed to provide a substantial degree of protection for the breeding seabirds in our sector of the North Atlantic.

Local problems can usually be identified and solved fairly quickly on a wardened reserve. Very often these arise from some sort of human disturbance or a simple conflict of human interests: a sensible compromise may then be the solution, a good example being the increasing co-operation we have from rock climbers in avoiding bird cliffs during the breeding season. Direct exploitation of seabirds for food is a thing of the past: gone are the days when the famous 'climmers' collected eggs in baskets from Bempton Cliffs, or when an intrepid local swarmed hand over hand along a rope above an awesome drop to the sea to reach the summit of the Great Stack on Handa. Nevertheless, there have been occasional

Opposite: Seabirds at Bempton Cliffs, the subject of the first British bird protection legislation and now an RSPB reserve.

raids by egg-collectors, or attempts by outlaw falconers to rob peregrine eyries, even on RSPB reserves. While we can never guarantee complete protection from these miscreants, a wardened reserve gives us a better than even chance of foiling their efforts.

Reserve status brings obvious advantages in terms of protecting individual sites, but there are also considerable benefits in owning or managing a whole chain of reserves. Not the least of these is an ability to speak from a position of strength whenever threats to single colonies, or whole areas containing colonies, come to our notice. The internationally recognised importance of Britain's seabird population is a crucial factor in any argument. The same applies when we are considering the increasingly alarming range of threats to the whole marine environment, all of which have their basis in various forms of pollution. For example, the boom in oil exploitation in the North Sea was something nobody foresaw in the 1960s, even though oil pollution itself was no new thing. The infamous *Torrey Canyon* disaster had taught us a great deal about how a major spillage might affect wintering concentrations and breeding populations of seabirds. The new oilfields and their shore bases and terminals, plus the knowledge that vast undertakings are operating perilously close to the limits of technological know-how and experience, have quite suddenly presented our densely-populated and no longer 'remote' seabird colonies with the prospect of oil pollution on a scale that scarcely bears contemplating. There have been several frightening incidents already. As reserve managers we can have an important voice on behalf of seabirds and can help our conservation planners to play their part in helping to formulate a sensible long-term strategy which, ideally, would exploit the oil resource with the minimum of damage to the environment.

Seabird reserves have another important function. Great seacliffs thronged with thousands of birds, where the whole experience is as much one of sound (and smell!) as of vision, are an obvious asset to the RSPB in the field of education, in its broadest sense. Committed birdwatchers will enjoy them, of course, but there can be few things more likely to impress the uncommitted. If we can use some of our more accessible reserves to show seabirds to people and to tell them about conservation we can foster sympathy and understanding for our cause — and in the end this is what conservation is all about. With this very much in mind we have already established safe viewing facilities on the huge chalk cliffs at Bempton and have opened the imaginative interpretative centre at Ellin's Tower on South Stack Cliffs in Anglesey.

So much, then, for the rationale, but what of the reserves themselves? The Gazetteer beginning on page 109 gives details of the individual sites, but what exactly *are* seabird cliffs? What birds live on them, and why?

The present character of our coastline results directly from the four Pleistocene Ice Ages, which began about 1,000,000 years ago, with the last great period of glaciation occurring 20,000 years ago. The southward movement of ice, which occurred on a scale so massive that we can scarcely begin to imagine what it must have been like, caused sea levels to drop by as much as 160 feet below those of the present day; the sea rose again as the ice retreated, but did not reach its present more or less stable level until about 5,000 years ago. This stability is relative, since we are still seeing the long-term effects of the last Ice Age. The land is still moving, imperceptibly, with the northernmost parts of our island rising and the southernmost parts sinking by roughly 2 mm every year. It is generally believed that there will be another great Ice Age at some time in the future and that we are currently in an 'interglacial' stage.

These colossal movements of ice and water affected the depth of the sea and shaped our coastline, the final results depending on the nature of the underlying rock and how readily it could be shaped, moved or pushed aside altogether. Steep-sided sea lochs were formed where the ice forced its way through hard rock; where softer rock could be worn away or

Opposite: Gannets on Grassholm Island

end and, apart from the
merge into the transition
sometimes, scarce and va
Herring gull colonies are
often with lesser black-ba
sea, as well as in seabird c
grab eggs or young birds;
steep or shallow slopes,
situations nesting herring
black-backed gulls are eve
tops and the flat summits
still, well able to capture fr

While these gulls then a
basis of their choice of ne
ecology of the more speci
preferring to nest some wa
more directly involved, e
arctic and great skuas (bor
and at our various Orkney
robbing incoming seabird
birds up to gannet size an
auks which appear on the s

Kittiwakes build their
impossibly tiny sites and t
they are increasing almost
available to them. These b
tribe and their wild calls ad
form the vocal accomplishn
to the extent that in Orkney
but will nest anywhere they
grass banks. To some exten
they tend to occupy broade
among auks and kittiwakes

Gannets nest in large, ev
stacks. In many cases their
tions, but because they to
founded at intervals: sightir
Ramna Stacks in Shetland m
long-established island site
at Bempton Cliffs in Yorksh

Most people's favourites
black-and-white birds whic
gannets match them for num
the three sea-going species,
prey to any great extent. Th
inshore. Competition for ne
crevices, or more typically ur
cliff, guillemots use open, e
seemingly impossible densit
for the most part. Both requi

ren
all
pill
sha
all r
and
Wh
rem
and
V
mos
nor
rich
Atla
Atla
ings
this
fooc
A
and
dep
dist
sho\
com
sea-
here
thei
soil
actu
O
mod
only
by t
drop
limit
inso
rath\
chara
and
annu
grow
must
perh
swar
abun
comr
fine k
often
mead
It i

Black guillemot

There is some overlap, as at Bempton Cliffs, between razorbills and puffins, but the classic puffin colony is usually higher still where the softer soil of broken clifftops or the grassy tops of cliffs and stacks enables them to make and use the burrows they like best.

The only British breeding bird to have become extinct in historical times, the great auk, must have used the lowest and most easily accessible parts of sea cliffs simply because it was flightless. It was also considerably bigger than the other auks and presumably fed on much larger fish. It deserves a mention here as our reserve at Papa Westray in Orkney was one of the last places it was seen alive in Britain, in the early years of the 19th century. By 1844 it had gone for all time.

Cormorants are seldom found with other seabirds, although they breed colonially on seacliffs and island tops, but shags are very much a part of the scene in many major colonies, nesting in caves and holes as well as in semi-sheltered and even fully exposed sites, usually at no great height above the sea. Shags may be the most grotesquely foul-mouthed seabirds of all, but somehow they manage to remain firm favourites with most ornithologists!

Shearwaters and petrels are still birds of mystery in that we really know very little about their numbers and still possess only incomplete knowledge of their distribution, mainly because they come ashore only after dark. Manx shearwaters breed on clifftops and even (as on Rhum) open mountains and nest in burrows, while storm and Leach's petrels nest either underground or beneath stones and boulders and in walls. Leach's petrel has the most restricted breeding distribution of all British seabirds, with only six confirmed breeding stations in Scotland: one, only recently discovered, is an RSPB reserve in Yell Sound.

Seacliffs provide a home for landbirds. Genuine wild rock doves still occur in Orkney and Shetland, and probably on Handa in Sutherland, where they breed in sea caves but feed on the machair and croft fields inland. Sadly, feral pigeons are infiltrating their ranks and have replaced them completely further south. Ravens breed on many sea-cliffs in Britain, as do jackdaws and both forage inland for most of their food. Even more interesting is the chough, a true sea-cliff inhabitant and another cave-nester, but nowadays something of a rarity. It still occurs in some numbers in Wales and Ireland and breeds on the RSPB reserves at South Stack in Anglesey and Rathlin Island in Ulster. Its scarcity seems linked to the disappearance of much of the grazed clifftop grasslands where it finds much of its food. Research on this species at South Stack has led to more studies elsewhere and, during 1982, a fuller survey of its status and problems in Western Europe.

Although there are none on RSPB reserves, some golden eagles nest on sea-cliffs, some-times in close proximity to big seabird colonies where they do much of their hunting. If, as looks increasingly likely, the present programme to re-introduce the white-tailed eagle to Scotland is successful, it will be interesting to watch its comeback in seabird areas where it once bred and also to see how it interacts with the golden eagle, which has replaced it in some areas. One is bound to wonder, too, if it will ever return to its ancestral site on our Handa reserve where it last bred 120 years ago. . . . One raptor which *has* made a definite comeback after a massive pesticide-induced decline (and despite much nest-robbing in recent years) is the peregrine. Due to increasing marine pollution presumably affecting its prey, its return has been slower on its traditional sea-cliff sites than elsewhere, but it is now encouraging to be able to report that it is nesting again at several RSPB reserves where it was but a memory a decade ago.

Many small birds appear on sea-cliffs, but have usually come in from adjoining habitats. Only the ubiquitous wren and the unobtrusive rock pipit are true residents, their songs contrasting with the cacophony of noise at a great seabird colony. They are as much a part of the scene as the pink thrift or white sea campion, or the relentless waves endlessly pounding on the rocks far below.

Peregrine

Terns on RSPB reserves

by Gareth Thomas

Terns regularly breed at twenty-four of the RSPB reserves, ten of which are of international importance in North-west Europe, with a further five holding nationally important colonies. All species nest colonially, ranging from the densely packed Sandwich tern colonies to the rather loose colonies or groups of little terns. This habit makes them ideal species to conserve at nature reserves which is as well when we remember that the roseate tern and little tern are the two rarest of the twenty-four species of seabirds that breed in Britain and Ireland.

It is mostly in April and May that terns arrive at the breeding colonies and leave again for their wintering quarters between July and September. Most winter off the western coasts of central and southern Africa, but arctic terns reach the furthest south, some covering the 14,000 kilometres to Antarctica. The northward journey to breed around the British and Irish coasts coincides with the availability of small shoaling fish, especially sand-eels, which appear in large numbers in summer and sustain the terns throughout the breeding season.

Excellent views of breeding terns are to be had from the hides at our reserves, many of which are positioned close to the colonies. Visiting, however, is not possible at some tern islands, especially the tiny Swan and Green Islands or the very densely populated low coastal island of Coquet. Visit a colony early in the breeding season and you will see the stylish courtship displays where birds strut around with heads held high and wings drooped. Rivals posture and squabble for the small areas of land which will hold the scrape or shallow nesting depression where the eggs are laid. Tern colonies are very noisy places and you will soon learn the distinguishing cries of each tern species. Later in the season, when the young terns have hatched, you will see endless journeys into the colony by the adults bearing food. Opportunist gulls often try and steal the fish from the terns and you may see aerial chases where small numbers of gulls will harry the terns and get them to drop their fish. When a sudden, serious threat appears the terns may all take to the air in a 'dread' flight and for a few eerie seconds everything seems very quiet. Recently fledged terns with their brownish markings gather together in separate little groups before leaving the colony.

Nesting in colonies enables terns to synchronise their breeding season. Courtship and egg-laying are all concluded in a short space of time. Birds may also nest near the best feeding areas or learn the best pathways to offshore fish supplies. Most of the large colonies of arctic terns, such as on Papa Westray, are in fact situated near to the tide rips and races where upwelling of water brings the shoaling fish into catching range. There are, however, a number of disadvantages to nesting in colonies. Predators find and exploit them: peregrines, kestrels and several species of owls all specialise in taking adult or juvenile terns from our terneries. Rogue oystercatchers sometimes become specialist egg-thieves at little terneries, whilst herring, lesser black-backed gulls and black-headed gulls all take the eggs and small young of the other terns. Probably the greatest predator to have exploited tern colonies was Victorian man. Nesting numbers were probably at their lowest in this era as many thousands of terns were taken, along with other colony nesting birds, to satisfy the millinery trade, which the RSPB was founded to fight.

You may notice that little terns feed just offshore or in creeks and gulleys, very near to the

Arctic tern

nest site, where they catch small fish and marine crustaceans. Common terns usually fly further out to sea. Sandwich terns fly from ten to fifteen miles out to sea, whilst roseate and arctic terns are thought to fly some 20 miles to find food. Food is caught after the terns take shallow plunge-dives into the water. They mainly catch sand eels but will take crustaceans and young herrings and sprats if they are available.

Most widespread of the terns breeding in Britain is the common tern. It nests on coastal islands, sand and shingle beaches, sand dunes and saltmarshes and small numbers have begun to choose inland sites on small islands in sand, clay and gravel pits. The British and Irish breeding birds probably number about 15,000 pairs and seem to have been stable over the last ten years. Large colonies are uncommon and Coquet Island, regularly holding more than 1,000 breeding pairs, is one of the largest and the small island of Inchmickery regularly holds over 500 breeding pairs. Reserves regularly holding between 100 and 500 pairs include Swan Island, Green Island, Strathbeg, Dungeness and, lately, Snettisham and Titchwell in Norfolk. Other reserves holding small numbers of breeding common terns are Shane's Castle, Horse Island, Langstone, Minsmere, Havergate, Elmley and Rye House Marsh.

Overall, our reserves have recently held about 3,300 pairs of breeding common terns each year which represents about 22 per cent of the numbers nesting in Britain and Ireland.

The most numerous of the British and Irish breeding terns is the arctic tern. Here it is at the southern edge of its breeding range. In 1980 the numbers were estimated at 77,000 pairs, 65,000 of which were found in Orkney and Shetland. Like the common terns, its breeding numbers seem to have maintained themselves over the last decade.

There are over 600 densely packed small colonies on sand, shingle and storm beaches in Orkney and Shetland, but the largest colonies occur inland on the unimproved sheep pastures. The largest colony is found at our reserve on the North Hill on Papa Westray in Orkney, where 4,000 to 7,000 pairs (but occasionally as few as 1,500 pairs) regularly nest in well-spaced groups over almost 500 acres of sub-arctic vegetation on the Hill, presenting a marked contrast to the agriculturally well-developed lower parts of the island. The RSPB reserve on Fetlar holds most of the 1,000 to 4,700 pairs that have nested on the island in recent years. Here they nest on parts of the heather moorland and amongst the emergent plants in some valley bogs. Between 100 and 200 pairs also nest on Samphrey, an island in Yell Sound and on the machair of Balranald in the Outer Hebrides. The most southerly colony on the east coast of Britain, holding 500 to 700 pairs, is at Coquet and at another colony on the west coast 200 to 300 pairs have nested in recent years. Other reserves holding small numbers of breeding arctic terns are Swan Island, Green Island, Horse Island, Strathbeg, Copinsay and Nairn Bar. In the last couple of years our reserves have held over 11,000 pairs of arctic terns which represents about 15 per cent of the numbers nesting in Britain and Ireland.

Breeding failures sometimes occur and are obvious at such large colonies as North Hill on Papa Westray. Many breeding pairs desert whether the weather is fair or foul. It is thought that the desertions are caused by the late or non-appearance of tern foods, mainly sand-eels.

Probably the most enigmatic and least understood of our terns, the roseate breeds at only about a dozen sites in Britain and Ireland. All but a few pairs nest on offshore islands. They usually, but not always, seek out areas with plenty of cover in which to nest. They are fond of nesting deep down in grassy tussocks or part of the way down old rabbit burrows where only the tips of their long tails remain visible. In all Europe there are only about 1,000 pairs. Apart from about 120 pairs in Brittany, all breed in Britain and Ireland and are, sadly, declining. Breeding numbers have dropped by about 60 per cent in the last ten years despite intensive management at the nesting colonies.

Sandwich tern

RSPB reserves currently hold about a half of the breeding numbers in Europe. Green

Island regularly holds 160 to 200 breeding pairs, a west coast reserve 130 to 180 pairs while thirty to forty pairs breed on Swan Island and twenty to thirty pairs on Coquet Island. The most northerly colony, on Inchmickery, has declined from between fifty to 100 pairs in the 1970s to less than ten pairs today, but small numbers, though, have recently colonised the islands on the gravel pits at Dungeness.

The reasons for the decline of the roseate tern in North-west Europe are not fully understood. The bulk of the world's nesting birds breed in warm latitudes and the breeding outposts in Europe may simply be contracting. The decline, however, could be closely connected with conditions at its winter quarters off the central West African coast. Most of the recoveries of British ringed roseate terns come from Ghana where they are trapped for food or sport by children from fishing villages. The terns are caught in nooses, baited with small fish, which are placed along the tide lines. Roseate terns, possibly hungry, seem more vulnerable to this method of capture than other sea terns. The decline in Europe has been mirrored in the New World. Most of the recoveries of roseate terns ringed in the eastern USA, where the breeding numbers have fallen from 5,000 pairs to about 2,500 pairs over the last two decades, have been from Guyana in South America where they are also extensively caught for food. Conservationists are trying to make the peoples who trap the terns aware of the possible consequences of their actions.

Little terns nest almost exclusively on sandy or shingly beaches, especially along the southern and eastern coasts of Britain. They nest within a few yards of the high tide-lines and are very vulnerable to having their nests washed away. They are very susceptible to disturbance from holiday-makers and unless special precautions are taken nesting numbers decline wherever the holiday industry develops. About 2,100 pairs of little terns breed in Britain and Ireland following a peak of about 3,000 pairs in the 1930s. Nowadays, about 80 per cent of the breeding numbers breed at reserved or protected areas in Britain and Ireland.

Our reserves at Tetney, Titchwell, Langstone and Minsmere usually hold between forty and 100 pairs, all nesting on shingle beaches. Small numbers breed on the machair at Balranald. In recent years about 225 pairs of little terns have bred on our reserves which represents about 14 per cent of the breeding numbers in Britain and Ireland. Additionally, the RSPB species protection department also runs three protection schemes at holiday areas along the North Wales coast allowing some sixty to eighty pairs to breed in areas where they would probably now be extinct.

Sandwich tern colonies are found along most coasts which have clear water and predominantly sandy bottoms. The preferred sites are offshore islands, sandbanks or coastal saltmarshes. Although several species of tern will breed close to black-headed gulls, there seems to be a special relationship between these gulls and Sandwich terns. The dense colonies of each seem to nest as close as possible to one another and often intermingle.

At the present time there are probably about 15,600 pairs of Sandwich terns breeding in Britain and Ireland and have probably increased by about 30 per cent in the last ten years. Almost all now breed at nature reserves or specially protected areas and this is thought to have helped increase the breeding numbers. In fact, there are probably more Sandwich terns breeding in Britain and Ireland now than at any other time this century.

One of the largest colonies is on Coquet Island where over 1,000 pairs regularly nest. They nest on the close rabbit-grazed turf especially alongside the large nettle beds which probably give some shelter. Sandwich terns nest only inches from each other and the ground within colonies becomes bared as a result of all the trampling and guano deposited. Vegetation is literally killed in this way and the island has several brown 'earthy' scars which are old colony sites recovering from past use.

Between 500 and 1,300 pairs nest on Green Island which is a small, bare shingle island of

Common tern

less than a quarter of an acre in Carlingford Lough in Northern Ireland. On Inchmickery 400 to 600 pairs regularly nest. Here, some of the birds nest on the flat, grassy roofs of the deserted wartime buildings. An interesting isolated colony of over 100 pairs is found on Screegan, one of our small island reserves on Lower Lough Erne, in Northern Ireland. This colony is about 10 miles from the sea to which the feeding birds have to commute. Between 100 and 200 pairs have recently begun to nest at Dungeness. Smaller numbers breed at Swan Island and on Havergate Island.

Our reserves have recently held about 2,600 pairs of breeding Sandwich terns which is about 16 per cent of the British and Irish breeding numbers but occasionally they hold up to 20 per cent of the total.

In contrast to the other five species of terns, which live largely at marine habitats throughout the year (they are known as sea terns), black terns (known as marsh terns) need wet marshes with reedy growths during the breeding season. They used to breed commonly in England, especially in the east, but became extinct in the mid-19th century largely as a result of the extensive drainage of freshwater marshes at this time. Since 1966 they have periodically nested at the Ouse Washes at times when there have been large expanses of spring flood-water and floating or submerged vegetation on which to anchor their nests. They feed extensively on insects. Black terns also winter in tropical African waters and, like roseate terns, are also trapped for food or sport.

Management on nature reserves is aimed at reducing or minimising a number of threats or constraints on terns, chief amongst which are human disturbance, the impact of certain predators and competition for nest space. Our objectives are to maximise the nesting numbers of terns and their breeding success.

With our expanding human population in Britain disturbance is probably the single biggest nuisance to breeding terns. The range of disturbances successfully tackled by our wardens to the benefit of terns have stemmed from holiday-makers, birdwatchers, vehicle trespassing, egg-collectors (still persisting at some sites), shooting and low-flying aircraft. Almost invariably our first task on acquiring a reserve with nesting terns is to regulate human disturbance by creating proper pathways and good observation facilities. This often has immediate impact. Before one tiny offshore island became a reserve in 1976 up to 350 pairs of terns inconsistently nested there and were continually disturbed by holiday-makers. Since 500 pairs have regularly nested including arctic, Sandwich, common and the largest colony of roseate terns on the British mainland. Terns may also have colonised from non-wardened sites nearby.

Little terns nesting along the public shingle beach at Minsmere used to suffer heavily from the pressure of holiday-makers. Most terns ignored the specially prepared shingle islands at the Minsmere scrape and tried, usually unsuccessfully, to continue nesting on the shore. Nesting numbers had dropped to ten pairs by 1979. Our wardens erected a single fence around an area of shingle about the size of a football field with courteous notices explaining this need to the public, asking them to keep out and above all pointing out the terns to be seen. Thirty-five pairs nested in 1980 and forty-five pairs in 1981. Just over one young per pair were reared in 1980 but this was halved in 1981 as a result of the local kestrels taking the young little terns.

Predation of eggs and young birds by gulls, crows, birds of prey and owls are by and large pressures that terns can stand and we have no serious problems on our reserves. The effects of foxes and rats can be more damaging. Foxes are deterred by digging deep ditches around the small tern islands at our mainland reserves. At two reserves we have had to eliminate rats in their holes as they were destroying virtually all egg-production and causing terns to desert.

Sand-eels

The provision of new islands in the gravel workings at Snettisham and Dungeness, the

Minsmere scrape, at Havergate and at the newly flooded marsh at Titchwell have benefited nesting terns, especially common terns. At Snettisham the creation of some tiny islands has allowed up to 160 pairs of common terns to nest. The complex series of islands at Minsmere currently holds up to 100 pairs of common terns and until recently up to 750 pairs of Sandwich terns. Some of these have moved to nearby Havergate where up to 250 pairs have nested recently. The island complex in the new bunded freshwater marsh at Titchwell, created in 1980, has allowed common terns to build up to 200 pairs in a couple of years. Rafts have been placed in lagoons just off the reserve at Rye House Marsh just outside London and about forty pairs of common terns nest on them.

One of our greatest joys has been to see the developments at Dungeness. Before 1939 there were large colonies of gulls and terns on the Dungeness peninsula — 350 to 700 pairs of herring, thirty to forty pairs of lesser black-backed and common gulls, and some 600 to 1,000 pairs of common terns, with a large colony of black-headed gulls. Between 1940 and 1952 when most of the area was in the hands of the War Department, there was an increase in egg-collecting and a large increase in ground predators, notably foxes. All the gulls and terns stopped breeding apart from about six pairs of herring and common gulls, which did not produce any young. The RSPB supervised the excavation of about 200 acres of gravel pits, which contained ten small islands by 1973 and then the provision of four island complexes in another 200 acres of pits which were fully available by 1976. These islands, which are beyond the range of foxes, have been a boon for nesting gulls and terns. At the present time they hold some 900 pairs of black-headed gulls, seventy pairs of herring and lesser black-backed gulls and 350 pairs of common terns. Up to five pairs of roseate terns have nested since 1976 and Sandwich terns, which colonised in 1975, now number 170 pairs. To a large extent the gull and tern potential of the peninsula has been restored.

We manage existing sites to make them more attractive to nesting terns. Our wardens prepare many islands by selective weeding and mowing to achieve a balance between shingle, short grass and taller herbs. Loads of shingle are laid on some islands, sometimes over heavy duty polythene sacks which check the growth of some perennial plants. By experience we know that if this management ceases then tall vegetation prevails at some islands at the expense of nesting terns and to the benefit of nesting gulls.

There was a large series of nettlebeds on Coquet which occupied up to a quarter of the island's area. Virtually no birds nested in the denser parts but there were significantly higher numbers of terns nesting around most edges of the nettlebed and in any gaps in the middle, where they probably benefited from the shelter or cover from predators. With the aid of a non-persistent herbicide, we have sprayed out large holes and rides in the nettlebeds and further increased the areas available to nesting terns, especially common and arctic. The trial spraying was only done in a 15 m×3 m rectangle. In the first year sixty pairs of common and arctic terns nested, but the area was taken over in the second year by almost 500 pairs of Sandwich terns.

Our Scottish staff have turfed more of the flat-roofed buildings on Inchmickery and induced more Sandwich and common terns to nest at these sites.

Management at Screegan is concerned with scrub clearance to keep part of the island grassy and open for the Sandwich terns. Previously this job was done by feral goats which once lived on many of the Lower Lough Erne islands. If we did not do this the island would be dominated by woody growth in a very few years and the Sandwich tern colony would be lost.

Little tern nests getting washed away on spring tides has been a perennial problem at Tetney and Titchwell. Many replacement clutches were laid and breeding success was only between 0·1 and 0·5 young/pair. Clutches at risk were removed and placed in labelled boxes for three-quarters of an hour to two and a half hours each time for three days around the

Roseate tern

highest tides. Little terns readily reincubate their clutches that have been moved in this way for up to ten times and are able to hatch them. An elevated chalk road at Tetney had been built up by 1980 to try and entice little terns to nest there without fear of flooding but so far only the replacement clutches have been laid there and unfortunately have been lost to predators. However, luck has been with us at Titchwell where dune accretion has occurred giving little terns a larger safe nesting area. In the last few years the breeding numbers have doubled to over fifty pairs with a breeding success of two young per pair in 1981.

There has been a great increase in the breeding numbers of gulls in Britain and elsewhere, especially herring and lesser black-backed, in the last forty years. Many coastal islands which formerly held important tern colonies have now been colonised and taken over by gulls. On some of our reserves competition for nest space from these large gulls and black-headed gulls towards terns has been acute. We have seen downward trends in breeding terns at some and seen the extinction of terns on Horse Island and Inchmickery.

Problems with black-headed gulls are effectively solved by the removal of their nests and eggs (under Government licence) on perhaps three occasions in April and May. Between a third and a half of the nesting gulls then move away from the colonies at such reserves as Havergate, Minsmere and Swan Island. This allows space for common, roseate and Sandwich terns to nest. Small numbers of breeding herring and lesser black-backed gulls can be deterred in this way. However, the large numbers of these gulls which nest all over Inchmickery for example had to be reduced in number by killing them (under Government licence) with a narcotic poison. Gulls increased on this two-and-a-half acre island at a rate of 28 per cent per annum between 1960 and 1970 and when they had reached about 200 pairs they caused the extinction of 1,500 pairs of terns, including a colony of roseate terns. In subsequent years after the control exercises the breeding terns returned to occupy their former colonies. On the six-acre Horse Island 1,000 pairs of herring and lesser black-backed gulls have been reduced and the island is being recolonised by terns.

Although we are able to provide and manage the nesting areas of terns there is very little we can do to manage their food supplies. Their major food is sand-eels, which spawn in mid winter, the young ones growing to about two inches by the following summer. Previous age classes have reached four to eight inches by this time, and all are taken by terns. After cold winters and springs sand eels do not enter coastal waters so early. Food shortages for terns can then arise and our wardens sometimes record large mortalities of young terns and parental desertions, especially of Arctic terns. We are concerned that the commercial catches of sand-eels and sprats in north-west Europe is rapidly increasing in the wake of the much depleted herring stocks. If they become as seriously fished there may be a serious shortage of tern foods.

Little tern at nest

Estuaries and saltmarsh

by Tony Prater

There can be few habitats in Britain and Northern Ireland that are more dynamic and continuously changeable than estuaries. Here the twice-daily ebb of the tide successively reveals the highly adapted plants of the saltmarshes, the sand and shingle spits and finally the sandy or muddy intertidal flats. Then as the tide flows in again, these areas are bathed by the water carrying its load of vital nutrients and finally completely submerged. The cyclical nature of the daily rhythm of tides overlays other patterns. Every fortnight, with each new or full moon, spring tides occur — these give the highest highwater levels when even the high saltmarshes are flooded. In contrast, the neap tides of each intermediate week can be so low that even at high tide only the lowest plants in the saltmarsh are reached by the water.

Estuarine birds are intimately aware of and have learnt to live with this variable habitat. They are specialists, many of them being restricted to estuaries or other coastal flats. Each species of bird occurs in a particular part of the estuary where it can exploit a niche that others do not occupy. To find the various waders and wildfowl we need to understand the physical nature of an estuary.

Most estuaries are formed where a substantial river reaches the sea. Typical of these are the Dee, dividing North Wales from England, and the Dyfi, in central Wales where the RSPB reserves of Gayton Sands and Ynys-hir are sited. More complex sites are where several rivers form a bay. In Britain, the most notable of these for birds are Morecambe Bay and the Wash; here too, the RSPB has substantial reserves, protecting some of the key parts. In southern England, the coast has sunk over the years and major estuaries have formed with very little freshwater flowing into them. The great harbours of Sussex, Hampshire and Dorset are the best examples, and here too we have large reserves, for example in Langstone Harbour or at Arne in Poole Harbour.

Inner parts of estuaries tend to be muddy; this is due to the fine sediments settling out. The fine silt brought in from the sea or down the rivers does not remain in suspension, but is deposited in the sheltered waters. As the silt builds up, the conditions become favourable for plants to colonise and eventually saltmarshes develop. Towards the sea, conditions become more marine and turbulent, so the lighter materials remain in suspension and the coarser sands are deposited. Finally, at the estuary mouth, only the most coarse material can settle, so that sand or shingle spits develop, areas much appreciated by roosting and breeding birds.

Freshwater entering from the rivers creates an increasing gradient of salinity towards the sea. This, plus the distance from highwater mark, affects the invertebrates, which in turn influence the distribution and species of waders present.

Estuaries are considered to be the most productive natural habitat, far more productive than even the most fertilised crop or woodland. In the mud enormous densities of invertebrates have been measured. In Morecambe Bay, small bivalve molluscs *Macoma* of up to 50,000 per square metre, have been recorded, while another small snail *Hydrobia* may reach 40,000 per square metre and ragworms *Nereis* up to 5,000 per square metre. It is quite possible to have up to 70,000 invertebrates in a square metre of muddy sand, with most of

Oystercatcher

these in the top four centimetres. Typical densities are probably nearer 10,000 per square metre with many fewer in the mobile sandy outer areas.

Saltmarshes are very variable in nature and value for birds. In north-western England and Wales, parts of the great saltmarshes are grazed by sheep, cattle or ponies. Here the close-grazed areas provide good goose or wigeon grazing areas in winter, while the tussocks that are left are used by breeding birds. Morecambe Bay and Ynys-hir provide good examples of this. However, in most areas grazing is not carried out, so the saltmarshes develop an interesting succession of flowering plants. Colonising the mudflats may be samphire, green at first, but becoming a striking golden-red as it matures in autumn. This is harvested for local consumption in places in eastern England, but not only man enjoys it, for its tiny seeds are eaten avidly by teal. Further up the shore, a variety of plants may be found, from the greyish-green sea purslane to such attractive flowering plants as sea lavender, sea aster or, in south-eastern England, golden samphire, which can provide carpets of pale mauve, blue or yellow respectively. As a marsh becomes higher and dryer, more grasses and larger shrubs appear.

Over much of the country another saltmarsh plant has become established during the last century. This is the cord grass (*Spartina*). This invasive plant was the result of a hybrid between a British and an American species and, like many hybrids, its growth was vigorous. Thousands of acres throughout British and Irish estuaries were swamped by it; sometimes it spread naturally, but often it was planted deliberately to aid reclamation of intertidal flats. It has very little direct value to birds, certainly much less value than the mudflats it replaced — but it is now with us for good, although there are signs that it is becoming more in balance with other estuarine forces than it seemed twenty years ago.

Two additional general features of saltmarshes should be recognised. These are that they trap much sediment, so reducing the need for dredging estuaries (and then the dumping of dredgings on valuable adjacent areas) and they put an enormous amount of organic matter back into the estuary, which then forms the food of invertebrates and subsequently, birds.

Before leaving the physical nature of an estuary some mention must be made of the adjacent inland habitats. At high spring tides waders generally resort to fields nearby; some superb views of waders can be obtained at Snettisham as birds pour to roost on the islands created in the lake there, or at Elmley where they join thousands of duck on the reflooded reclaimed saltmarsh.

Contrasts can be very large between the seasons for birds on estuaries. Passage migrants, moulting birds in autumn, wintering hordes and specialist breeding birds, give estuaries a flavour matched by few other habitats.

Already, before the end of January, some of the breeding species will be displaying and cementing the pair bonds, particularly in the southern half of England. Redshank commence their drifting song flight on down-curved quivering wings, while mallard start their head-bobbing displays. Even some of the winter visitors, still present in very large numbers, appear to be present in pairs within the flocks. By mid-February, other species, such as ringed plover, oystercatchers and goldeneye, are displaying in earnest. On mild calm days, the beaches and marshes ring with display calls.

Birds cannot breed on the intertidal flats nor in the colonising plant zones because these are covered even by neap tides every week. They can, however, breed in the higher saltmarshes and for some species, this forms an important breeding habitat.

Opposite: Bar-tailed godwits and dunlin winter on several reserves

Of the wildfowl only shelduck and mallard have significant breeding populations on estuaries, indeed the great majority of shelduck find the higher saltmarshes suitable. In early spring they gather in groups for their communal display before splitting up to find rabbit burrows or deep vegetation in which they can build their nests and obtain camouflage

for their striking black, white and chestnut plumage. A wide variety of duck will breed in the ditches and dykes of grazing marsh just behind the seawall.

Management of the marshes can modify the diversity and density of waders. The extensive areas on the Morecambe Bay reserve illustrate several factors — here there are variations in the grazing intensity by sheep and cattle and turf-cutting activities. Indeed it is rumoured that Morecambe Bay turf has been laid at Wembley. Turf cutting is not a particularly helpful activity for breeding birds because the aim is to mow regularly to provide a low dense sward. However, strips of less intensively managed grass nearby can be productive.

Similar grass can be obtained by sheep and, especially in the Burry Inlet, pony grazing. In these cases the many tussocks left provide sites for redshank, while lapwing and oyster-catchers nest on the more open positions. Rougher ground caused by the feet of cattle or floristically diverse areas are favoured by redshank; here nests and, subsequently, chicks are protected against predators. In such areas, average densities of over 150 per square kilometre can be reached with much denser 'hot spots' where the marsh is ideal. The downy wader chicks make for the wetter areas almost as soon as they hatch, so the maintenance of shallow muddy depressions or creeks can be important. The young which have to feed themselves need the combination of wet mud and nearby vegetation for the three to four weeks they take to reach the flying stage. Although they may be obvious when feeding, alarm calls of the parents soon make them rush for cover where they remain crouching motionless until released by the adults.

All waders, gulls or terns which wish to breed on saltmarshes are strictly constrained by the tidal pattern. These birds lay their eggs every other day so a clutch takes between four and eight days to complete; then the incubation period is just about four weeks. Thus from starting to lay to hatching takes about five weeks — just longer than the monthly interval between the highest spring tides! In general, high tides are lower in May and June than in other months, so nesting birds have a good chance of success on the higher levels, but almost every other year, weather conditions conspire to push one tide higher than predicted, so swamping nests and eggs. Breeding on saltmarshes must be sufficiently attractive, for despite all the problems, many birds still try!

Black-headed gulls usually risk their nests most often because the majority of them in England choose the mid-marsh. The notable colonies, each of over 10,000 pairs, at the mouth of the Beaulieu River, on the Wash and the Ribble, as well as dozens of other smaller colonies, suffer regular loss, but they are very persistent and try, try, try again. Usually one attempt is reasonably successful.

By mid-July estuaries start to change their nature; the saltmarshes are in flower while where excess organic matter is found, usually from sewage inflow, a dense green carpet of seaweed blankets the mud. The birds, too, are changing. The young are now on the wing and move out onto the intertidal areas to find food. Here they are joined by the first waves of migrants — some curlew and redshanks coming from nearby inland breeding areas, but some already appearing from Iceland, Scandinavia or even further afield. Packed together on high tide roosts, waders in summer plumage are superb; here the very striking grey plovers, with their black underparts gleaming in contrast to the spangled grey and white upperparts, may stand against the buff-brown and chestnut male bar-tailed godwit and the pied oystercatcher whose orange bill and brilliant red eye really gleam in the sun.

Autumn is the easy time for estuary birds. Food is at its most abundant, the temperature is warm and life is unhurried. Few birds have a tremendous urgency to fly down to winter quarters. However, this is the time when they moult; the replacement of feathers is an energy sapping process and the birds need estuaries with especially plentiful supplies of food and security from undue disturbance. Corners of our major estuaries are chosen for the

Shelduck

moult and tens of thousands congregate at Gayton Sands and Snettisham, two of the most important moulting areas. Very few duck moult here although small groups of shelduck have recently taken to moulting at Skinflats on the Firth of Forth and the mouth of the Ouse on the Wash, in addition to the well-known group in Bridgwater Bay.

Soon, however, the autumn storms start to encourage those birds which winter further south, to leave on their migration. Some which pass through our estuaries will eventually end up in southern Africa although many more will stop further north in the great coastal complexes in Morocco, Mauritania and Guinea-Bissau. By November most of the moult has been completed and the main winter influx starts of birds which spent autumn on the Danish, German and Dutch Wadden Sea. Numbers of dunlin, knot, bar-tailed godwit, shelduck, wigeon, brent geese and many other birds, build up to mid-winter maxima and at this time most of our estuaries are at their most crowded.

Britain, and especially Ireland, is fortunate, although we do not always appreciate it, in being relatively mild in winter. This, combined with a large tidal range, allows the productive estuarine flats to support birds which breed as far away as north-eastern USSR or northern Canada.

Although the British Isles are mild on average, some winters have had spells of severe weather, the most recent examples being in 1962/63, February 1979 and 1981/82. In these conditions, estuaries become extremely important as refuges for birds which are rapidly forced away from frozen inland sites and also from adjacent continental coasts. For example, in the last cold spell in 1981, the Elmley reserve hosted 20,000 wigeon — about 4 per cent of those wintering in Europe. Despite the value of estuaries at this time, birds there still suffer greatly from less food being available and more competition to eat it. Of the waders, redshank, because they feed fairly high up the shore and on food which is on the mud surface, are particularly vulnerable to cold. In 1981/82 their death rate increased by at least five times as the mud surface froze and their energy demands increased.

Overlapping with the start of display from resident birds in late winter, a great exodus of wintering birds takes place. The winter duck and waders start to move back to Wadden Sea shores in order to start the slow build-up of condition and weight which will eventually allow migration back to the breeding areas. By the end of March numbers in most estuaries are well down. It is only on certain major areas that numbers remain high. A particularly valuable site is the Morecambe Bay reserve where up to 50,000 knot may congregate to put on fat as fuel for their crossing of the North Atlantic. These birds start to gain the chestnut underparts of summer plumage and form a dense, rippling flock of grey and chestnut which, combined with the sound of their wings, makes an unforgettable spectacle.

The lull in migration is, however, only short-lived, for during April summer-plumaged waders start to arrive. These birds have wintered far to the south in Africa and are in a much greater rush to reach their breeding grounds than those we have seen before. Flocks of sanderling, dunlin and ringed plovers which will breed in Iceland, Greenland and Canada, seek out the western estuaries. Notable, particularly during May, are the Dee, Ribble, Solway, Morecambe Bay and the Dyfi. East coast estuaries receive relatively few birds although the Wash, Teesmouth and the Firth of Forth do see some migrants. There can be few more pleasant experiences than standing on the large Morecambe Bay saltmarshes on a warm late May day listening to the beautiful, soft, trilling song of dunlin, a species which sings readily on migration. Then, as dusk approaches, birds fly round calling excitedly, pulling more and more up with them to gain height and eventually head north-westwards over the Atlantic on the final leg of their long journey to breeding grounds.

Suddenly, by the first week of June, just as dramatically as it started three to four weeks earlier, virtually everything has departed. Only the breeding birds on the marshes and the small numbers of immature, non-breeding birds remain. The intertidal flats are quiet, awaiting the autumn influx which is only six or seven weeks away.

Grey plover

Overleaf: Marsh harrier over reeds at Minsmere

John Reaney — 1977

Despite the great physical forces operating in estuaries, the habitat is one which is under immense threat. Man has the power to destroy much nowadays, usually with the excuse of progress. One has frequently heard the remark about estuaries and marshes, "they are only wasteland, we should use them." It is important to realise that many birds are dependent on estuaries and it is one habitat that cannot be created — no one is likely to breach seawalls around the Wash to re-create the vast marshes of the past.

Threats come in all forms, from reclamation to pollution. Perhaps reclamation is the most significant for this leads to physical loss. Major schemes have been put forward for most large estuaries, notably Morecambe Bay, Dee, Wash and the Severn estuary. Initial proposals for all tend to be expansive, but even when smaller, more practical suggestions eventually appear, these still involve losses of tens of square kilometres of mud. It is probably a significant observation that very rarely do these schemes proceed; normally this is because they are based on grossly biased assumptions of their value which do not stand up to critical appraisal. However, they are real threats.

More disturbing perhaps are the many smaller schemes for reclaiming mud for yacht marinas, docks, oil refineries, agriculture and industrial workings. Individually they may appear less damaging, but together they provide an enormous threat. Death by a thousand cuts is certainly true for estuaries. In many of the south coast harbours and estuaries, intertidal flats are being lost at the rate of about one per cent per annum. Without vigorous defence, much more could easily go.

On the Ribble and on the Wash, agricultural reclamation of saltmarsh has been projected; on the former it was prevented, as were recent schemes on the Wash, although during the early 1970s this area lost several important sections of saltmarsh on the south and west shores.

Few estuaries have yet disappeared under modern developments, but some have come very close. The most dramatic has been port, industrial and, especially, petrochemical activities at Teesmouth, which have transformed a large, important estuary virtually into a small patch of mud with two sandy beaches. The scale of loss during the last two decades has been frightening here and it provides a classic example of what can happen if ill-intentioned man is left to his own devices.

Despite the pressure that estuaries are under all over Europe, they still provide one of the most exciting places to see birds. The vast numbers of duck resting out among the saltmarshes, the grebes and diving duck in the channels and the waders on the mudflats, give the patient observer unparalleled sights. The sounds of an estuary too are impressive; the hiss of the incoming tide as it inundates the dry flats, the lapping of water at high tide against the saltmarsh and particularly the intermingling of calls from thousands of birds driven in front of the tide, all combine together to make most estuaries places which still retain some of the feeling of wilderness so lacking in the countryside nowadays.

Bar-tailed godwit

Reedswamps

by Colin J Bibby

The reed is one of the very few plants in Britain to occur in extensive single species stands. A large reedbed has a superficial appearance of uniformity that belies the considerable richness and variety of life to be found there. Several of the bird species are specialists, confined to reedy areas. Additionally, because really good reedbeds are rare, so are some of the birds with more exacting requirements and no keen birdwatcher would want to leave this habitat out of the year's field trips.

Reed is a very widely distributed plant, but it most favours rich wet places which may also provide a variety of habitats for different plants, birds and other wildlife. Open water, perhaps both fresh and brackish, reedbeds, fen, watermeadows and wet scrubland or carr may all occur adjacently. If interesting dry land habitats adjoin the marsh, so much the better. This combination of habitats occurs at some of Britain's most exciting nature reserves such as Minsmere or Leighton Moss.

Wetlands as a whole are not only of great richness and interest but also pose some of the thorniest difficulties to conservationists. Drainage for agriculture has either destroyed or eroded innumerable sites. Many that remain are now surrounded by such well-drained land that it is increasingly difficult both to get enough water to keep them wet and then to retain it without damaging adjoining farmland by flooding. At the worst extreme the famous National Trust reserve at Wicken Fen is now several feet higher than surrounding drained land which has shrunk through farming. How on earth can a wetland be managed in these circumstances? Further problems arise from fertilisers running off farmland.

So how are we to look after Britain's reedbeds and their birds for the future? First we must have knowledge of the state of the resource and an understanding of the ecology of reedbeds and the requirements of the specific birds and other creatures that inhabit them. Secondly we need a strategy based on this knowledge which must cover both the maintenance of reedbeds at large and also the more detailed management possible on those that are nature reserves. Thirdly we need the will to execute the conservation strategy, where a major difficulty is the cost.

In 1979 and 1980, the RSPB conducted a survey of the status of reedbeds in England and Wales. Scotland was excluded because although it has what is probably the largest bed in the British Isles, most of the interesting birds, including the reed warbler, do not breed this far north. Taking a minimum size of 2 ha (5 acres), 109 reedswamp sites were found totalling 2,300 ha (5,683 acres). Most were small with three-quarters being of less than 20 ha (50 acres), but the largest fifteen sites accounted for half the total area.

Beds of reeds occur in five kinds of situation. Reeds may be early colonists of artificially created areas of shallow fresh water such as on the clay-pits at Barton, Humberside, or the margins of Chew Valley Lake, Avon. Such beds are likely to be short-lived because of the vegetational successions described later. Natural lakes may have marginal reedbeds but these are not abundant, partly because lakes of sufficient fertility in lowland Britain are rather scarce and partly because the area of suitable margin is often rather small and narrow. The best examples are at Slapton Ley, Devon, and the Fleet at Abbotsbury, Dorset. A rather distinct kind of reedbed occurs on the upper reaches of estuaries and tidal sections of rivers where salinity is too high to be tolerated by many plants. These sites are damp with periodic

Marsh harrier

Overleaf: Black-headed gulls mob a bittern at Leighton Moss

Marsh harrier

floods of brackish water at spring tides. Floods deposit silts which raise land levels and lead to a progressive drying out of the reeds and succession to other vegetations. One of the best examples is at Blacktoft Sands, where silt accretion resulted from the construction of a training wall at the junction of the Humber and the Ouse and a superb bed of reeds has developed as an early phase of succession.

The most commonly imagined location of reedbeds is probably the flood-plains of the lower reaches of rivers and I divide them into two types. Most of the wholly natural flood-plain marshes have been drained. The best were the classic fens. Imagine what birds might now occur at Whittlesey Mere had it not been drained in the middle of the last century. Instead, this is now one of the richest arable areas of Britain with a native flora and fauna about as poor as it is possible to achieve. The best surviving fenland areas which still include some superb reedbeds are in the Norfolk Broads, though their natural history is much enhanced by the fact that they were extensively dug for peat in the Middle Ages. The second kind of flood-plain reedbed occurs where coastal flood-land has been protected from encroachments by the sea but drainage has never been completed or has even reverted. Some of Britain's best reedbeds now occur in these circumstances at Minsmere, Leighton Moss or Oxwich, Glamorgan. In all three cases, drainage and coastal defence works produced grazing land that was flooded in winter. For various reasons, these 'improvements' fell into disrepair and reeds were rapidly able to spread from the ditches to cover the old meadows. Minsmere was flooded during the war as a protection measure and in about twenty years transformed from an area of shallow open water with reed fringes to a state like the present, an area of reed with patches of remaining water.

Two things stand out in this view of our present reedbeds; the natural succession of vegetation of wetlands and the impact of man. Left to itself, an area of shallow fertile water will rapidly be colonised by reeds if the summer water level is below two or three feet. Reeds will not however hold their dominance for long. A combination of the annual production of dead plant material and importation of silt from tides or rivers will steadily raise the ground level so making the water shallower. A range of other plants may then flourish. Once the ground is no more than damp in summer, trees such as alder or willows can invade and speed the drying out. Left to itself a glorious reedbed may become a dense tangle of scrubby vegetation in no more than a few decades. Though this succession is a process in time, its nature can be seen by looking at almost any reedbed. Open water might have a reedy margin and further back there will be a drier vegetation with sparser reeds and a mixture of other plants perhaps including the odd bush. On the slightly higher ground there may be a dense carr grading into a deciduous wood.

How then, if the succession is so rapid, do any reedbeds survive to the present at all? The answer is largely at the hand of man. I have previously described how the construction of a reservoir at Chew or a training wall at Blacktoft and the abandonment of a drainage system at Minsmere have all produced reedbeds. A high proportion of the reedbeds in Britain are of such recent and artificial origins. More important is the fact that reeds have been of commercial use mainly as a thatching material. Exploitation for thatch has meant that invasion by scrub has been controlled during the harvest. In addition, removal of the crop and burning of the litter slows the rate of drying from accumulation of dead plant material. In several places, the reed crop is so important that beds have been embanked and subjected to artificial water control. By this means, the future of the reedbed is extended. A decline in rural crafts during this century has resulted in the abandonment of many commercial beds some of which, especially on the Broads, as at Strumpshaw Fen, are now dense carr. There are welcome signs of renewal of interest in thatching and the crop is again valuable. The modern tendency is, however, to favour larger beds which are machine-harvested with

Reed almost agricultural thoroughness. Although the most intensive harvesting of reeds may not

be ideal for birds, the long-term survival of thatching would help nature conservation.

Knowledge of reed management for thatching has been of direct use to nature reserve management though for this purpose, we also need to manage for the particular birds as well. Four characteristic reedbed birds are rare in Britain: marsh harrier, bittern, bearded tit and Savi's warbler. Historically these birds have had problems with human persecution but their present rarity is largely due to habitat scarcity. In the case of the marsh harrier the main habitat requirement is probably for extensive areas of rough vegetation in the vicinity of the reedbed nesting site. From Minsmere for instance, marsh harriers range widely on the adjoining heaths from which rabbits are the major prey. Some wetland birds are taken and marsh harriers are more likely to breed in the larger sites with an ample supply of such prey. Overall, management for a bird of such wide needs is difficult.

The situation with the bittern is rather different. Bitterns are mainly fish-eaters and prefer to hunt in dense cover where they are superbly camouflaged. These conditions are best met in places where reedbeds have taken over seasonal pasture-land which would have had a drainage ditch system. The remnants of such old ditches provide the bittern with access to open water with fish in the depths of cover. Minsmere and Leighton Moss which together hold nearly half of Britain's bitterns have been able to keep them as a result of a programme of clearing out the ditches as they become overgrown and drier. Another site which once held several pairs has lost them at the same time as the disappearance of the remains of the old ditch system within the reeds. The limitation for bitterns in Britain is simply lack of sufficiently wet reedbeds. It is encouraging that management work at Titchwell has attracted this species which can only maintain or increase its numbers because of such help.

The bearded tit is more dependent on reeds than any other bird, both nesting there and feeding on the seeds when insects are scarce in winter. Bearded tits nest near the ground and need an understorey of sedges or litter for support and elevation above the water in wet periods. Much of the food during the breeding season consists of insects dependent on water, so the best feeding places are often at the edge where reeds abut the open water and the birds can collect such things as emerging midges. Another important food may be the larvae of various stem-boring moths which are regarded as pests to a thatch crop and may be controlled by burning in commercial beds. Management can aid the bearded tit by providing a mixture of the wetter feeding places and the drier areas needed for nesting.

The Savi's warbler is a very scarce migrant with a foothold in some of the larger reedbeds. Its requirements are rather similar to those of the bearded tit with a need for safe nesting sites, often in sedge tussocks below the reeds. Cetti's warbler is another rare bird but its numbers are steadily increasing after its colonisation of Britain in the early 1970s. This warbler is unusual in being resident throughout the year. It is also one of the very small number of passerines in Europe with a regularly polygynous breeding system (one male with several females). Cetti's warblers inhabit the patches of damp scrub often found at the edges of reedbeds, though in winter they may make more use of the reeds themselves. There are probably plenty of suitable places for this species to colonise in the next few years and its extraordinary song should soon become a feature of most reedbeds in southern Britain.

Several more warblers arrive just for the summer. Reed warblers are very numerous and build finely woven nests suspended to escape from flooding and ground predators, though they may be badly plagued by cuckoos which parasitise some nests and predate others. Amongst other features, reed warblers much favour the scattered bushes as feeding places. Sedge and grasshopper warblers prefer the drier edges of the reeds, filling the early summer mornings with their two very different songs. Reed buntings are also most numerous in these drier areas though they may fly long distances to feeding places especially when they have young. The caterpillars on alders are much sought after.

In winter, the reeds may provide roosting sites for huge numbers of birds such as

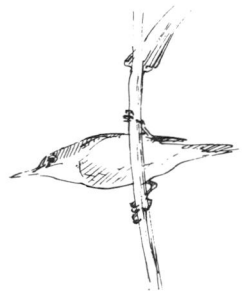

Reed warbler

starlings, pied wagtails, corn and reed buntings. In autumn, migrating yellow wagtails, swallows and sand martins may also be found roosting in great flocks during overnight stops. A remarkable autumn feature is the pre-migratory gathering of fattening sedge warblers, especially on the south coast sites of which Radipole is the most famous. These birds feed on the plum-reed aphid which may plague reeds in numbers like some of the familiar pests in the garden. In a few weeks, a sedge warbler can double its weight on this rich diet and will then take a single non-stop flight to sub-Saharan Africa. Suitable fattening sites are rather few and the aphids are local in abundance, favouring the better reeds in water or on fertile silts.

Several birds use reedbeds more incidentally. They may provide nesting sites and cover for feeding birds more dependent on the open water. So there might be great crested grebes or pochards nesting in fringing reeds or a variety of ducks feeding in their shelter. In winter there may be blue tits cracking open the stems in pursuit of the over-wintering larvae of various gall flies, or wrens hunting the small insects that shelter in the dead reeds.

Taking the birds overall, it is clear that different species have different requirements so a well-managed reedbed on a nature reserve will have a variety of conditions. The open water elements are particularly important for ducks and other water birds as well as providing fish as food for bitterns or insects for bearded tits and other small birds. A well-managed reserve would thus have some reed in deep water with open pools and ditches within these areas. The drier phases of the succession would be controlled but by no means eliminated. Invading trees might have to be thinned but some would be left to provide sources of food and song perches for a variety of birds. There would also be damp areas where a tangle of other plants occurred within the reeds so providing nesting sites for bearded tits or sedge warblers. On the drier margins, carr might adjoin drier scrub or even woodland so Cetti's warblers might be heard singing besides blackcaps.

The greatest difficulty in such a scenario is raising water levels in the short term and then maintaining them in the face of inexorable succession. The reedbeds which survive for the future will need an adequate supply of water and the means of controlling it so that at least some of the areas are kept wet throughout the summer when the need for water is greatest and the supply poorest. A particularly successful example of management has been at Titchwell where a huge earth bank had to be constructed to keep sufficient water in, but bitterns and marsh harriers bred as a result. As shorter term expedients, things can be improved by clearing out pools and ditches within the reeds. A herbicide may have to be used to repel reeds or control their spread. Alternatively, ditches may be mechanically excavated. Apart from the large cost this has the problem of what to do with the spoil. Dumping it alongside will raise the ground too high for good reed growth and thus destroy half the purpose of the exercise. Eventually a way will have to be found actually to remove material from these sites to keep the ground level low enough. I envisage that reedbeds might be rotated, maybe cropping or grazing sections periodically or even excavating them. Perhaps visitors to these reserves could all take away a few bags for their gardens. New beds might be created in areas presently used for summer grazing such as the Ouse Washes. In some places it would only be necessary to prevent grazing to allow the spread of reeds, while elsewhere some embankment may also be required. Such new beds could be started off with pools and ditches which would remain free of reeds for several years. With management, there is no reason why populations of reedbed birds should not be flourishing for all to see in the next century. With luck, we might even get a few new species. Possibilities include spoonbill, purple heron, little bittern, great reed warbler or penduline tit. Without management on a large scale, no such rosy future is in sight.

Opposite: Bearded tit, a species dependent on reedbeds

Lagoons and open water

by Bob Scott

Water, which has always held a fascination for man, is especially attractive to modern man with his steadily increasing leisure time. From the days when the Victorians discovered the pleasures of a holiday by the seaside, man has continually increased his interest in, and pressure on, bodies of open water. The scenic attraction of holidays in the Lake District or Scottish Highlands is largely a result of the extensive lakes and lochs which provide the postcard views. Elsewhere, in sites more readily accessible to the dense populations of southern England, any small lake, reservoir or gravel pit will attract the attention of fisherman, birdwatcher, sailor or water-skier.

The history of water bodies in Britain is one of considerable change; change which has accelerated greatly in recent years. The formation of the different lakes and ponds varies considerably, from the acid upland water area left by the last retreating glaciation to the most recently excavated quarry in a southern river valley.

The largest area of freshwater in the United Kingdom is Lough Neagh in Northern Ireland with an area of a little over 150 square miles, but for its size it is very shallow, no more than 56 feet at its deepest. Differing from virtually all other water areas, Lough Neagh was formed by volcanic action which covered a large area with solidified larva that subsequently subsided, more or less centrally, to form a basin that resulted in the present-day Lough.

By contrast, Loch Ness is one of the deepest freshwater bodies, over 750 feet at its greatest depth and lies in the natural fault in the earth's surface resulting from a movement of the crust that has left a steep-sided, long, deep, yet relatively narrow water area.

Elsewhere in the Scottish Highlands the large number of mountain lochs were formed by great sheets of ice cutting ravines and blocking entrances to leave huge water bodies trapped within the granite as the ice retreated. At the same time, other less mountainous glacial lakes were formed when huge ice blocks slowly melted in vast open plains or river valleys and were surrounded by accumulated debris. Often such features were accompanied by land subsidence and areas such as the Cheshire Meres, now greatly enhanced by mining subsidence, and Loch Leven, Tayside were formed.

Glacial action was also responsible for the lakes in the Welsh mountains and English Lake District, while in contrast, on the east coast the silting up of river mouths or estuaries resulted in coastal lagoons such as Loch of Strathbeg, Grampian where extensive sand dunes now separate the loch from the North Sea following a sand storm in the early 18th century. Further south, in Humberside, Hornsea Mere is now divided from the North Sea by some half mile of land which holds the Hornsea seaside resort. Even further south the fens and meres of East Anglia were separated from the tidal Wash, their outlet to the North Sea, by a mass of deposited silt that resulted in a series of inland water areas on highly fertile ground. Agricultural man converted this soil and the modern Fenlands of East Anglia are now intensive farmland where once lagoons and open water areas existed.

Until the end of the 19th century, lagoons and open water areas in Britain were generally declining. Man was reclaiming and draining at a steady rate; only in the more mountainous areas where farming or development prospects were poor were the water bodies safe. One major exception to this was the Norfolk Broads, where extensive peat-cutting in the early 14th century resulted in the network of interconnected Broads now beloved by modern

Common scoter

leisure-seeking man. Many of these Broads however have become either choked by encroaching vegetation or made lifeless by high pollution levels. Only recently have modern conservation methods started to redress the balance.

Modern industrial man's demands upon the environment have been the saviour of the open water. Since the late 19th century a steadily increasing necessity for water in the densely populated industrial centres has created the need for reservoirs and the damming of rivers from Kent and Somerset in the south to Scotland in the north has more than replaced areas lost through silting and drainage. Some are patently artificial, like the Metropolitan Water Board sites in London, with their concrete banks, while others such as the Severn Trent Water Authority's reservoir at Lake Vyrnwy are flooded river valleys with 'natural' edges.

In addition, man has created fish ponds, ornamental lakes and, as a result of mineral excavations, a series of pits, frequently in river valleys, where their after use ranges widely from all forms of water sports to nature reserves and country parks. Somewhat similar features, but usually shallower, result from subsidence following mining or tunnelling. The activities of the National Coal Board in such widely separated sites as Stodmarsh in the valley of the River Stour, Kent and the various riverside meadows or 'ings' in the valley of the River Aire in Yorkshire, have produced water bodies similar no doubt to the meres that were once cut off from the sea by the silting process.

The growth in water areas is reflected in the population levels of a typical freshwater species, the great crested grebe. Shallow lakes in southern Britain are the favoured habitat, but in the latter part of the 19th century the population was devastated by shooting to collect the fashionable 'grebe fur', and the remnant breeding pairs were confined to the Cheshire meres, Norfolk Broads, and a few large lakes on private estates. When the birds eventually received legal protection at the turn of the century the tremendous growth in the development of reservoirs and gravel pits had begun. The grebes responded to greater protection and increased availability of habitat and in a period of some fifty years the population grew from approximately thirty breeding pairs to over 1,200 pairs with the dramatic increase continuing as each new water body was colonised.

Although the grebe is just one of several species which now exploits and maintains healthy populations on Britain's lagoons and open waters, the threats still exist, although in different forms. Very few shallow lagoons that are suitable for large scale drainage still remain, but small water bodies can still be lost in this way. In cases where the creation of a gravel pit has meant the destruction of valuable agricultural land, the pit can be back-filled with waste and rubble and then reclaimed. Increasingly, planning permission for schemes that will result in areas of open water is only granted after careful consideration of the after use. With care, the numerous demands, often highly incompatible, can be accommodated and the quieter requirements of nature conservation kept separate from the noisier, more intensely active pastimes, such as power boats and water-skiers.

Unfortunately, many of the threats now facing waterbirds are not readily visible. The period of wide use of various agricultural toxic chemicals of the organochlorine group in the 1950s and 1960s posed a threat to many species, particularly fish-eaters at the end of the food chain. Although the position has certainly improved following various legal and voluntary bans on chemicals, the pollution of water courses and the various lakes associated with them still continues, with high concentrations of various fertilisers seriously affecting plant growth and consequently the animal life in the water. Ineffectively treated sewage and industrial effluent can still raise pollutant levels to create virtually lifeless water areas, and the excessive human use of the Norfolk Broads has resulted in some of the most polluted water in Britain. To safeguard the wildlife of one area of the Broads, Strumpshaw Fen (a site of a one-time broad, but now a silted reedbed), it has been necessary to isolate the area from

Little grebe

the surrounding polluted water by building embankments to trap unpolluted water within, before reopening, by digging out, the old broad system.

Popular leisure activities, too, create their own pollution and disturbance problems. Recent studies have shown that considerable quantities of lead, both as pellets from shotgun cartridges and split-shot from fishing weights, are swallowed by wildfowl species when obtaining grit from the mud or margins of the water. The result is that lead poisoning is now considered a major conservation problem in wetlands. Clearly it is essential within any area of water bodies, be it reservoirs, gravel pits or natural lakes, that part is available as a safe undisturbed refuge to which birds can retreat when pressures become too high at other sites, and from which they can spread to colonise or feed at times of least disturbance. An excellent example of such a principle are the various gravel pits in the Dungeness area, Kent, where in addition to an established reserve, there are other water areas available for various water sports, while on other sites shooting or fishing are allowed. At weekends the majority of the birds are to be found in the reserve areas, while during the week they are more widely spread over the total area.

The value of a water area to birds will vary from site to site, depending on the quality of the water and its richness in plant and animal life. Most upland water bodies, surrounded by granite and peat with steep rocky shores, are acidic and relatively lifeless. Ironically, this is the case with many of our 'natural' areas of open water which as a result hold very few birds indeed. The visiting birdwatcher will find many of these northern lakes and lochs a very poor place in the summer months, with a meagre scattering of breeding wildfowl, such as goosander and goldeneye and small numbers of divers and grebes. Generally the waters are too deep and cold, but associated species will be present with grey wagtails and common sandpipers on the banks, while the ospreys of the Scottish Highlands use them as a food source where large fish surface in the shallower waters. The lack of food means that wintering populations must seek a feeding site elsewhere, although the open water may provide a secure roosting or moulting ground if food is close at hand.

Water areas with an underlying basic soil, such as limestone or chalk, are the most fertile and ornithologically the most productive. A rich aquatic flora and associated fauna, from the smallest larvae to the largest fish, will provide a food source for a range of species from the little grebe to the grey heron. The actual species at any one site will depend upon its structure. Key factors such as water depth, presence of islands, surrounding vegetation, gradation of the banking and variation of water levels will all play their part in the behaviour patterns of the various bird species at different sites. Fringe or overhanging vegetation will allow nesting by coots and grebes; dense bank vegetation will provide sites for wildfowl, while islands provide safe places for nesting colonies of gulls or such obvious nests as the feral population of Canada and greylag geese. Surrounding trees with holes will house nesting mandarin and goldeneye, both relatively restricted species in the lakes of Berkshire and the lochs of the Highlands respectively.

The islands of Lough Erne, Co. Fermanagh, provide nesting sites for red-breasted mergansers and virtually the entire breeding population of British common scoters, while the gravel pits and their islands in south-east England have seen a tremendous growth in nesting tufted duck, to the extent that on a considerable number of open water sites they now outnumber the more familiar mallard.

Once incubation has commenced among wildfowl, many drakes, which take no further part in the breeding cycle, will congregate on open areas to commence their moult, the annual renewal of feathers which water birds undertake as quickly as possible by shedding all their flight feathers at the same time and enduring a period of flightlessness. This requires a secure feeding and roosting water, and many sites now attract a regular con-gregation during July and August, but of course a food supply must be available to take

Opposite: Great crested grebe must have open water to thrive

them through this period. As the autumn progresses the importance of a site will change as it becomes the temporary home to large numbers of migrant waterbirds. In the shallow areas, waders from the high Arctic breeding grounds, spotted redshanks and green sandpipers, move south towards the African wintering sites. In the northern sites the increasingly inhospitable open waters are being deserted as the birds leave for a more maritime life during the winter months; but in the south garganey leave the ditches and marshes where they have nested and congregate, often with the closely related teal, on the more open sites prior to their southward departure for the winter. Amongst the British wildfowl only the garganey is a summer visitor. The majority are winter visitors, leaving northern and eastern European nesting grounds for the milder, more maritime climate of Britain's waters. As a result, at the height of the winter, there are huge numbers of wildfowl in Britain. Many wildfowl species winter here in internationally important numbers with a significant proportion of the north-west European population. The open waters provide a permanent winter home for many of the duck, particularly the diving species such as pochard and tufted duck, between forty and fifty thousand of each at their peak. The geese, wild swans, and grazing duck such as wigeon, will use the sites for roosting and drinking, flighting each dawn and dusk to their feeding grounds on nearby saltmarshes or grazing meadows, although increasingly use is being made of arable crops.

Coastal sites, water bodies separated from the sea by just a narrow strip of land, have an additional value during the mid-winter period. Severe gales and storms at sea will drive sea fowl, such as red-breasted merganser, scoters, eider, divers and grebes close inshore to seek shelter on such sites. Similarly, when inland waters freeze during extreme cold, the coastal sites frequently remain open and thus provide a site for the many water birds which move towards the coast at these times. Severe winters with prolonged freezing conditions will have a marked effect on the population of water birds. Many are forced to undertake weather migrations which take them further south and west in search of unfrozen waters. There is a general movement towards the coast where estuaries and bays will hold temporary security for a species normally associated with fresh water. Flocks of coots will appear on the sea and the great crested grebe population becomes even more marine. It is the fringe species of the open waters, the kingfishers, snipe and herons that are particularly likely to be the first to suffer actual mortality, the direct result of being unable to feed.

Of all water bodies, it is the shallow freshwater lagoons that are the most dynamic and have suffered the greatest loss. Not only do the fertile soils in such sites allow a rapid plant growth and encroachment that turns lagoons into fen or reedswamp, and subsequently willow scrub and woodland as the site dries out, but such sites are ideal for drainage and conversion into highly productive farmland. Because these shallow waters change so rapidly there are few, if any, well established sites, but subsidences following mining activities create replacements, although without active management these new sites will also be lost.

Perhaps the best known, ornithologically, of all shallow water lagoons, is the Minsmere 'scrape' in Suffolk, where not only was the site created by extensive management work, but a continuing work programme is necessary to maintain the area. On such a site dense populations of birds breed, feed, roost, winter and summer, exploiting the rich food supplies held in the mud and water, and nesting on the small islands which gently shelve above the surface. Water level is critical and a series of sluices controls the amount of fresh water let on to or removed from the site. Levels have to be constantly monitored and checked for flash flooding which could seriously damage an entire season's breeding potential.

These 'ideal' conditions produce a rich vegetation which if allowed to develop unchecked will create the next stage in the natural succession and the open water will be lost. 'Safe'

Goldeneye   chemicals on reed growth, make the maintenance of such large areas a possibility, but occasionally it is necessary to use heavy machinery to 're-scrape' the surface and remove the accumulating silt and humus that threatens to reclaim the site. Alternatively it may be possible to rotovate the site to break down the developing vegetation and this requires access to the site with tractor and machinery.

Because the maintenance of such sites is so delicately balanced, virtually all such localities that are likely to remain are safeguarded as nature reserves. Sites such as Havergate Island in Suffolk; Cley and Titchwell, Norfolk; Blacktoft in Humberside; and Leighton Moss in Lancashire. In all cases an important management factor is the ability to control the water level and by this means or by subsidiary work to control any developing vegetation. Each site has its own unique management problems. At Titchwell it is necessary to keep at bay the North Sea and large-scale banking works have been necessary while at Blacktoft the rather high land beside the Rivers Ouse and Trent can only be flooded at times of spring tide and a system of embankments and sluices has been constructed to make this possible.

The luxury of creating an open water area for bird life from the very beginning is a rare event, but our experience has shown that various features are most important if the widest possible range of species is to be supported. Diversity is the key factor with variable water depths and irregular water edges that shelve gently from dry land to deep water. The feeding margins are most important and shelving banks allow for drought years when the water level may drop or very wet seasons when levels may rise. An indented water line with numerous bays and peninsulas allows many extra bird territories because many species really prefer not to see their neighbours and islands provide secure nesting and roosting sites safe from foxes, stoats and other ground predators.

The very nature of lagoons and open water areas is such that it is possible to allow people to view the many species that are attracted to such a 'honey-pot'. Covered access and carefully sited observation hides enable visitors to watch the roosting waders at Blacktoft, when they are forced to leave the mud of the Humber by the steadily rising tide; to see the summering flock of little gulls at Hornsea Mere, rare visitors to Britain that have made this site a regular summering locality; to observe the huge winter concentrations of wild geese and swans that visit Loch of Strathbeg, Loch of Kinnordy and Loch Leven each winter.

Man's ever increasing need for water will ensure that water areas remain, reserves will ensure that they remain in a condition suitable for the wealth of wildlife that inhabits and is dependent upon them.

Wigeon grazing

Flood meadows

by John Day

On its way to the sea, the river leaves the urgency of the hills and moves in a more leisurely fashion, swaying through winding channels across the flat hinterlands. There, after the rains, the swollen waters slowly overtop the banks and quietly spread across the flat meadows, depositing their rich silts and invigorating the herb-rich natural turf. For centuries man has lived with this natural rhythm, grazing his herds and cutting hay amongst the rich flush of summer grass and leaving the wet, winter swards to the fishermen, wildfowlers, eelcatchers, and, of course, the birds. In some places the natural waterways were harnessed and, using sophisticated sluice systems and channels, the meadows could be flooded artificially after the first hay cut or early bite. Later, the rejuvenated fields were drained, enabling a second crop to be gathered. These were the managed water meadows, now largely gone, the artistry of their cycles forgotten.

Over the years, man has constantly sought to improve on this natural system, rivers have been canalised, their banks raised and the meadows ditched and pumped. By maintaining lower, and constant, water tables, it was possible to plough up the old turf with its rich mixture of water-loving herbs and grasses, and plant the improved ryegrass mixtures, without fear of winter floods.

Improved drainage with field drains supplementing the ditches, allowed crops to be grown over thousands of acres. With the advent of modern electric pumps in the 1930s and 1940s this process was speeded up. Corn, barley and potatoes flourished in the reclaimed meadowland and the birds, their numbers sadly reduced by the effect of earlier drainage and improvement, were finally forced to leave for good. But in a few, a very few places, this process has not reached finality, and the traditional farming patterns are still followed. West Sedgemoor is such a place.

At the beginning of the 12th century much of that part of Somerset known as the Somerset Levels, which includes West Sedgemoor, was owned by the Bishopric of Bath and Wells, and the Abbot of Glastonbury. For over 200 years successive Bishops and successive Abbots disputed the ownership of the Levels; pursuing their quarrel with a disregard for law and order that would have done credit to a range war in the old American Mid-West. Cattle were rustled, stock slaughtered, houses and other buildings burnt to the ground, and, more importantly for the Levels, sluices, ditches and other drainage works were broken up and destroyed. No serious attempts to drain a major part of the Levels were made until Sir Cornelius Vermuyden, a Dutchman, arrived on the scene in 1655. He had already been instrumental in partly draining the Cambridgeshire fens (a job he was to finish after the Civil Wars), and he was also to be responsible for further major drainage works in Lincolnshire and Yorkshire. In Somerset though, a lack of funds, and the opposition of the local people, many of whom had common rights of grazing out on the Levels, successfully deflected this threat.

Opposite: Winter flooding turns the Ouse Washes into a major wildfowl refuge

By the end of the 1700s the influence of the commoners was declining, the more prosperous farmers owned or rented their own farms, and common rights were largely restricted to the labouring classes. A campaign to discredit these rights by those landowners who had most to gain, preceded the extensive enclosures and improvement of open land which took place throughout the country at this time, and many parts of the Levels were drained.

West Sedgemoor was one of the last areas to be affected, but in 1816 a ditch system was installed which marginally reduced the depth and frequency of summer floods, but did little to stop winter inundations or the flash flooding in the summer following heavy rainfall in the surrounding hills. These ditches still form the backbone of the drainage system today, 165 years later, although by themselves, they were not very effective.

Over huge areas of grazing marsh, hay fields and wet meadows the installation of diesel, and later, electric pumps, sounded the death knell for their rich plant, animal and bird communities. At West Sedgemoor, a diesel powered pump was installed in 1944, but fortunately the need to pump water into the tidal Parrett river, which itself cannot cope with extra water when it is in spate and the tides are high, meant that winter flooding still occurred regularly and occasionally in spring and summer too; although inevitably the area became drier than formerly.

Although the flooding regime of another famous wetland, the Ouse Washes in Cambridgeshire, is artificial, this is another site where the difficulties of disposing of floodwater through sluices into tidal river channels have been a factor in preventing improvements. The Cambridgeshire fens covered an estimated 1,300 square miles in 1650, but by 1976 this was reduced to a remnant of only 10 square miles of undrained land, much of it on the Ouse Washes. By 1600 the problem of disposing quickly of the floodwater had long been recognised; the winding channels of the Great Ouse and the Nene rivers moved sluggishly through the flat lands of East Anglia covering a considerable distance, but only slowly falling towards the sea. Vermuyden went a long way towards solving this by digging the Old Bedford river. This channel, some 70 feet wide and 21 miles long, reduced the length of the Great Ouse by some 20 miles by cutting across a great arc in the river. Although summer flooding was greatly reduced, regular winter floods still occurred. After the Civil Wars in 1651 he cut a second channel, parallel to the first but some half mile distant. The Banks on each side of these two rivers contained the washlands where to quote Vermuyden, "the water in time of extremity may goe in a large roome to keep it from rising too high". This is now one of our most important wetlands and with some 1,750 acres under RSPB control; and with other areas owned by the Cambridgeshire and Isle of Ely Naturalists' Trust, and the Wildfowl Trust, its future is now secure. Huge numbers of duck and wild swans come here in winter making this a site of international importance. It has also been designated as a Ramsar site by HM Government which means that major changes can only be made if there is an over-riding national interest, and in such circumstances alternative wetland must be provided.

For many people the true character of an old wet grassland site like this is most evident in the spring, when the startling green washlands have emerged from their winter covering of floodwater and stretch like an emerald sword, cutting through the monotonous brown fens, where the spring wheat is just beginning to cover the dark soils in a thin, blue-green film. The winter wildfowl have gone. Huge flocks of noisy, self-confident wigeon, the graceful pintail and swift flights of teal have left. Gone too are the wild swans — whoopers and Bewick's — which until a few weeks ago could be seen in unhurried family groups, breasting the brown floodwaters or flighting over the wash banks. Nearly seven months will pass before they return from their breeding grounds in the northern wastes. The resident ducks are left behind; mallard and shoveler, gadwall, teal and tufted duck, now in pairs along the ditches or by the receding flashes of water.

Some birds are already making their nests in the long grass tussocks, and will soon be launching their ducklings on the quiet waters of the rivers and dykes. The air is full of sound. Larks are singing, high above the bank, their song interrupted by the drumming of a snipe, as the bird knifes through the sky with a sound like tearing cloth. Below, the redshank call from the gatepost tops and the nuptial 'wicka-wicka' of black-tailed godwits

Marsh marigold

carries across the river. Later in the summer these washfields will be grazed by cattle or, later still, cut for hay. Wader chicks will crouch in the shadow of the sedge tussocks left by the slow-moving bullocks, while anxious parents drive off the sharp-eyed crow, as it too looks for food for its own chicks in the nest back in the riverside willow.

The ditches and dykes are alive with colour — water forget-me-not, yellow flag, comfrey and loosestrife — a bewildering mixture of blues and yellows, whites and purples, lining the watersides. Down in the clear depths, pondweeds and hornworts reach upwards towards the platelike leaves of fringed water lily, or the water-piercing spears of arrowhead. The plants are food and shelter to a myriad of tiny animals which give life to the ducklings, in their turn prey to the lurking jack pike. This habitat, rich in colourful wildlife and once such a common sight, is now restricted to a few remnants. You can almost count them on your fingers. Pevensey Levels and Amberley Wild Brooks in Sussex, the meadows of the Hampshire Avon and the 'Ings' of the River Derwent in Yorkshire, The Nene and the Ouse Washes in Cambridgeshire and West Sedgemoor in Somerset.

Their survival has largely been due to the physical difficulties of drainage; tidal rivers, deep treacherous peats, sudden floods, and the high cost of drainage, all of which have, over the centuries persuaded the engineer and agricultural improver to look elsewhere. Sadly, there is now nowhere else to look except perhaps tidal saltings and mudflats where huge profits can be made by large reclamation and drainage schemes. For many years we have all been paying as tax and ratepayers to destroy our own heritage. Grants paid by the Ministry of Agriculture for field drainage increased by 45 per cent between 1975 and 1979 to over £17 million. Water authorities up and down the country are preparing comprehensive schemes for the drainage of the last vestiges of wetland in their regions. In twenty years' time, apart from those saved as reserves, all our wet meadows will probably be gone.

At Amberley Wild Brooks, a comprehensive drainage scheme proposed by the water authority was, for the first time in Britain, subjected to the scrutiny of a public enquiry. The 700 acres of the Wild Brooks constitute the largest and most important wetland left in West Sussex, a county where only two per cent of the land surface is now wet meadowland.

The scheme was to cost £339,000 of which some 90 per cent was to be paid out of the public purse. A careful analysis of the financial aspects of the scheme found that for every £1 spent the benefit would be 95 pence; the Inspector concluded, and the Minister confirmed, that the scheme should be abandoned. Unfortunately though, it is not only the major schemes that threaten the integrity of such sites.

At West Sedgemoor, the turf has not been underdrained or ploughed in 700 years. The spring carpet of flowers has an unsurpassable beauty; fields full of early flowering yellow kingcups give way to the whites and browns of meadow rue and sedge intermixed with the delicate pinks of the scarce green winged and southern marsh orchids and the bolder purples of meadow thistle. Waders breed in large numbers, snipe, redshank, the black-tailed godwit, and curlew, their beautiful song reminiscent of the wild open moors of the north. Herons from the nearby heronry stand motionless in the ditches waiting for unwary eels or minnows, and the mewing of buzzards is a reminder of the West Country setting for this most attractive of wetlands.

But nearly a third of the moor has now been underdrained and grows carrots and potatoes, or modern grass leys; whilst new schemes to underdrain and pump dry small blocks of pasture are constantly coming forward. In 1979 the Minister rejected the argument for retaining the established low cost farming system over 50 acres and grant-aided a drainage scheme which destroyed its ecological interest.

The recommendation of the Nature Conservancy Council, that this, the richest wetland in south-west England, should not be destroyed piecemeal in this way, was ignored. On the brighter side, in 1977 a comprehensive scheme, proposed by the water authority, for

Bewick's swan

improving the drainage of the whole site, was thrown out by the farmers on the moor, partly because those around the drier edges, who would have derived little benefit, outnumbered the 'improvers' in the wet central areas.

Still flooded in most winters, West Sedgemoor attracts many duck together with huge flocks of waders, up to 15,000 lapwing, 10,000 dunlin and 500 golden plover as well as passage waders like whimbrel and green sandpipers and a small flock of wintering Bewick's swans. But to see wildfowl in really impressive numbers one must go back to the Ouse Washes where between 30,000 and 40,000 wigeon, up to 7,000 mallard and teal with lesser numbers of pintail, shoveler, gadwall, tufted duck and pochard, coupled with over 2,000 Bewick's swans, make up one of the largest and most exciting assemblages of wildfowl to be seen anywhere in the United Kingdom.

Of course wetlands can be created, where large numbers of birds can be attracted to new areas. In Kent, on the island of Sheppey, some 4,000 acres of grassland constitute the largest block of unimproved rough grazings left in the county. Dry and flat, protected from the sea by clay banks, and grazed by thousands of sheep, such an area may at first sight look unprepossessing. On closer acquaintance, however, it becomes apparent that much of this area has been reclaimed from the sea during the last few hundred years. The meandering tidal creeks that once let the tides silently rise and fall over the mudflats and saltings have now become water-filled fleets lined with sea club rush and reed. A few duck breed around these — mallard, tufted, pochard and an occasional pair of garganey — whilst, settled sparsely over the marsh, lapwing and redshank pairs nest in the odd tussocks of grass left by the close grazing flocks of sheep.

Here, in 1975, the Society established a reserve of 650 acres, intent on creating a new stopping-off and wintering wetland site for the thousands of wildfowl which pass through the Medway and Swale in the winter. The construction of dams, sluices, and new ditch systems captured and held the rainwater that fell on the area, and this was supplemented by the run-off from some 2,000 acres of adjoining marsh. Pumped into holding areas or onto the flood during each winter, this water would otherwise run out through sluices into the sea.

This first experimental project has been wildly successful. Elmley has become a feeding, roosting and sanctuary area for many of the duck from the two estuaries. Wigeon, teal, mallard and pintail, shelduck from the nearby mudflats as well as dunlin, curlew, whimbrel and redshank all use the flood in good numbers throughout the winter. Particularly spectacular are the autumn flocks of teal and shoveler, up to 10,000 of each species, and recently the Sheppey flock of white-fronted geese has also been attracted by the shallow water and freedom from disturbance.

Perhaps in some ways more exciting, though, are the breeding birds, since it is always more difficult to satisfy the fastidious requirements of breeding ducks or waders than those of the throngs of greedy wildfowl spending the winter away from their own breeding sites in the far north. Snipe, lapwing, and possibly the densest population of breeding redshank in southern Britain, together with gadwall, teal, shoveler, tufted duck, mallard and a nationally important population of breeding pochard have been the reward.

Despite this success, it is second best; the rich dyke flora, the meadows ablaze with flowers, the array of colourful invertebrates in the waters of the ditches and shallow pools that are a feature of West Sedgemoor simply do not occur at Elmley.

Certainly there are flowers, among them the seaside crowfoot, adapted to growing in the slightly saline waters of the borrow dykes, or the knotted hedge parsley and grass vetchling, interesting features in an otherwise rather restricted meadow flora. The aquatic insects too are limited to rather few common species, although they occur in large numbers. But the paucity of species means that food chains are short and simple: the failure of one of the few common invertebrate prey species could leave breeding birds with no alternatives to fall

Opposite: Black-tailed godwit, a rare breeding bird of flood meadows

back on for food. This means that richness and variety have to be replaced by careful and precise management, coupled with constant monitoring to ensure early warning of any problems in this simple ecosystem.

Management is a vital component of all these wetland reserves. Take ditch systems for instance. Work by the Society's staff on the Ouse Washes has established that 58 per cent of the aquatic plant species growing in the ditches become less frequent as the ditch gets older, and a similar picture emerges from work done on aquatic invertebrates in the dykes at Strumpshaw in Norfolk. To maintain the richness and variety of plants and insects in the ditch systems, they must be cleared out regularly every five to seven years. With over 35 miles of ditches on our land holding on the Ouse Washes alone, this is a costly but essential task.

Ditches not only provide safe and productive nursery areas for the many broods of ducklings, they are also an essential factor in providing drinking water and wet fences for the hundreds of cattle which graze these wet meadow systems. Grazing cattle remove the dense vegetation alongside the ditches, delaying the inevitable spread of coarse vegetation such as great water grass and sweet reed grass but more importantly creating the right sward structure for breeding waders and duck.

Waders need thick tussocks of grass in which to nest and lay their eggs, but once the chicks have hatched, they require short grass to feed and move about in. This structure can be achieved by grazing with cattle which are kept at the right densities on each field the previous summer. Small wader chicks covered in a thin layer of down soon get soaked and chilled in long rank vegetation, but sufficient long grass is essential nearby in which they can hide when crows or other predators are about. Ducks, too, need a mosaic of tussock and short grass for much the same reasons, and research on the Ouse Washes shows that the nesting requirements of different species are closely linked to the grazing regime in the previous year. Mallard and shoveler prefer lightly to moderately grazed ground; whereas pintail, a duck which nests in some years in good numbers on the Washes, prefer heavily grazed or hayed fields.

Heavy grazing is also necessary to establish 'lawns' of short grass on which wigeon will graze in large numbers in the winter, and this is often achieved by a late cutting of cattle grazed sward, or by autumn after-grazing with sheep.

All this implies the necessity for grazing or haying on all these wet meadow reserves, and with some 5,000 acres let for the summer every year the RSPB must be one of the biggest grass farmers in the country, particularly since over a large part of this area our wardens manage the cattle as well!

Of equal importance is the management of the water regimes on the meadows themselves. In early spring large areas of shallow water are necessary to attract and hold wintering and passage duck and waders. Later in the summer when the birds are breeding but these shallow flashes are drying out ready for the summer grazing, permanent pools are needed for the adult birds to feed, bathe and preen and, later, bring their young to feed.

Management of such sites, however, is a skilled and expensive undertaking. At our broadland reserve at Strumpshaw Fen where we lease some 110 acres of wet meadow along with the reedbeds, ditch and sward management is doubly important. With only two of the forty-two broads now containing a full complement of aquatic plants, due to pollution and intensive use of the broadland river systems, the richness of the dyke flora is of particular importance. This poses yet another problem common to many wetlands, the threat of polluted water. Close monitoring of water quality and the isolation of the sweet water ditches from the turbid and over-enriched river water is essential. Otherwise the nitrates and phosphates from agricultural run-off or the sewage outfalls further upstream result in massive algal 'blooms'. These simple plants multiply until the waterways are choked,

Yellow iris

cutting out the light and, when they decay, the resulting bacterial attack depletes the water of oxygen. First the fish and then the aquatic invertebrates die or leave and the delicate plant life, struggling for light and deprived of the precise balance of nutrients, minerals and dissolved gases which they need, are eliminated.

Sometimes this cycle is short-lived and seasonal; nutrients leached out of cereal crops during heavy rains in the spring for example. Where this can happen, and a normally pure water supply can become polluted for a short time, by-pass sluices and ditches need to be designed and constructed to divert the flow harmlessly past the reserve.

Alongside the water meadows at Strumpshaw are the alder woods which are such a feature of the broadland scene. Management here borrows from the practices of woodland management elsewhere, with the creation of woodland rides, clearing of ditches and ponds, and a programme of coppicing.

Elsewhere, on the Washes and in Somerset, their place is taken by willow 'holts'; areas of planted osier willow, never growing higher than about fifteen feet, but able to reach this height in only three seasons, starting from shoots sprouting on the side of the cut stumps. These osier beds are the breeding places of ducks like mallard, shoveler and gadwall, together with sedge and reed warblers, the latter stringing their tiny nest by 'handles' from the thin willow stems, so like the more familiar reedstems in which they commonly nest. In Somerset these osiers are managed commercially to produce the raw material for basket making but on our reserves, management is aimed at producing a constant crop of new stems, to provide food and nesting cover for the birds.

The establishment of these wetland reserves is not easy. Lowland meadowland, with its potential for reclamation, is a valuable commodity. With multiple ownership (over 150 different owners on the Ouse Washes and nearly ninety on West Sedgemoor when the Society started to buy land), it is expensive both in money and time to establish a viable block of land as a reserve. Such an area needs to be large enough to contain its own water regime, regardless of what is happening on adjoining land, and also of sufficient size to allow the birds to breed, or flocks of waterfowl to feed and rest in the winter, free from human disturbance. Fishermen, wildfowlers, birdwatchers as well as agricultural operations, can all cause unease to the nervous flocks of teal, mallard and shoveler, or the watchful wigeon and pintail. Birdwatching hides with concealed approaches like those on the floodbanks overlooking the washes or in the wood at Strumpshaw not only conceal the watchers, but provide comfortable vantage points from which to see the wildfowl behaving naturally on their wintering grounds. The provision of sanctuary areas where no human activities are allowed during critical times will also help to engender confidence in the birds, which will return year after year, to the same safe areas.

From time to time new threats arise. Recently concern has increased at the number of deaths caused to both ducks and swans by lead poisoning. The birds pick up fishermen's weights or spent lead from shotgun users as they grub about for food, and this is ground down in the birds' gizzard before being absorbed into the system, causing partial paralysis and death. The ingestion of even a single lead pellet can be enough to cause death in up to 70 per cent of mallard.

Research, constant monitoring of water quality, the careful management of grazing and water regimes and control of disturbance, all play their part in the maintenance of these wetland reserves. But more important than all these is their establishment in the first instance, preferably by land purchase; and for the few remaining areas, time is running out. At Pevensey drainage and improvement is far advanced, and nearby at Amberley, small pumping schemes are starting to achieve piecemeal what the water authority failed to do in a single step. On the Derwent Ings two internal drainage boards are considering plans for wholesale drainage and on the Nene Washes, the balance is tilting towards agricultural

Teal

Breeding waders of flood meadows include lapwing (this page) and snipe (opposite) for which flood meadows on nature reserves are becoming increasingly important.

improvement as more and more farmers move away from traditional grazings and plough their wash fields. The drainage and improvement of these areas would destroy the scientifically interesting and important flower rich meadows, and wetland bird communities, and transform the colourful dykes into unsightly noisesome gutters.

But also lost would be the chance to experience the sense of wonder and serenity such places can give.

Lowland deciduous woodland

by Michael Walter

The eerie quietness in the frosty stillness of a winter's wood; the exuberance of spring when woodland is decked in blue, white and yellow flowers and the morning air is brimming with birdsong; the mellower, sultry charms of a walk in the cool sanctuary of summer woodland; or, most poignant of all, the yellowing trees in autumn, leaves tumbling out of the sky. Such sensations must be so familiar to millions of people as to scarcely need description; yet, because it is such a commonplace, the local wood is too often taken for granted, and we do not stop to think whether our grandchildren will be able to show their children the same bluebell dell or the hideaway in the hollow bole of the massive beech.

When Britain's ice cover melted away after the last glaciation some 10,000 years ago, a gaunt, treeless landscape was exposed. Lowland Britain, which includes most of England apart from the Pennines, escaped the worst ravages, but even those favoured southern counties which were never covered with ice were too cold to support tree growth. So our present lowland woods are relatively young. The natural lifespan of an oak is three or four hundred years, so the woodlands' interdependent communities of birds and insects, plants and mammals, have evolved in the course of a mere 25 or so oak generations.

As the climate gradually improved, the harsh landscape was soon softened by vegetation and it was not long before the first trees, pines and birches, re-established themselves. No remnant of those early pine woods remains in the lowland region, so this account will be confined to deciduous woodland. As the climate continued to change, now warmer, now wetter, the pioneer birches and pines were replaced by other species, and there is no reason to suppose that woodland is not still subtly adapting to long-term meteorological trends. It has been suggested that the natural tree cover in Britain is oakwood, but this is probably an over-simplification and it is more likely that, prior to man's intervention, the woods were a mosaic of different species. Even today, it is obvious to a casual observer that all woods are not the same: it may be that one wood is a haze of bluebells when another shimmers with wood anemones: Wellington boots may be essential all year round in one wood, yet in a nearby copse it may be possible to walk dry-shod in most months: or there may be a dramatic difference in the species composition of the woodland trees.

Although the mixture of trees in a wood can be very varied, it is often possible to pick out different types of woodland. For example, on low-lying, waterlogged soil, alder and willow will tend to predominate, and in the days before drainage work was undertaken this sort of woodland would have been much more extensive. Here woodcock can probe deeply for worms, mallard and moorhen nest, and the soft wood of mouldering alder trees provides an ideal site in which the willow tit can excavate a nest-hole. Enriched with minerals washed in by floods or springs, the soil supports a lush growth of plants; hazel, guelder rose and other shrubs flourish here, providing plenty of cover for species like blackcap, wren, dunnock and nightingale; whilst above, in the tree canopy, siskin, redpoll and goldfinch feed on the seeds trapped in the little cone-like alder fruits.

On nearby, slightly higher ground the soil is better drained, but still enriched by occasional floods. Here you may find ashwoods, beneath whose light shade hazel and other

Lesser spotted woodpecker

shrubs can thrive, providing habitat for many woodland birds. Ash seeds are taken by bullfinches and hawfinches.

On infertile or dry soils few trees do really well and woods are likely to be dominated by birch, beech or oak. The heavy shade of beech, which is usually the principal tree on chalk downs, tends to suppress plant growth and consequently the variety of birds, but the crop of beech mast is a favourite with great tits and winter-visiting bramblings. If the soil is very infertile the woodland may have an open, heathy character, and on such ground birch is often the only coloniser, though scattered oaks may later grow up in the birches' shelter. These woods have some of the characteristics of the upland woods, so it is not surprising to find that species such as redstart, wood warbler and tree pipit occur in the oakwoods growing on poor soil at Church Wood, Blean. Birches produce vast quantities of tiny seeds, and these are relished by redpolls; blue tits revel in their acrobatic prowess, swinging upside down from the delicate twigs in order to reach insects lurking in the catkins or buds — whilst their heavier cousins, the great tits, must content themselves with a less athletic search amongst sturdier branches or else on the ground, attacking nuts with their stout bills.

On soils ranging from damp clay to fertile loam other trees may be dominant in different woods — elm in parts of Northward Hill, aspen at Wolves Wood, and hornbeam at Fore Wood, for example. Hornbeam is often found covering large areas of southern woodland to the exclusion of other trees, and its very dense shade excludes most other vegetation, giving such woods a resemblance to the clean-floored beech woods. Its small, hard seeds are a particular favourite with hawfinches and greenfinches.

This very general account of some of the trees to be found in lowland woods shows that certain birds tend to be associated with particular trees, but it has already been seen that presence or absence of a good shrub layer can be crucial in determining whether or not some birds will occur in a wood. And, in fact, it is the general structure of a wood rather than its component tree species which determines what species will be present. Old trees are important to many hole-nesting birds, but trees are usually felled before they have developed natural holes, so species such as tits and nuthatches may be fairly scarce even though there is an abundance of food. A wood with an uninterrupted tree canopy will support a less interesting range of birds than one which is broken up by clearings or glades where dense undergrowth can become established, enabling species such as garden warblers and white-throats to breed. The whitethroat barely qualifies for inclusion in the category of woodland species, being very much a bird of young scrub; it must have been quite rare when lowland Britain was covered in woods, but today's landscape with hedges, copses and tangled margins of countless small woods, provides plenty of scope for colonisation by this warbler. However, this pattern of fragmented woodland is not suitable for some larger species such as honey buzzard and goshawk, birds which must have been far commoner in the ancient, extensive woods. Another factor which should not be forgotten is geographical location: nightingales will not be heard in apparently ideal woodland habitat in the Midlands, for they are at the northern edge of their breeding range in Southern England; and we will listen in vain for the stentorian drilling of woodpeckers in Ireland.

A wood is a private, self-contained world. On entering one you are enfolded by its trees, their foliage filtering out the tiresome noise of human activity. On a windy day the wood will seem a sheltered haven; during drought there will still be damp places; in hot weather it will be deliciously cool in the heavy shade; and in the depths of winter frosts are less likely to penetrate. The wood's climate is more equable than in the exposed fields and marshes, and birds are not slow to appreciate the advantage this confers; when the open ground is baked hard in summer or frozen solid in winter, birds like woodcock, redwing and blackbird will be drawn to the woods.

Woodcock

This page: Woodland at Northward Hill Opposite: Nightingale, a bird for whom woodland reserves are specially managed.

Relatively few birds spend their entire lives within the wood's confines: among these might be listed treecreeper, lesser spotted woodpecker and tawny owl. Many species, such as tits, robins and great spotted woodpeckers, often spend part of the winter foraging further afield in hedgerows and gardens. The reason for this ebb and flow of birds is bound up with the availability of food: insect breeding ceases in the winter months, so predation by birds gradually depletes the stock of food, whereas the advent of warmer spring weather initiates a rapid increase in insect numbers, the most conspicuous manifestation of which is the abundance of defoliating caterpillars in the trees in late May and June. At this time seed-eating species abandon their specialised diet in favour of the easy pickings, which are fed to their nestlings. It is this seasonal abundance of food that enables woods to support not only the resident birds but also the summer visitors such as warblers, spotted flycatchers and cuckoos. During this period of plenty some birds like house sparrows and crows, which are not normally associated with woodland, may venture in to claim their share of the spoils. All these species feed in woods to a certain extent but herons and rooks are exceptional, nesting in woods but feeding exclusively in open land.

To appreciate how woods came to assume their present form it is necessary to know something about man's influence on them in the past 5,000 years or more. Ever since he returned to these islands after the last glaciation he has been modifying the woodland cover, initially by creating small clearings in which to practise his primitive farming, latterly by managing the remaining woodland as a source of material for multifarious domestic, agricultural and industrial requirements. Even by Saxon times so much woodland had been destroyed that some parishes were short of wood and it may have been then that man began to conserve this precious resource. Early woodcutters clearing the woods with their brittle flint axes must have noticed that the cut stumps sent up a fresh crop of shoots, or coppice. In their competition for light the shoots grow up quickly into thin poles which, after as little as ten years' growth, are sturdy enough to be put to a variety of uses. Medieval woodmen could crop the trees' coppice growth indefinitely, so there was no need to replant, and the only extra work involved some form of fencing or ditching to safeguard the young, palatable shoots from the attentions of deer or livestock.

Most lowland woods have been managed as coppice for hundreds of years, though a scattering of oak trees were often retained for felling at longer intervals to satisfy the demand for the larger timber needed in buildings and boats. These coppices, cut fairly regularly, were therefore in a permanently young state, with an abundance of shrubby growth for at least half of the cycle. But the practice fell into decline early in the twentieth century and today most of these woods, formerly providing employment for thousands of woodcutters and their felling-axes, stand derelict — too old to form workable coppice, yet too young to have developed into mature, diversified woodland.

Such woods tend to be rather dull, heavily shaded and poor in birdlife. Fore Wood was in just such a state when it was bought in 1976. It supported a fair number of species like treecreepers and tits, but held few wrens or warblers, which need a certain amount of cover. Management there since 1978 has concentrated on opening up the wood by creating glades and rides, by thinning and coppicing. Many birds soon benefited — two pairs of willow warblers bred for the first time in 1980, eleven pairs in 1981 and twenty-two in 1982. Carried out up and down the country, such simple management could revitalise the thousands of abandoned coppices, large and small.

Birds are by no means the sole beneficiaries of all this work: following coppicing a dazzling array of flowers — primroses, violets, orchids, wood anemones, bluebells and others — appear, their dormant seed or buried rootstocks suddenly prodded into life by the sunlight flooding the earth for the first time in fifteen years or more. After two or three years the growth of more aggressive plants like bramble chokes out the delicate spring flowers,

Sparrowhawk

but subsequent coppice growth gradually shades out the brambles, so that by the time the area is cut again the ground is fairly bare and ready for the flowers.

The even rhythm of coppicing and regrowth conjures up an image of an unruffled, unchanging rural craft: but man must long ago have found himself dissatisfied with the often crooked poles that would become brittle with rot within a year of harvesting, and the problem was overcome by planting coppice that better suited his purposes. Sweet chestnut, a native of southern Europe, can grow into a fine, massive-boled tree, but when treated as coppice it sends up a cluster of straight poles which are remarkably resistant to decay. In recent centuries thousands of acres of native coppice in the warmer counties of Southern England have been replanted with this alien tree. Unfortunately, it lacks the wealth of insect life associated with many indigenous trees, so chestnut coppices are barren areas, their sterility emphasised by the way birds are drawn to any oaks which may be present amongst the coppice. Nearly half of Fore Wood was dominated by chestnut coppice and a start has been made on clearing it away, then replanting with oak, hornbeam, and other native species.

So natural woodland has passed to native coppice and then through to deciduous plantations; now a further step has been taken in fundamentally altering woods — the planting of exotic conifers. These fast-growing trees are readily converted into accurately-machined planks which suit modern requirements better than the imprecisely straight, thin coppice poles. Huge acreages of lowland coppice have been grubbed up and replaced by spruce from North America, pine from Corsica and larch from Japan — their dark, spiky profiles in stark contrast to the undulating lowland scenery. Once the canopy has closed in, the number and variety of birds choosing to stay in the perpetual gloom plummets and little can thrive apart from fungi. Gone are the spring flowers, the small mammals, warblers and butterflies that make deciduous woodland such a joy; even if deciduous trees are replanted once the conifers have been felled (as will be done on our reserve at Arne) it will be many centuries before all the specialised flora and fauna can recolonise.

Conifer-planting is a major threat to our remaining woodland, but there are others. The least worrying is neglect — an abandoned coppice will, over the years, mature and its wildlife value increase without any intervention by man. Nor is disease likely to prove a serious problem: at Northward Hill all the elms were killed by Dutch elm disease, forcing the large heronry to shift into the nearby oaks; but now fresh shoots are springing from the still-healthy tree roots and elm woodland will eventually heal the scars.

More worrying is the destruction of woodland to make way for new roads, housing estates and factories. Since this development usually occurs on the periphery of towns, the lost woods are the ones most valued by the local populace for recreation. But the area lost in this way is small by comparison with the acreages grubbed out each year by farmers eager to gain a little extra land: the process is as old as farming itself, for by 1086 as much as 85 per cent of our woodland had been cleared for agriculture; in the succeeding 900 years half of the medieval remnant has been lost, much of it this century, and yet we are still hungry for land. Naturally, earlier farmers reclaimed the more fertile and better-drained land centuries ago, so today's woodland generally stands on barren or waterlogged ground which will produce indifferent pasture, and then only after the farmer has extensively drained the land, a process which, along with grubbing out, is encouraged by Ministry of Agriculture grants. Faced with such overwhelming threats, what safeguards are there for woods? Very few, alas: the usual planning controls do not apply to those wishing to radically alter our countryside by ripping out age-old deciduous woodland. The only safeguard lies with Tree Preservation Orders; but the local council imposing such an order on a tree or wood must be prepared to pay the owner compensation, and in times of austerity there is an understandable reluctance on the part of councils to invoke this power. Thankfully though, just such an

Hawfinch

*This page:
Sparrowhawk
Opposite: Great
spotted woodpecker
and young*

order prevented Wolves Wood from becoming a 90-acre barley field prior to its purchase by the RSPB.

Our woods are in retreat, and nothing short of the miraculous enlightenment of their owners or a massive programme of acquisition by conservation bodies will do more than enable us to preserve a sample of a former inheritance. But nature is very resilient, and will fight back, given a chance: in times of agricultural depression some farmland is abandoned and it soon tumbles down to scrub or woodland as seedlings invade the ungrazed, untilled soil. One fifth of the wood at Northward Hill was farmland before the First World War: the fields were invaded by hawthorn, and recent management has turned this area into a haven for wildlife. Having lost its links with the primaeval woodland, this secondary woodland cannot be expected to harbour the same wealth of animals and plants, but it is still a great improvement on a featureless field.

Primary woodland, which has supported tree growth ever since the recolonisation of these islands by trees, is a living link with our past, a priceless heritage to be treasured, not squandered. When 93 per cent of the lowlands are already devoted to agriculture, housing and industry, is it really too much to ask that a mere seven per cent should be kept as woodland where future generations may thrill to the rich tones of the nightingale and gaze in wonder on a seemingly endless carpet of bluebells?

Nightingale

Lowland heathland

by John Day

There is something special about our English heathlands. Whether it is the air of desolate abandonment on a mist wreathed evening, or the bright yellow of the gorse on a spring day and the swish of the heather about your legs, it's a landscape which has both attracted and repelled men for generations. The very words, 'waste of the manor', seem to conjure up a picture of a treeless, heather-covered tract, where the only occupation is the cutting of furze for the poor man's fire, and the only signs of activity are the commoner's sheep and ponies huddled beside a lightning-blasted tree for shelter. But to the naturalist, heathlands are the home for a rich and diverse assemblage of animals and plants, many of which are to be found nowhere else, and the apparent uniformity is belied by the different natural communities found in the dry, heather-covered banks, the moisture laden boggy hollows and the dark peaty pools.

Sadly, the heathlands of today are but a shadow of their former glory. The day is over, when, in the words of Thomas Hardy, the road "was quite open to the heath on each side, and bisected that vast dark surface like the parting line of a head of black hair, diminishing and bending away on the furthest horizon". When Hardy was thus immortalising the countryside of his native Dorset in the 1890s, there were some 56,000 acres of heathland in that county and in Hampshire west of the Avon. Until 1934, the rate of heathland loss was small (only some 0·5 per cent per year), but since then afforestation and reclamation have quickened up the rate of destruction. By 1960 only 24,500 acres were left, and today this total has been reduced to 14,000 acres of which nearly 15 per cent is actively threatened by proposals for development or reclamation. If the destruction of the last forty years were to continue at the same rate, then there would be nothing left by the end of this century.

To a greater or lesser extent, this story has been paralleled in Surrey, Sussex, Devon and Cornwall, and although the great heathlands of the New Forest have been largely protected against reclamation; many of them have been degraded by overgrazing and repeated fires. The story is also repeated on the continent of Europe, where only small pockets are left of the once extensive heathlands which stretched from Denmark down to the maritime heaths of Spain. The great heaths of Jutland have been so reduced that virtually all the remaining fragments are in protected nature reserves, in Lower Saxony, only one to two per cent has survived from 1800, while in France, the once extensive coastal heaths are now largely pine forest, and little is left elsewhere of a habitat that occurs nowhere outside Western Europe.

Of those that are left, some of the best examples are here in our southern counties. Nowhere else in Britain can one hear the song of the elusive and colourful Dartford warbler, or see the rare smooth snake, sunning itself on a sandy bank. The Purbecks are the headquarters of the Dorset heath, the finest native *Erica*, with its raspberry coloured bells, and here also is the very local marsh gentian, pushing up its dark blue funnel-shaped flowers from the reds and yellows of the bog grasses.

From a car window on the main road, the open heathland may have an uninviting look of sameness, but there is a surprising diversity of habitat, and a whole range of beautiful and unusual creatures. Take the heather plant itself: it has a life span of thirty to forty years and

Cross-leaved heath

Overleaf: Dartford warbler at Arne

during this time it passes through various stages, each of which has a far-reaching effect on the other plant and animal species with which it is associated. On bare ground the heather seedlings once established, usually take about five years to form a bushy habitat, then, for a further ten years the plants are growing and increasing in size, slowly shading out other plants and lichens, until they reach maturity in about eighteen years. For the next seven or eight years, the heather is not increasing in height but individuals are spreading in diameter and the central branches are showing a tendency to die back and let more light in. This die back will continue so that the central part of the plant becomes quite dead and the remaining live branches are spread out flat on the ground like the spokes of a wheel. At each stage, the ground beneath is colonised by a whole range of moss and lichen communities with their attendant insect populations, and each community is adapted to the differing conditions of light and shade, heat, cold and humidity provided by the dominant heather. On damper ground the heather gives way to cross-leaved heath, with purple moor grass and heath rush. But it is in the really wet boggy areas where the sphagnum moss oozes water and the plant roots hang down from the quaking mass of vegetation into the peat-laden water beneath that many of the most exciting plants may be found. In the wettest the yellow spikes of bog asphodel cover the ground in mid-July and the leaves of bog myrtle fill the air with scent.

On the edges of the bog the white plumes of cotton grass stand out against the green and orange of the *Sphagnum*, and on the bare patches the small red leaves of the sundew hug the ground, the treacherously attractive, sticky leaves adhering to any insect that alights and, glued securely in place, the hapless creature will be slowly digested by the plant, which has evolved this way of supplementing the meagre nutrients it derives from the acid bog waters.

Here, too, some of the most exciting insects have their home, the splendid multi-coloured dragonflies, darting on gauze-shimmering wings, their huge, many-faceted eyes alive to every movement, and the dainty feeble flying damselflies, resting with wings folded in butterfly fashion on the water-fringing vegetation. On the still water, the chocolate and cream striped wolf spider stalks the unwary pond-skater over the surface film, and at any disturbance, dives out of sight under the water, and swims up into its lair beneath the fringing moss.

Leaving the bog and walking into the dry heath, the most noticeable plant apart from the heather itself is the gorse. All three British species of gorse grow on lowland heathland — the two species of dwarf furze, and the spring-flowering gorse, which can often be seen growing in rough lines across the heath, marking old trackways and boundary banks into which it has seeded when the ground was disturbed many years ago. These gorse clumps are habitat for a number of scrub-loving birds, the most noticeable of which is the yellow-hammer, wheezing its monotonous song from the topmost spray. Linnets fly twittering from one bush to the next, and stonechats sit on favoured perches watching for insects.

The dry gorsy heath is also the favoured area for the Dartford warbler, the bird which, more than any other, characterises the heathlands, although it is often far from easy to see, as it creeps mouselike through the gorse and long heather searching out spiders and small insects. An odd little bird, it stays here all the year round, unlike most other warblers which leave us for warmer climes each autumn and, as a result, its population suffers severely in cold winters.

After the very cold winters of 1961/2 and 1962/3 only ten pairs could be found on all the lowland heaths, but a succession of mild winters since then allowed the birds to recolonise many of their former haunts. A census undertaken in 1975 revealed some 600 pairs, but another cold winter in 1978/9 again reduced their numbers, and although a few survived at the RSPB reserve in Dorset, at another, Aylesbeare in Devon, they disappeared.

Common sundew

Looking out over a stretch of open heathland one is struck by the odd clumps of pine, standing isolated amongst the ground-hugging vegetation, the landscape looking for all the world like a scene in some African travelogue. It is for this reason that ecologists call this habitat 'pine savanna'; islands of pine in a sea of heather. These isolated stands of trees provide nest sites for one of our rarer birds of prey, the hobby, a bird so fast and agile, it catches dragonflies and other insects, as well as swifts and swallows, in flight. It must make the most of its brief summer sojourn, for like the warblers, this too is a migrant. Tree pipits sing their plaintive song notes as they parachute into the pine tops, and from the dead branches, stretched out like fingerposts over the heath, the nightjar croons its summer song.

This mysterious bird, seldom seen during the day, flies in the gloaming catching moths and other insects in its wide-gaped beak, and on warm still evenings in June, its song, now soft, now loud, rolls across the heather like the distant purr of a cat. On the East Anglian heaths like that at Minsmere, this bird is associated with scrub birch, nesting on the barer patches under the trees and using the birches as songposts.

The future of areas like these and the rare and beautiful plants and animals which depend on them is in the balance. Continual nibbling away at the edges for agriculture, reclamation and the planting of blocks of Scots and Corsican pine are making inroads into what is left.

Sand and gravel working and, in Dorset, china clay mining are all threats. Proposals for golf courses, housing estates and caravan parks also need constant surveillance if the opportunity for stating the case against further encroachment is not to be missed. Sadly, too many heaths are still regarded as wasteland, a convenient dumping ground for sewage or a site for a council tip, a place to accommodate gypsy encampments, motor-bike trials and any other use which is inimical to existing urban or rural settlements. But it is not only these threats to the very survival of some heathland areas which is worrying, it is also the very real threat to the fabric of what is left.

In the past, heathland has been maintained by cutting, grazing and burning, and providing these were kept at a reasonable level, the system maintained itself. Changing land use practices have drastically altered this picture however; in Surrey, a lack of management on many areas has meant invasion of the heathland by dense birch. This will eventually signal the end of the heather on many areas, where it will be replaced by woodland; probably only the bogs would survive. In the New Forest burning and over-grazing has meant the replacement of the heather over large areas by tough and unpalatable grasses, resulting in a down-grading not only of the quality of the wildlife, but of the grazing too.

But by far the biggest and most widespread threat is fire. It seems ironic that the very factor which has in the past prevented so many heaths from disappearing beneath trees, should now be threatening the survival, not so much of the heaths themselves, but of the diverse and complex animal communities they support. Different aged stands of heather support different types of animal, bird and insect communities. In the past, on large heathlands, this uneven aging has often been brought about by occasional small fires started deliberately by commoners in order to improve the spring grazing. These fires sometimes got out of control and consumed large areas, but when this happened the plants and animals would quickly recolonise the area from surrounding heaths.

Nowadays recolonisation becomes increasingly difficult, as heathland areas become more and more fragmented and the distances between them become greater.

Following the severe 1963 winter, Dartford warblers have not recolonised some of the Surrey heaths. Sand lizards have disappeared from the New Forest, probably as the result of heather burning, and many other birds and insects have declined in numbers and disappeared from former sites. In 1975 Godlingstone in Dorset, one of the five largest heaths

Dartford warbler

*Some characteristic
heathland species —
nightjar (opposite),
silver-studded blue
(top left), bilberry
(top middle), bell
heather (top above),
natterjack (left) and
smooth snake (above)*

left in the county, and a conservation site of national importance, was almost completely burnt and this was followed in 1976 by a spate of fires during the summer on other sites.

Very few heaths escaped without some fire damage, and on one, Colony Bog, an army range near Pirbright, about 800 acres of the 1,000-acre heath was destroyed in one fire, while in Surrey as much as one-fifth of the entire heathland area in the county was burnt in 1976. Such fires can have a devastating effect on wildlife, with temperatures up to 500 deg C a few inches above ground level, no animal life survives on the surface and even small birds flying too near can be sucked into the flames by the vortex set up by the intense heat.

Recolonisation is taking longer and meanwhile the frequency with which heaths are getting burnt is increasing. What can be done? First and foremost of course is the acquisition of heaths by the conservation bodies, and strenuous efforts by the County Trusts, Nature Conservancy Council and National Trust, as well as the RSPB now mean that many of the larger heaths are nature reserves. The RSPB was one of the first in the field when it leased 308 acres at Arne in Dorset in 1965, and following further leases and a long period during which some 740 acres were managed as a reserve, the Society was able to buy over 1,100 acres in 1978, the largest area of southern heathland owned by a conservation body. Since then the acquisition of leases by NCC and a major gift to the National Trust has resulted in much greater protection for the Dorset heaths.

In Surrey, Sussex and Hampshire conservationists have also been active although many heaths are still unprotected and in Devon the RSPB was fortunate in being able to lease the most important of the pebblebed commons at Aylesbeare, near Exeter. But purchase or lease is not enough, since these heaths must be actively managed if they are to survive.

The first priority is to protect against accidental fire, by constructing firebreaks, controlling public access and maintaining a close liaison and a full contingency plan with the fire services. A two-way radio system, backed up by emergency fire-fighting equipment amongst the conservation bodies themselves has also been set up in Dorset, and at Arne water supplies have been provided at many points by the excavation of heathland ponds. This has a double benefit, for besides providing emergency water close to the points where it may be most needed, these ponds provide a rich habitat for wildlife, particularly for dragonflies, for which Arne is one of the most important sites in Britain. All these precautions have paid off; the few fires which have caught hold in recent years have been quickly extinguished, and in 1976 the Arne peninsular was unscathed by fire.

Much of the heather was killed by the fierce heat of that summer though, and it is here that the careful use of fire as a management tool can help, by burning off the dead and dying plants to expose the mineral soils underneath, which heather seed must have if it is to germinate. Another problem is the spread of pine seedlings over the heathland, in time shading out the heather and turning the open heath into sombre pine woods with only moss and fungi growing on the open floor. Since acquiring Arne, tens of acres of pine regeneration has been cleared, so that in a small way, we are increasing the acreage of heath to replace some of that which has been lost elsewhere.

Management is undertaken too for the birds. Following detailed research on the Dartford warbler by our research department, the close link with gorse, both as a nesting site, and as a reservoir of food at all times of the year, was conclusively shown. Since then new stands of gorse have been established, management of the older more straggly stands has also been undertaken, by cutting or burning to encourage the dense young growth to regenerate again at ground level. This gives thick stands of gorse, so important to act as feeding sites for Dartford warblers, particularly in harsh winter weather, when snow is lying over the heather.

At Minsmere the problem is birch and here too open heath is being maintained and enlarged by cutting back into the line of encroaching scrub, but taking care to leave suitable

Sand lizard

areas of trees for breeding and singing nightjars. Future generations of unwanted seedlings from these parent trees and their removal is the price we shall have to pay, then, for keeping our nightjars now.

Visitor control is vital on a heathland reserve, with its rare and sensitive plants and animals, and the ever-present danger of fire. Carefully sited paths and the provision of look-out points and hides can go a long way to minimising potential problems, but this has to be backed up by constant surveillance by wardens and volunteers. The acquisition and management of these heathland reserves is a splendid achievement, but while heathland reclamation goes on at the rate of an acre a day on average in Dorset alone, there is still much to be done.

Even on established reserves the threats are still there. As recently as 1976, and just before the Society bought the rest of the reserve, planning consent for clay workings was granted on a part of the Arne peninsula and now planning applications have been made to prospect for oil on the reserve boundary. But the rewards for the time and resources spent fighting these and other threats to our remnant heathlands are enormous, since nowhere else in Britain is it possible to enjoy their unique assemblage of colourful plants, insects and birds. We want future generations to be able to appreciate and understand George Borrow when he said "there's night and day brother, both sweet things, sun, moon and stars brother, all sweet things, there's likewise a wind on the heath".

Stonechat

Native pinewoods

by Stewart Taylor

Of all the conifer woodland in Britain at the present time only a very small proportion is native pinewood. Throughout the country, conifer plantations are usually made up of a variety of species of three main types of conifer, namely pine, larch and spruce, and if the native pinewood area is considered along with the pine-only plantations, its 26,000 acres would still account for only five per cent of the total. Part of this small area is the largest component of continuous woodland in Scotland and Britain, having been in existence in the surviving areas for the last 8,000 years.

In the pine plantations in Britain, four species are regularly planted. Three are quick-growing species, introduced to this country, but the fourth, Scots pine, is native. Although it is now naturalised in many parts of Britain, it is only in Scotland that it has grown continuously since trees began to recolonise the bare landscape left at the end of the Ice Age some 10,000 years ago. Successions of trees re-colonised the bare landscape and between 6800 and 5000 BC pine and birch forests covered much of Britain. However, climatic changes during 5000-3000 BC brought a warmer, wetter climate, with a reduction in the area of pine and birch forests and an increase in alder. Then, between 3000 and 500 BC, the climate became drier, and in the south of Britain a broadleaved forest of oak and elm developed to replace the former forest. The pine and birch forest became restricted to Scotland, though covering a smaller area than in its heyday a few thousand years earlier. Early man, whose needs at this time were not great, was having very little effect on these vast forests, clearing only small areas for building materials and areas to cultivate.

During the Roman occupation of Britain there is very little evidence of any mass pinewood destruction, and in AD 2 we have the first mention of a *Caledonia Silva* between Loch Long and the Beauly Firth. There followed very little written historical evidence about the Forest of Caledon, until about 1400, when, as lowland timber supplies became depleted, people looked further afield for supplies. Even so, many of the Highland pine forests survived intact into the 17th century, a period during which the iron industry began to grow dramatically. Its appetite for charcoal to fuel its furnaces seemed insatiable: in 1613, smelting 180,000 tons of iron required about 3·6 million tons of timber for charcoal.

By 1800 many of the Highland forests had lost their primeval character, as timber was extracted in vast amounts to supply the iron industry and, by floating timber down the rivers, maintaining ship-building industries at the coast.

Exploitation of the Caledonian pine-forest had reached a peak and, but for the remoteness at that time of some of the outlying forests, would probably have disappeared altogether during this period.

Further heavy felling took place during the two world wars, and though there was a lull in exploitation of what little remained after the second war, in recent years conversion of open mature pine forest into plantation type forest has been nibbling around the edges and, in some cases, right in the very heart of some of the last major areas.

The Loch Garten reserve was established in 1975 by the Society, in one of the larger surviving remnants — Abernethy Forest. The 1,517 acres of the reserve comprising a

Opposite: Capercaillie, a species that breeds at Loch Garten

mixture of pine forest, loch, bog and moorland habitats, centre around the famous Speyside osprey site.

Abernethy Forest is the largest of 35 recognised native pinewood sites in Scotland, and is one of the Speyside group of six sites, which, along with the three of the Deeside group, make up over half of the total remaining woodland. Other major areas occur in the Great Glen, at Rannoch and in Glen Affric. In comparison with these areas, many of the other sites comprise only scattered fragments of mainly old trees. The massive reduction in total forest area over the last 250 years has led to a decrease in diversity of tree and shrub species. Birch, rowan, aspen and juniper were once more abundant, and in some areas there was a mixture of oak. The distribution of plant species has also been modified and several species, which are common in Scandinavian pine forests, are rare or absent in Scotland.

Despite this decreased and modified area, the Scottish pinewoods support a characteristic bird population that contains several species that are uncommon elsewhere in Britain. Scottish crossbill, crested tit and capercaillie all come into this category, and along with other conifer-dwelling species, probably owe their survival in this country for the last few thousand years to the existence of the Scottish pinewoods.

One of the major characteristics of the native pinewoods is the variety of habitats with dense and open mature woodland, heathery openings, natural regeneration onto burnt or wind-blown areas, and on the valley floor sites like parts of Abernethy, boggy hollows, streams and open water areas. This variety helps to diversify the bird population, so that at Loch Garten, fifty to sixty different species breed, and over 100 species are recorded annually. Taking the pinewoods as a whole, about eighty species regularly breed. Of these, seventeen are associated directly with open water, two nest in woodland but use water for feeding, seven with marsh, forty-one directly with woodland, eleven with woodland and moorland, and two with woodland and farmland. The commonest breeding ducks are mallard and teal, but tufted duck, wigeon and goosander all regularly breed. A few small heronries occur in the pinewoods, and in common with the tree-nesting ospreys, they require reasonable amounts of open water over which to hunt for their food.

Among the birds of prey, kestrel, buzzard and sparrowhawk are fairly widespread, whilst golden eagle and merlin occasionally breed only near the tree limit. Ospreys bred for the first time in fifty years during the 1950s at a pinewood site by Loch Garten. From this one site in 1959 the recolonisation of Scotland started and over the years 45 young have been reared, and the Scottish population over the same period has increased to twenty-two pairs. The importance of moorland within the forest can be seen by the presence of red and black grouse. But the largest member of the grouse family, the capercaillie, can only be found in the larger, mature woodlands, and though originally a native species, it became extinct in Britain in 1770. Early attempts to re-introduce Swedish birds to the Deeside pinewoods between 1827 and 1829 failed, but later attempts at Taymouth in 1837 and 1838 were successful. Birds from this area were later introduced successfully to other parts of Scotland, and though they are now well established in many pinewood areas in Scotland, they are still absent from the south and west.

A good variety of waders breed, from woodcock in the woods, to curlew, redshank, common sandpiper and snipe in the boggy woodlands. Greenshank used to breed regularly within the pinewoods, but are now mainly confined to the open moor. Of the smaller woodland breeders, census work over the last six years at Loch Garten, and in the past in other areas of Abernethy and Wester Ross, has shown that chaffinches are the commonest breeder. Six other finches regularly breed: greenfinch and goldfinch around farmland, redpoll in areas of birch within the pines, bullfinch occasionally in the woodland, whilst the numbers of Scottish crossbill and siskin fluctuate with the abundance of the pine cone crop. In good cone years up to thirty pairs of siskin and twenty-five pairs of crossbill have been

Scots pine

recorded at Garten. Both of these species were formerly restricted to the northern pinewoods, but with extensive conifer plantations established elsewhere, have increased their range. The siskin now breeds wherever there is a large plantation, more or less throughout Britain. Scottish crossbills were recorded from most of the larger pinewoods during the 1968-72 breeding bird survey. Up until a few years ago the crossbills of northern Scotland were thought to be just a sub-species of the common crossbill of northern Europe *Loxia curvirostra*, but extensive work by Dr Alan Knox at Aberdeen University showed that there were both bill size differences and evidence of reproductive isolation between the Scottish and European birds, and hence they were separate species. The Scottish birds have now been designated *Loxia scotica*, becoming Britain's only indigenous bird species, and one of very few birds dependent on one specific food item.

Other common birds in the pinewoods are willow warbler, coal tit, treecreeper, goldcrest and wren, though numbers of the last two species can vary a great deal depending on the severity of the previous winter. Crested tits, the rarest of the British tits, are restricted in their distribution in the pinewoods to the Spey group, and to out-lyers in the Strathglass group. Of the two, coal tits are twice as common, according to surveys carried out at Loch Garten. Though crested tits have started to colonise recent plantation outside the older woods, lack of suitable dead tree nest sites in these areas probably restricts their wider distribution. Blue and great tits also occur, but are mainly restricted to areas with a mixture of deciduous woodland, and whilst long-tailed tits are most commonly found in similar habitat, they will nest in mature pines and in juniper bushes.

Tawny is probably the commonest owl, but both long-eared and short-eared are regular breeders. Redwing and wryneck, two sporadic breeders in Scotland, have bred within pinewood areas, and one species on the edge of its British range, the pied flycatcher, has bred occasionally. Great spotted woodpecker is the only member of the family to breed, but green woodpeckers have been seen in the Deeside and Speyside woods in recent years. Cuckoos, on the lookout for meadow and tree pipit nests, are regularly encountered in the more open woodland in summer.

The larger mammals are plentifully represented by both red and roe deer, and in some of the pinewoods of Ardgour and Loch Maree feral goats exist. Red squirrels are quite numerous in the Speyside, Deeside and Rannoch woods. Rabbits and brown hares will be found around most of the areas, though not commonly within them. Several small carnivores occur, the commonest being stoat, weasel and fox. Badgers occur close to some of the woods, and otters are to be found in associated lochs and water courses. Two species which are less common and not often encountered because of their nocturnal habits are the wildcat, which is recorded from all the pinewood groups, and the pine marten which is fairly common in the Wester Ross woods, and uncommon but present in many of the others.

The pinewoods support a characteristic beetle fauna, with ninety-one dependent species recorded. This may seem poor compared with oak woodlands, the richest insect habitat in Britain, with 284 dependent species. However, many of the oak species are also found on other tree species, so if all the oaks were lost, many of the beetles would survive. The pine species though are more vulnerable in that they do not have alternative tree species, and many have not, in Britain, been recorded from any other trees.

Large numbers of anthills occur, mainly made up of forest floor litter by the wood ant *Formica lugubris*. These are commonest in Deeside and Speyside. The Spey woods are also a noted area for a good variety of moths, butterflies and dragonflies, some of which are restricted in Scotland to this particular area.

Because of the reduction in area of the pinewoods, several once common plants are now quite local in their distribution. Of five orchids regularly found, creeping ladies tresses and

Scottish crossbill

Overleaf: Osprey at Loch Garten

lesser twayblade are the most typical. The tresses, though common in most sites, are scarce in the western woods, whilst lesser twayblade is common throughout, though probably overlooked because of its small size and habit of growing under heather. Four species of wintergreens occur, with one-flowered wintergreen, restricted to only the Speyside woods, being the rarest of all the pinewood plants. Of the others intermediate wintergreen is found in most of the woods, whilst the common and serrated wintergreens are much more local in their distribution. Chickweed wintergreen on the other hand is not a true wintergreen, and is most common in woodlands with an element of birch. It is a vernal plant and is common in Deeside, and thinly spread over the other areas. But the plant that is perhaps the bonniest of all the pinewood species is twinflower, forming dense patches of hanging, pink, bell-shaped flowers in June and July. This plant, along with one-flowered wintergreen, is probably the one that has suffered most due to the reduction in pinewood area, and is restricted within them to Speyside and Deeside.

The dominant ground vegetation in most of the woods will be a mixture of heather, cowberry and bilberry, the latter two producing an abundant crop of berries in late summer.

In Britain, Scots pine is at the western extremity of its natural distribution, and, as the largest surviving remnant of continuous woodland in Britain, with a dependent flora and fauna, appropriate steps must be taken to help ensure the survival of what remains.

Apart from the RSPB's reserve at Loch Garten, which is less than one per cent of the total, very little of this habitat is actually owned by any other conservation body. The NCC does own some, and has management agreements with owners in several others, but the Forestry Commission owns or manages twelve of the thirty-five listed sites, and though they have carried out much research, not least into problems affecting the continued existence of their woods by establishment of natural regeneration, they have in the main tended to manage them in the same way as their other commercial woodlands. In some cases, scattered open woods have been underplanted with other conifers, and plantations of unrestricted species have been established up to and around the remnant stands, restricting the area for possible natural regeneration to take place.

Although many recognised sites are owned or managed by Government departments, 75 per cent of the pinewood habitat is still in private ownership. Many of the owners recognise that they own a unique part of the national heritage, but with large estates needing income from as many quarters as possible, more and more previously untouched areas are being managed to meet this requirement.

Recent grant aid schemes aimed at helping these woodlands have been badly worked out and, because of the rigid rules governing what qualifies for grant, really provide a charter for the conversion of the open scattered woodlands into commercial forestry plantations. Because so many of these pine forests are in private ownership, the current grant aid system could encourage even more intensive management within these areas.

Already, during the last twenty years, large areas within one of our largest pinewoods, Abernethy Forest, have been converted to plantation forest. We can only hope, therefore, that a scheme can be worked out which recognises the natural make-up of the native pinewood habitat, and one which will encourage the owners of these woodlands to manage them in a way which will ensure their survival — in their entirety.

Capercaillie

Upland oakwoods

by John Day

Although from a distance upland woods are superficially similar to those in the lowlands, on a closer inspection they can be seen to be quite different in a number of ways. To start with, the dominant tree, the oak, is a different species from that usually found in many of the woods in the Midlands and South-East England. This lowland tree, which sometimes grows to a huge size, is the pedunculate oak whose acorns grow on stalks, called "peduncles" by botanists. By contrast, the oaks of the upland woods are usually shorter, their branches starting higher up, and making smaller crowns, and with their acorns unstalked or 'sessile'. This is a different species, the durmast or sessile oak. The shorter, often distorted growth of the hill country trees is not a characteristic of the species, but rather a reflection of the harsh conditions in which they are growing. Sessile oaks can grow into magnificent trees, as a visit to the reserve at Nagshead, in the Forest of Dean, will confirm.

In this country, oaks will only grow to an altitude of 1,500 feet, and at this height the trees, bent and twisted by the winds, reach no more than twelve feet, bearing little resemblance to their sturdier cousins lower down the valley sides. Aspect is important, too; south-facing slopes receive more sun than those facing north, and the steeper slopes also benefit if they face the sun, since the light intensity is greater. This is of real importance in the mountains, where life is a hard struggle against the elements, since a difference of only ten degrees in slope may increase the growing season by several days.

In addition, of course, rainfall in the uplands is much higher; in some parts of Wales, it reaches 200 inches a year, and the constant washing effect creates huge blanket flows, where the ground is constantly saturated and only sphagnum mosses and sedges will grow.

On steeper slopes, where trees will grow, one effect of this constant throughflow of water is that soil nutrients are washed away, so that the thin and stony upland soils tend to have little humus and few nutrients and make a poor medium for growing plants.

Walking up the grass or bracken-covered slopes beneath a Welsh or Pennine woodland, another difference is strikingly apparent. The profusion of shrubs, the tall woodland plants, the trailing honeysuckle and dense thickets of blackthorn and bramble under the openings in the tree canopy above, so characteristic of lowland woods, are practically absent. Instead of this lush undergrowth, the trees are growing on a bare hillside, where rocky boulders thrust up through the thin covering of grass and bilberry; ferns sprout from pockets of soil on rock ledges, and the only shrubs are stunted hawthorns or hazels, marking the ancient boundary banks of long forgotten and abandoned fields at the wood edge. But as if in compensation for this bare and open woodland floor the oaks themselves are festooned with ferns and lichens. Broad buckler ferns, common polypodies, and even young rowan trees find a foothold in the angles and crutches of the moss encrusted branches; the flat plates of dog lichen cover the stumps of a dying limb, and everywhere the *Usnia* lichens hang from branches and trunks like miniature seaweeds.

These lichens, sensitive to polluted air, are practically absent from the woods in the industrialised counties further east, since few species can tolerate the sulphur dioxide-laden air; the result of innumerable coal- and oil-burning appliances in homes and factories. But up here in the mountains, open to the fresh Atlantic winds, the air is clean and the

Red kite

*Opposite: Coombes
Valley, an upland
oakwood reserve
This page: Redstart*

lichens flourish. Sometimes, where the soils are a little deeper, an understorey of hazel will grow, and has been coppiced in the past, so that the stems now shoot up from massive stools which, due to repeated cutting over the centuries have never been able to reach their natural form, and remain grotesque and squat reminders of their former value as providers of sheep hurdles and crook handles. Elsewhere the oaks are many stemmed, showing that they too have been coppiced, and sometimes they give way to birch woodland with only a few ancient oaks, standing like hulks amidst the delicate greys and silvers of the birch trunks. Here, wholesale felling or coppicing of the oak in former times, and lack of regeneration, has led to its replacement by the quicker growing, but shorter-lived birch.

Scattered through the woods, rowans are growing, huge twisted trees some as large as the oaks themselves, and providers of innumerable scarlet berries to the winter thrushes, who in their turn, broadcast the seed through the woods as they fly to their evening roost. In damper hollows ash and alders grow, a favourite spot for siskins in winter, and occasionally where an outcrop of less acid rocks protrude, or a lime-rich flush of water breaks the surface, wych elm and small-leaved lime might be found. Nearly all the woods show signs of past use by man. Timber and coppice for fuel, agricultural implements, vehicles, and buildings, had been extracted since before medieval times, but as the industrial revolution got underway charcoal for smelting, timber for pitprops, and oakbark, used to extract tannin for the leather trade, were also much in demand.

However, industrialists rapidly found better substitutes — coke replaced charcoal, softwoods replaced oak as pitprops and house timber, and wooden ships gave way to iron and steel. Country crafts based on timber products declined, and even on the farm, galvanised iron, barbed wire and softwoods have combined to make the native woods redundant, except as sources of firewood, and as shelter for stock in winter. Despite this decline in their economic value to man, these woods are still, as they always have been, a vital part of the framework of habitats for the wildlife of the hills.

As the buds break after the silent desolation of an upland winter, and the valleys are filled with the calls of the ewes and their lambs, the migrant birds return to the woods. Amongst the boisterous calls of the resident blue and great tits, the delicate trill of wood warblers can now be heard, and the repetitive note of the tree pipit, parachuting down from his song flight, to land in the tree tops.

Black and white cock pied flycatchers return to set up breeding territories as they await the arrival of their mates, and handsome male redstarts display their rich tawny tail colours as they flit from tree to tree, disappointing the listener with a brief song which never seems to realise the promise of the first few bars. Overhead the buzzards soar on the thermals of the spring sunshine, sparrowhawks dash among the small birds at the wood edge, and the ravens, now feeding the young hatched from eggs laid during the snows of February, call harshly from their nest in the top of a solitary oak.

On the woodland floor, anemones and wood sorrels produce a profusion of delicate white flowers amongst the green stems of early vernal grass, and thin green bracken stems with unopened fronds, looking like miniature walking sticks thrust randomly in the ground, give a promise of high summer.

The woods are full of the sound of running water, as the upland mosses and peats, full of meltwater after the winter snows, swell the innumerable streams, coursing down their boulder strewn beds to the river in the valley below. Water loving plants find a precarious foothold along the banks and amongst the spray soaked stones; the flat overlapping plates of liverworts and moss-like sprays of filmy ferns cling to the rock crevices, bog pimpernels clamber on the wet banks and saxifrages enliven the sombre green of the mosses and ferns with white and yellow flowers.

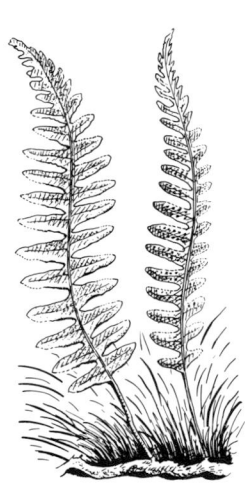

Polypody fern

In remote Welsh valleys these woods are the breeding place of the red kite, a very special bird for ornithologists, since within living memory it has been brought back from the verge of extinction in Britain. By 1900, due to human persecution by poison, trap and gun, the kite was reduced to a remnant of only a few pairs. Due to the protection afforded by conservationists and a few hill farmers, the numbers stopped declining and slowly and painfully built up to nearly a dozen pairs by the Second World War, and this population maintained a precarious hold until the early sixties. Further efforts by conservation bodies including the RSPB, and the help and interest of hill farming folk at last began to bear fruit and numbers increased.

Now there are about forty pairs of this superb bird of prey, and its breeding range is spreading. Protection against egg-collectors is still needed though, and threats still remain from the illegal use of poison, secreted in carcases and eggs put out on the hills to kill crows, but indiscriminately poisoning buzzards, ravens, kites and other animals which also eat carrion.

Another species which has increased in numbers and distribution, following a decline in persecution by man, is the polecat. Like the kite, its stronghold is in mid-Wales, where it lives in a variety of habitats in and around the woodland and small farms. Rarely seen, the presence of the partly nocturnal polecat is most often apparent as a road casualty. It is quite common on the Gwenffrwd reserve in Dyfed, but has been recorded as far east as the steep wooded valley of the Coombes Valley reserve in Staffordshire, having spread to some English counties bordering the Welsh marches during the last thirty years.

Despite these successes, all is not well. Hanging oak woodland is under threat and is rapidly disappearing in some areas. In Wales, where probably as much as 90 per cent of the land area was once covered by woodland a few thousand years ago, gradual clearance over the centuries had reduced this to only about four per cent by 1870. Since then, this remnant broadleaf has been progressively removed or replaced by conifers, and now only about one per cent of the country is covered by privately owned deciduous woodland. The story is repeated elsewhere, and the pace of destruction has quickened in the last forty years.

In Devon, 20 per cent of the woodland was destroyed between 1952 and 1972; in one area of Yorkshire, over 23 per cent of the woodland has been lost in the seventeen years to 1978, while in the Scottish borders, 80 per cent of the deciduous woodland has gone in the last thirty years. As landowners seek to maximise the productivity of their land, many small woods have been felled, and replanted with conifers, sometimes leaving a scattering of oaks to provide some protection to young trees from frost and wind, but often after removing all traces of the oakwoods. In the narrow coombes of Devon and Cornwall and the remnant river valley woods of the Pennines, this destruction has been widespread.

Tragically, in many cases landowners, badly advised by land agents and others, have felled the native woods, so well adapted to the soils and weather conditions, and replanted with conifers which have failed to grow well under the adverse conditions or, after a promising start, have suffered widespread damage as the wind has blown down the trees, whose roots have insufficient anchorage in the thin soils. Too often the result has been the replacement of the ecologically rich hanging oakwoods, which for centuries have been so characteristic of the scenery of our uplands, with ugly blocks of conifers to the immeasurable detriment of both wildlife and landscape.

A change of this sort has an immediate and measurable impact but, in the long term, a greater and more insidious problem threatens the woods. Looking closely at almost any piece of upland woodland, one is immediately struck by the absence of tree seedlings and young trees. As the bitter upland winter closes in, the sheep move down from the high ground to the shelter of the woods, and in the ensuing months, the hungry animals will eat everything they can reach. Tree seedlings from the previous year stand little chance, except

Buzzard

Overleaf: A red kite flies above the Gwenffrwd

on inaccessible ledges or block scree, and as the spring returns to the woods, the ground is once again swept clean, only the low growing grasses and herbs, the ferns and mosses, surviving.

Year after year this pattern is repeated, and as the trees get older and begin to die off and fall, gaps appear in the canopy overhead, but no young trees spring up to fill them. The process is accelerated by the removal of the odd tree for firewood or fence stakes, or sometimes by the wholesale removal of trees to satisfy the growing demands of wood-burning stoves. Gradually the wood changes from a compact block of trees, providing continuous cover, to more disjointed woodland, park-like in appearance with clumps of trees or individuals scattered over the hillside, and bounded by the hawthorns of an old remnant hedge. Finally even these disappear, and the only signs that there was once a woodland on the bracken-covered hillside are a few ancient thorns and a clump or two of bluebells in a grassy hollow.

Sadly, many upland farmers are aware of these changes but they have neither the time or resources to halt the process which, in many cases, will not make an impact for one or two human generations to come, since the oaks take a long time to die and fall.

The loss is not solely to the wildlife and the scenery; to the farmer the winter shelter is of considerable value. The number of lambs the sheep produce in the spring is a reflection of how well the animals have withstood the winter, and this in turn depends on the availability of shelter and food, as well as the weather. So the decline of the woods will in due course prompt many farmers to construct expensive modern buildings to in-winter their ewes on the more exposed farms. In addition, the shade of the trees previously kept out the invasive bracken and allowed the growth of nutritious grasses and herbs. With the trees gone, the hillside becomes covered with a thick growth of unpalatable bracken, and the farmer is forced into the expense of spraying and reseeding, a difficult and often unsuccessful operation, or into accepting the loss of productivity on a part of his farm. Thus, the farmer loses, the wildlife is diminished, and the woods which have been the delight of naturalists and walkers for generations are lost for ever.

The only answer to the problem is to fence the sheep out of the wood for the seven to twelve years that it takes for the trees to regenerate and for the seedlings to grow above the reach of browsing sheep. This is an expensive operation, as only a part of the wood can be fenced out at any one time, because the remainder is still needed for shelter. In addition, the fence must often follow an uneconomic line, since it must avoid corners which will trap sheep in blind alleys when they are driven through the woods at gathering time. Fencing on the steep, boulder-strewn slopes is expensive, and the fencing, once erected, must be regularly maintained; sheep which get inside an enclosure can be trapped by their fleeces amongst the tangle of briars which often spring up soon after enclosure and, if left, will starve to death.

Despite the obvious long-term economic value of such woods, no grants are payable either by the Forestry Commission or Ministry of Agriculture for this type of exclusion fencing, although replanting with conifers, or replacement by modern buildings will readily attract grant-aid. Some planning authorities in the National Parks, aware of the problem, will make grants available, but their resources are not sufficient to tackle the problem on a large enough scale.

The RSPB, too, is doing all it can on its reserves to guarantee the future of its woods. At the Gwenffrwd and Ynys-hir in Dyfed, and at Lake Vyrnwy in Powys, where an enormous upland area, containing many small broad-leaved woods, has been established as a reserve by agreement with the Severn Trent Water Authority, fencing exclosures and individually guarded trees have been erected and planted. Another technique which can be used to establish trees in open areas at less cost, is to plant individual trees amongst the dense

Pied flycatcher

stands of bracken into which the sheep will rarely wander away from the paths, and this has achieved limited success.

Additionally the Society is making every effort to identify and acquire the richest of the remaining woods. Surveys of upland woods have been carried out in Wales, the West Country, and the Pennines, and a number of new reserves are being sought or established. Research is also needed into the best way to regenerate and manage the woods for birds and other wildlife. For many years it has been known that pied flycatchers readily respond to the provision of nestboxes, and when these are put up, their numbers often sharply increase. The first boxes at Nagshead, a reserve recently established by agreement with the Forestry Commission in an area within the Forest of Dean, were put up in 1928 and at the Gwenffrwd several hundred boxes have been supplied. But despite this, pied flycatcher numbers can once again decline, and in some years, as in 1981, very few young are produced, when the usual abundance of caterpillars fails.

These caterpillars, notably of the winter moth and oak roller moth, sometimes occur in huge numbers on the oaks, stripping the trees as bare of leaves as if winter had arrived in mid-summer. Fortunately, the oaks, like some other forest trees, can produce a second crop of leaves in the summer, called lammas shoots, and this carries them through to the next year, when the caterpillars have returned to their usual numbers. These caterpillars are the main food for many woodland birds, whose breeding cycle coincides with their emergence on the oak leaves.

Another problem which is receiving attention is the implication of inclosures on the bird community. Pied flycatchers and redstarts catch some of their food on the ground, where scurrying insects are easily seen amongst the short grass stems. Wood warblers and willow warblers nest on the ground in low clumps of grass. The effects of inclosure will include a great increase in the height of the vegetation, and while blackcaps and thrushes may like the dense clumps of bramble as nesting sites, the effect on the more specialised birds of these woodlands is less well known.

With its programme of acquisition management and research, the Society is doing everything it can to safeguard our hanging oakwoods. But without a massive injection of public funds to help farmers and landowners to save their woods, there is little doubt that at the present rate of destruction and degradation, very few of them will survive to the next century.

Long-tailed tit

Highland birchwoods

by John Hunt

The Scottish Highlands has been described by Frank Fraser-Darling as a 'devastated area'. He and many other naturalists have pointed out the serious damage which man has inflicted on the natural environment of this unique area to the detriment of both its human and wild inhabitants. Few of the many tourists who flock to the Highlands each year to admire the splendid scenery will be troubled by such considerations and, indeed, it is not easy for anyone to realise that the great bare hills and moors were once clothed by woodland up to the natural treeline which in the eastern Highlands was over 2,500 feet above sea level. But this was the case until well into the Middle Ages with forests of pine, oak and birch covering most of the Highlands and Islands. Even the windswept Hebrides and the northen isles of Orkney and Shetland once supported some natural woodland and scrub, now almost entirely gone.

The destruction of the ancient forests by man is well documented and makes a long, dismal story of ignorance and greed. The final seal was set with the introduction of extensive sheep farming in the late 18th century. The grazing of sheep and deer, combined with the widespread practice of burning grass and heather to 'improve' the grazing or maximise grouse stocks, has effectively prevented any significant regeneration of native woodland. This is seen most clearly in the north-west Highlands where enormous tracts of countryside are now entirely treeless and one has to look on crags and islands in the lochs to find a few trees, clinging on where hungry mouths cannot reach them.

Fortunately there are still some small fragments of the ancient forests surviving today albeit in a much modified form. These are a very precious part of our heritage and their future must be protected. Included amongst these are a number of birchwoods, particularly in the far north and west of Scotland where birch can be regarded as the true climax tree cover. Birch also features prominently elsewhere, not just as a remnant of old native woodland, but as an opportunist tree, able to take advantage of any chance to establish itself. In the past, birch, which is not a long-lived tree, would often have acted as a coloniser giving way eventually to oak or pine. Today that process is rarely possible, though woods containing a mixture of these trees are not uncommon.

Belying its graceful and almost fragile appearance, birch is one of the great survivors of the tree world. Producing abundant seed, it colonises bare or disturbed ground with great vigour and, if ungrazed, thick scrub develops rapidly. This is often seen within forestry plantations where birch will fill in gaps left around the edges of the conifers. More commonly birch seedlings wage a losing battle against rabbits, sheep and deer as each year the new growth is bitten back. Occasionally a dense area of seedlings is able to develop into a thicket which eventually provides sufficient protection from grazing for some trees to grow. More often before it can reach that stage, a grass or heather fire destroys the seedlings. But birch never gives up trying and its widespread distribution through the Highlands is a tribute to its resilience and success against all the odds.

Three species of birch occur in Scotland. The dwarf birch is an arctic-alpine shrub which is found only sparsely in mountain areas and never forms anything approaching woodland. It is silver birch and downy birch which separately or together make up the Highland

Downy birch

birchwoods. These are not always easy to tell apart though a mature silver birch will often stand out with its silver-white bark and graceful drooping tips to its branches. Silver birch prefers drier, richer soils than downy birch so the latter is usually more common in the wet, acid areas and in the far north and west.

Highland birchwoods support a good density of breeding woodland birds. Most typical of all and often the most numerous is the willow warbler, a species which seems to prefer birch above all other trees. The silvery descending song of the willow warbler proclaims its summer presence from even the smallest stand of birch. Most of the other common woodland birds also nest, taking advantage of the very large number of insect species which are dependent on birch. In particular the life-cycle of a wide range of moths is linked with birch of which the Rannoch sprawler and Kentish glory are two of the more memorably named. Few rare plants are likely to be found under birch though a fine display of woodland flowers will develop in the absence of grazing. In undisturbed birchwoods mosses and lichens can form a luxuriant woodland floor whilst fungi attack the various stages of dead and dying trees.

In the poor soils and harsh climate of the Scottish Highlands, birchwoods cannot match the lush profusion of plant and animal life of a southern oakwood. Nevertheless, they provide a most valuable wildlife habitat, often in marked contrast to the surrounding moors and hills. This is seen clearly in the far north of Sutherland where three fine birchwoods survive in Strath Beag and on the rocky slopes of Ben Hope and Ben Loyal. Amongst the birch are rowan, aspen and holly with willow and alder on the wetter ground. For a few brief weeks in summer these trees resound to the song of willow warbler, chaffinch and redstart. Spotted flycatcher and redpoll are also quite common and tree pipits song flight splendidly in the clearings. The evocative song of the occasional wood warbler proves the exception to the rule that this species will only nest in oakwoods. These woods are truly a green oasis amongst the bare flows and hills of Sutherland.

The most northerly remnant of natural woodland in Britain is at Berriedale on the island of Hoy in Orkney. This is a tiny wood of birch, aspen and rowan but with its honeysuckle and rose it captures the atmosphere of woodland in much milder latitudes. It is most encouraging that in the absence of sheep the trees are regenerating well and the wood is slowly spreading.

There are some splendid examples of birchwood on both Speyside and Deeside, occasionally with pine or oak present. Juniper and hazel frequently provide a valuable understorey though both appear to be declining under the pressure of grazing. Not far from Ballater, on Deeside, the Muir of Dinnet National Nature Reserve has several hundred acres of birchwood, mostly young trees that have developed since the war with the cessation of muirburn. Here can be seen the succession from seedling trees on the heather moor through thick scrub to mature trees above a grassy woodland floor with plants such as dogs mercury and chickweed wintergreen.

On Speyside, at the RSPB's Insh Marshes reserve, birch fringes much of the wetlands and one fine birchwood section is included within the reserve. It is, perhaps, unfortunate that birch logs make excellent firewood and the power-saw is making considerable inroads into the birchwoods in this area, in order to feed the growing number of wood-burning stoves. On the reserve the trees are safe from this fate and fenced enclosures will encourage birch to regenerate into new areas.

Birchwoods provide a valuable shelter for stock during the winter but this may prove their eventual undoing because the grazing prevents any regeneration. Sadly there are many woods today which are so obviously on their last legs — a thin scattering of elderly trees waiting for their inevitable end at the hands of the winter gales. The woodland flowers such as wood anemone, wood sorrel and violet will linger on, sometimes for years, as a

Redpoll

reminder of what had once been but eventually grazing and burning will remove even these traces of former woodland.

Bleak though the birchwoods can seem in the long winter months they still provide a climate of their own which is a little warmer and less windswept than elsewhere. The occasional flocks of tits, redpolls or siskins move through the trees brightening a dull winter's day. Amazingly they can find sufficient insects and seeds to survive even when the frost bites hard and snow lies deep.

In the past foresters have tended to treat birch as a weed which interferes with the efficient establishment of conifer plantations. A more sympathetic attitude has been shown in recent years and birch may now be left until the plantations are thinned or harvested. Birch grows quickly and could produce excellent pulp wood. Moreover it will do so on our poor upland soils without the care that the foresters lavish on exotic conifers with their drainage, ploughing, weeding and fertilising. On the Continent birch can be a valued forest tree and one wonders why in Britain foresters have so completely ignored its potential.

Research has shown that birch can help to restore the fertility of soils impoverished by generations of overgrazing and burning. Given time, its leaf litter will gradually replace the lost humus and retain nutrients previously washed away by the heavy rains. Many ecologists have pointed out how bad land use has turned much of the Scottish Highlands, beautiful though they may be, into as near desert as it is possible to get in our climate. Such a view is not popular with the agricultural establishment which is understandably reluctant to admit past mistakes or to face up to the remedial action that is needed. So, sadly, unwise practices continue in our uplands with overgrazing and uncontrolled burning still widespread over huge areas.

The problem of depopulation in the Highlands and Islands has been of great concern for many years. The difficulty of maintaining the small and fragile human communities is frequently discussed but the ecological factors rarely receive any attention. Agriculture is still the most important source of employment in the region and we should recognise that the hill ground could be so much more productive than it is. The country could well afford to redirect the present system of agricultural grants and subsidies in the Highlands into a long-term scheme of land improvement that initially reduced sheep numbers in the hills and encouraged the partial restoration of native woodlands. Birch would play a major part in such a scheme where for once agriculture would be working with nature on its side. It would take many years to bring back some of the lost fertility to the uplands but what an exciting project this could be with great long-term benefits for people and wildlife alike. All that is needed is sufficient vision and determination.

Silver birch

Birch is one of the few native British species widely planted for its ornamental value and would be a top contender for the prize of Britain's most beautiful tree. It adds enormously to the landscape of the Highlands with its changing hues from the purple haze of its winter branches through the fresh green of spring and the gold of autumn. Birch does not live to a great age and many birchwoods will probably have only a limited life before they disappear in the face of pressures from grazing and the power-saw. It is likely that other birchwoods will spring up elsewhere to take their place and all those who love the Scottish Highlands will hope that they can continue to do so.

Moorland in Scotland and Wales

by Graham Williams

Above the mountain wall or boundary of enclosed land there lies, throughout highland Britain, an extensive and desolate landscape dominated by peat-covered, gently undulating plateaux interspersed with small lakes, pools and boggy areas, the source of many major rivers. Higher still in altitude is a zone of bare rock faces and tangled screes which are the worn down remnants of once much greater mountain ranges.

In winter, the moorlands, remote from human habitation, are more isolated than ever in continuous periods of low-hanging cloud, driving snow and fierce winds; there are few birds or animals adapted to eke out an existence in such a harsh environment, but in spring the scene changes with almost startling suddenness with the return of the migrants and birds which have wintered in milder climes at lower altitudes. It is now that the moorland is at its most appealing to birdwatchers, when the far-reaching and evocative display calls of golden plover, curlew and other waders mingle with the less musical calls of the resident red grouse and hen harriers and merlins perform marvels of aerobatics in the full ritual of their display flights. Set against a wide, open landscape receding gently into a distant view of far hills, this is an exhilarating and spiritually uplifting scene for those devotees of wild places who seek it out.

The types of vegetation which occur on moorlands in Britain are very varied and whilst there are some areas where one plant may be dominant (for example some heather moors) it is often more usual to find a complex mosaic of vegetation communities reflecting local differences in the physical environment, especially variations in climatic and soil characteristics. The peat soil which supports the moorland communities often contains remains of tree trunks and seeds from long-departed trees, evidence of the period after the last Ice Age when an improvement in climate permitted native trees to establish themselves at much higher altitudes than now. Man's influence has also been very marked on areas which are now moorland, through a combination of tree-felling, burning and subsequent grazing by his livestock which has prevented tree regeneration. Drastic changes are taking place to moorland through man's activities at present day and these are described later in this section.

There are three main categories of vegetation: dwarf shrub heath, blanket bog and grass moorland. The first two are far more productive in terms of their flora and fauna than the latter, but all categories support communities of rare and specialised birds which generally occur in small numbers compared to bird populations of many other habitats. This is hardly surprising since most moorland is acid, infertile ground (as on the siliceous rocks of much of north and west Britain): wherever the base status and fertility of the soil increases, however, as in parts of the Pennines, the population density of breeding birds can show a marked increase.

Dwarf shrub heath is dominated by heather or ling, and to a lesser extent bilberry; the latter, together with the handsome purple bell heather, is particularly conspicuous as an early coloniser of recently burnt heather moorland. Pure, dense stands of heather are specially well developed on drier ground in central and eastern parts of Britain where they are often managed intensively in the interests of grouse shooting, but heather is also

Golden plover

distributed widely in the wetter moorland of the west. The sheets of colour provided by square miles of heather and its associated plants in late summer are hard to match in visual beauty, especially when stirred by a warm gentle wind and against a background of blue sky interspersed with occasional clouds which send shadows dancing across the moor in a scene of sharp clarity.

The eminently hardy red grouse is one of the very few birds which is adapted to spend the whole year on the moors; the shoots of young heather are its main source of food and its numbers and breeding success are dependent on the quantity and quality of edible heather available. Other foods are taken, however, especially the flowers, berries, leaves and stalks of bilberry, crowberry, and other like plants. The even hardier ptarmigan breeds in Scotland, principally at heights above 3,000 feet but also at lower elevations in the north-west; found on higher ground than the red grouse, the food taken is nevertheless similar, chiefly shoots of heather, crowberry and bilberry. During especially severe winters, ptarmigan may descend to lower slopes but even then they very rarely mix with the flocks of red grouse that occupy the same terrain.

Two birds of prey, merlins and hen harriers, are also particularly associated with heather moorland; the former is a dashing sharp-winged scimitar of a bird which takes its prey by sheer speed and agility while the latter is a casual but elegant hunter which floats in leisurely fashion low over the ground on the lookout for suitable prey. In both cases the most favoured nesting site is long, rank heather which provides good protection from the onset of short periods of harsh weather that can characterise the moorland even in early summer. The status of the two species is very contrasting at present. Hen harriers are enjoying a marked increase in breeding range, having re-colonised suitable breeding habitats on the Scottish mainland, northern England and Wales since the 1950s. Merlins, sadly, are experiencing a marked decline in numbers and have disappeared from several moorland areas where they formerly bred.

Blanket bogs, too, have their own special breeding birds. Wildernesses of eroded peat hags interspersed with numerous wet hollows and pools support a variety of plants such as cotton grass, heather, cross-leaved heath, deer sedge and a variety of *Sphagnum* mosses and form a major breeding habitat for wading birds. Where the ground is particularly wet, there is a chance of finding a small colony of elegant, black-breasted dunlin with a pleasing, purring trill of a display song contrasting with the more strident but equally musical fluting of the greenshank in Scotland and haunting melodious notes of golden plover in Wales, England and Scotland.

The third major type of moorland is the grass moorland which covers extensive areas of the northern and western hills of Britain and is the least productive in terms of the fauna it supports. Deserts of acidic grassland dominated by the mat-grass or white bent *Nardus stricta* are generally of low palatability to grazing stock and similar vast tracts of purple moor grass are scarcely better except where burning encourages new growth which is then grazed by cattle or sheep. Where mineral nutrient status is better, short-cropped grassland, consisting chiefly of common bent and sheep's fescue, provides better grazing for animals. Apart, however, from the ubiquitous meadow pipits (the most abundant moorland bird) and skylarks, the grass moorland is largely devoid of bird life except where there are small oases of different vegetational and topographical features, such as where a scattering of outcropping boulders attract a pair of wheatears to breed.

Resulting from a happy blend of the effects of a harsh physical environment coupled with the influence of man's activities, the moorland of Britain may seem a limitless resource in which its own specialised plants, like the delectable little orchid, the lesser twayblade, found growing underneath heather, and rare moths and butterflies whose larvae feed on

Wheatear heather will continue to flourish undisturbed. This, sadly, cannot be taken for granted as

the rate of loss of this specialised habitat is proceeding apace in modern Britain.

There are several land use changes which are having a profound effect on the moorlands, but two in particular, hill farming improvement schemes and afforestation, are specially serious. New techniques have recently been developed for the re-seeding of moorland areas using relatively simple surface seeding techniques involving the application of appropriate quantities of lime, basic slag and nitrogen, flail mowing and spike rotovation. In this way heather and other moorland forms are readily converted into rye grass-clover pastures, resulting in higher sheep stocking rates per acre (from one to two sheep per acre before re-seeding to four to five per acre afterwards), an increase in the lambs reared per ewe and reduced ewe mortality. There is therefore a considerable impetus in moorland reclamation, especially in Wales, where recent statistics show that there are now no less than 2·8 million hill ewes, which compares with a figure of only 2·9 million in Scotland where the hill area is almost five times greater. The enclosure, ploughing and re-seeding of more than 250,000 acres of moorland is the main reason for an increase of no less than 300 per cent in hill sheep and cattle numbers in Wales within the past thirty years.

Afforestation in many areas of Britain is also a major influence and cause of concern for the future survival of the very extensive areas which are needed to ensure the survival of the characteristic moorland flora and fauna. In areas such as Galloway and the Borders, the planting of conifers is having a profound effect on moorland populations. During the first stages of tree planting, the moorland habitat is scarcely affected, and indeed can be improved quite substantially as reflected in the number and variety of birds it supports. As soon, however, as the forest begins to mature, the moorland birds are forced to move out and are replaced by a rather limited and much less interesting woodland bird fauna. Research on both golden eagle and raven in southern Scotland has correlated declines in breeding success with increased afforestation. Both species require large expanses of open moorland as hunting range.

With a national policy leaning towards a significant escalation in timber production, it is inevitable that the economically marginal moorland areas of Britain will come under increased consideration for afforestation. Whilst there are still very extensive moorland areas left in Britain, and especially in Scotland, it would be unwise to be complacent about the very real threats this poses to the specialised bird communities of the moorland. The scale of the threat is indicated by *Strategy for the UK Forestry Industry*, the report published in 1980 by the Centre for Agricultural Strategy at Reading University. The report suggested four possible planting programmes, the most ambitious of which would double the forest area of Britain and Ireland by the year 2030 and would, it is admitted, mean the loss of up to a third of the 16 million acres of open hills and uplands. Planting on a similar scale, which would roughly double the existing area of woodland, was also recently proposed by the Forestry Commission. Virtually all this increase would have to be on agriculturally unproductive moorland areas.

There are, of course, many moorland areas with little ecological interest where agricultural improvements and afforestation have little impact on valued bird communities; the RSPB is not opposed to afforestation and agricultural improvement, but we do feel that there is a great need for more research and survey work to be carried out and the results used to integrate the needs of bird protection with new land use policies and strategies. In this context, the Society is pursuing two lines of enquiry which will be very beneficial. Firstly, survey work to identify the most important moorland sites (the work has virtually been completed in Wales and has been extended to other parts of Britain) and secondly research into the feeding requirements of the key species at risk (a three-year programme is under way on the ecology of the merlin in Wales).

Although moorland is not as well represented among its reserves as some habitat types,

Hen harrier

the Society does have some very exciting moorland reserves with contrasting features. At Lake Vyrnwy, the Society's largest reserve, there are no less than 8,000 acres of open hill land which form part of the Berwyn Mountains, the largest remaining block of heather moorland in Wales. Here the key feature of the main management aim to retain the heather moor is a fifteen-year rotational burning programme to provide a varied age structure and to maintain the dominance of heather at the expense of other plant species which might replace it. This aim is common to many other moorland areas of Britain, especially where there is management of red grouse for sporting purposes. Besides being the correct form of management for red grouse in giving a mosaic of young heather to provide nutritious young shoots for feeding and older heather for nesting sites, this benefits other bird species by, for example, giving good breeding areas for golden plover on newly burnt ground with sparse vegetation cover and for merlin and hen harrier in patches of dense, older heather. The management of moorland for sporting interests (red grouse in Wales, Northern England and Scotland and red deer in Scotland) is supremely important as an economic factor which helps to retain the habitat.

At the Gwenffrwd reserve in Dyfed there are also some areas of heather moorland, more than 300 acres in extent, which are burnt on a rotation basis. Although relatively small in extent, this block is of significance in that it is one of the few residual heather moorland areas remaining in South Wales, a reflection of the fact that the number of sheep grazing there and the existing vegetation cover are in balance; it is well known that above certain densities the number of sheep will radically change the plant communities on which they feed, in many cases causing a marked deterioration both in the nutritional quality of the sheep walk and in the wildlife interest of the site.

The avifauna of the Orkney moorland reserves is covered in a separate chapter and is different in some respects from the Welsh reserves although there are species common to both areas such as dunlin, golden plover, merlin and hen harrier. Further north still, in the Shetlands, are two further moorland reserves, Fetlar and Lumbister. Here the moorland vegetation is down virtually to sea level and there are vast expanses of blanket bog with many small lochs and pools. These wildernesses attract a wide variety of breeding birds and the usual species are joined by specialities of northern latitudes such as whimbrel, great and arctic skuas and red-throated divers. Lumbister and Fetlar are wild and remote and the Society plans to retain this essential freedom from human disturbance; this is an important management element in an era in which the desolate moorlands throughout Britain are under increasing threat not only from land use changes but also from the pressure caused by an increasing demand for a variety of leisure pursuits.

Opposite: Birchwood and moorland at Killiecrankie

There are further plans in hand for the acquisition of moorland reserves at important sites in Britain to give protection to a wildlife resource which is greatly esteemed not only for its rarity value but also for the integral part it plays, visually and in sound, in the aesthetic appeal of a dramatic and wild landscape.

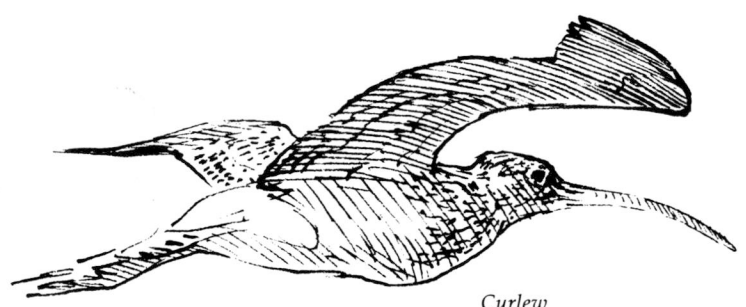

Curlew

Orkney moorland

by Eric Meek

The Orkney moors, long famous for their bird communities and especially for their population of hen harriers, represent yet one more type of habitat under threat. The threat in this case comes not from afforestation as in other parts of Britain, but from agricultural reclamation which is steadily converting the heather moorland into pasture to provide grazing for beef cattle, Orkney's main source of income. To anyone who has visited the island over a period of years the process is frighteningly obvious. The moorland edge, starkly conspicuous as a result of the contrast between the brown heather and bright green pasture, retreats higher and higher each year. As I write, occasionally gazing out of my window onto Pullan, one of the Stenness hills, the threat is brought forcefully home once more, for here a strip, almost a kilometre in length and over 100 metres wide, was reclaimed in 1979. This great green scar on the hillside is visible from up to sixteen miles away and the once-thriving common gull colony which existed there is reduced to a small number of pairs outside the enclosure fence. This then is the situation which is worrying conservationists but why do we need worry? What is so special about the moorlands of the Orkney archipelago? Let us take a closer look at this particular type of habitat in order to understand the urgent need for conservation measures to be taken.

Geologically Orkney is, in the main, made up of flagstones of Middle Old Red Sandstone age. These rocks produce a landscape of rounded hills, nowhere exceeding 270 metres in height. Only in Hoy where these rocks are overlain by younger, more resistant sandstone are the hills at all spectacular. Here they rise via very steep slopes to as much as 477 metres above sea level and, in addition, produce a precipitous coastline of high cliffs and rock stacks, including the Old Man of Hoy.

Despite lying at a latitude of 59 degrees, similar to that of Stockholm, Sweden, and just south of that of Cape Farewell, Greenland, Orkney has a remarkably equable climate, lying as it does in the path of the warm ocean current, the North Atlantic Drift. However, its position also means that it lies in the track of the depressions moving across the Atlantic so that strong winds are frequent. Assessing climatic conditions throughout Scotland, E L Birse described those parts of Orkney below 300 feet as 'very exposed' and those areas above as 'extremely exposed', his two highest categories. On average twenty-four gales a year occur in the islands and no part of them is free from the salt they carry with them.

It is now generally accepted that the lack of trees in Orkney is as much the result of human activity as of the climate. We may imagine that, prior to the coming of the Norsemen, the moorlands that we know today would have a covering of hazel, birch and willow scrub. During the next thousand years this natural vegetation gradually all but disappeared, burning probably being the main method by which this was achieved. Thus by the early 19th century most of the scrub woodland had been converted into moorland and, from the 1830s on, the process of reclaiming the moors for agriculture gained pace. At this time the moors were still used as summer pasture for livestock (including pigs!) but this ended abruptly early in this century with the introduction of a low-growing, perennial variety of white clover. The increased fertility and carrying capacity of the lower, in-bye land meant that all livestock could now be kept on this improved pasture and that all hill grazing became

Short-eared owl

unnecessary. This situation has persisted to the present time and even today those areas of moorland which are used for grazing livestock are, in general, lightly stocked. We may now, however, be witnessing the first signs of change with Shetland sheep having been introduced to a large part of a moorland SSSI in Evie and cattle to a similar area in Orphir.

At present though, it is reclamation, more than overgrazing, which is the major threat to Orkney's moors, moors which are ornithologically unique in the British Isles. Perhaps their most famous occupant is the hen harrier which, as a result of the lack of game preservation interests in the islands, was never wiped out as it was over much of the Scottish mainland in the late 19th and early 20th centuries. It did, however, decline in numbers and it needed the dedicated efforts of several Orkney naturalists, notably Eddie Balfour, to see the birds through this lean period. Today, in a good year as many as 100 breeding females may occupy the Mainland moors with, because of the prevalence of polygyny, something less than half that number of males. Over fifty pairs of short-eared owls also breed and they, together with the unique ground-nesting population of kestrels, depend to a large extent for their food on the Orkney vole. This large vole, a race of the common vole of continental Europe, is now believed to have been introduced to the islands by Neolithic or early Bronze Age man and is today common on the Mainland and some of the other larger islands.

The other important bird of prey to be found on the Orkney moorlands is the merlin, a species which has declined over much of Britain, perhaps at least partly as a result of organo-chlorine pesticide pollution, but about a dozen pairs still nest on the Mainland. Feeding chiefly on meadow pipits and skylarks but also hunting out over arable areas and into farmyards to find species such as house sparrows, the merlins' dependence on heather moorland here is for nest sites. They use only long, old heather, a commodity which, because of reclamation and indiscriminate burning, is in increasingly short supply. The practice of peat-cutting, carried on for centuries on the Orkney hills has, despite creating a certain amount of disturbance on the moors during the summer, helped the merlins in one way. The old, disused peat banks become overgrown with long heather and provide ideal nest sites.

Other characteristic species of the moors are golden plovers, preferring the shorter vegetation of the hill-tops, and the red-throated divers, confined as a breeding bird to the often tiny moorland lochans although flighting noisily down to nearby sea areas to feed. Both great and arctic skuas also nest in small numbers as do a few pairs of dunlins and almost unbelievable numbers of curlews, a species with a good claim to being Orkney's 'national' bird!

When all of these species are considered together the importance of Orkney's moors can be clearly seen and it was this together with the subjective impression of rapid moorland loss which caused the RSPB to map carefully whatever remained of the Mainland moors during the summers of 1980 and 1981. With the completion of this exercise we now have an accurate baseline from which to measure future change. The moors of the East Mainland, once so extensive, have now been reduced to under four square miles and are much fragmented; their reclamation has been accelerated by their relatively thin covering of peat. This is in direct contrast to the West Mainland where consequently the moors have survived longer. In the West Mainland today the moors are in two major blocks. The area remaining to the south of the main Kirkwall-Stromness road extends to barely seventeen square miles while that to the north has an area of little over twenty-one square miles. In the former, protection is afforded by RSPB reserve status to under three square miles at Hobbister while in the latter the reserve area extends to under seven and a half square miles in the areas known as the Birsay Moors, Cottasgarth and Greenay Hill. However, only four square miles are actually owned and thus permanently protected. SSSIs have been designated in the past in the southern area (two square miles) and in the north (6·22 square miles) but neither is

Orkney vole

extensive enough to conserve effectively the moors and their bird populations. Reserves and SSSIs all badly need to be extended if viable populations of the characteristic species are to be maintained.

Of all Orkney's outlying islands it is Hoy which has so far been least affected by the reclamation process. Here reclamation is chiefly confined to the eastern coastal fringe and the great majority of the island is still dominated by moorland in one form or another. Unfortunately, however, Hoy does not possess that major food source for birds of prey, the Orkney vole. Densities of small moorland birds such as meadow pipits and skylarks are particularly low and hence their main predator, the merlin, is present in much smaller numbers than would otherwise be expected. The moors of Hoy are thus not typical of Orkney as a whole. Nevertheless they are far from unimportant with a scattering of golden plovers and dunlins, red-throated divers on the hill-top lochans and large colonies of great and arctic skuas.

Rousay, too, has so far been little affected by agricultural 'improvement'. Here Orkney voles are found and in consequence there are several pairs of hen harriers, short-eared owls and kestrels. However, again, small bird densities appear to be decidedly low in comparison with the Mainland and support, at present, only one pair of merlins. There are good populations of waders, a 1981 census by David Lea for NCC revealing, for example, nineteen pairs of golden plovers and 145 pairs of curlews.

Parts of Eday are also dominated by heather moorland and hold the characteristic Orkney species. These moors, however, are eminently suitable for reclamation and major changes in habitat appear imminent. The nearby island of Sanday is, in general, flat and low-lying, the only area of heathland occurring in the south-west where the land rises to some 150 feet above sea-level on the Gump of Spurness. This area, too, with its colony of over fifty pairs of arctic skuas, is soon to be lost. On Stronsay, only in the south-western peninsula of Rothiesholm has heather moorland survived. Here, in an area of one and a half square miles can be found a delightful bird community of between thirty-five and forty breeding species, a mixture of those dependent on the moors and those dependent on the sea.

The extent to which moorland has disappeared or is about to disappear on some of these outlying islands illustrates clearly what might happen on the Mainland. With improved technology it would appear that virtually none of the moorland area is safe from the reclamation process. Efforts must be made to conserve as much as possible of what remains.

Gazetteer of RSPB reserves

Details of the most notable RSPB reserves are included in the following pages. Entries are arranged in alphabetical order and are intended to give an impression of each reserve.

Geographical position: indicated on one of the maps on pages 110 to 120 and as a six-figure grid reference (for use with Ordnance Survey Maps) under the entry for each reserve.

Status: the various gradings of reserves are shown under individual entries and include Sites of Special Scientific Interest (SSSI) notified by the Nature Conservancy Council under the Wildlife and Countryside Act, 1981, and sites included in the NCC's comprehensive list of major sites of conservation importance, the *Nature Conservation Review* (NCR1* — of international importance, NCR1 of national importance and NCR2 — prime sites of only slightly less value than grade 1 sites).

Access: has to be limited at many reserves for the sake of the wildlife and the human visitors. Before visiting it is, therefore, *important* to check that the reserve will be open and that advance permits are not required. Visiting details are usually published in the Winter issue of *Birds*. Members of the RSPB and YOC are admitted free to all reserves, where visiting is permitted.

These maps are based on the
Bartholomew British Isles Motoring Map
Scale 1:1,000,000

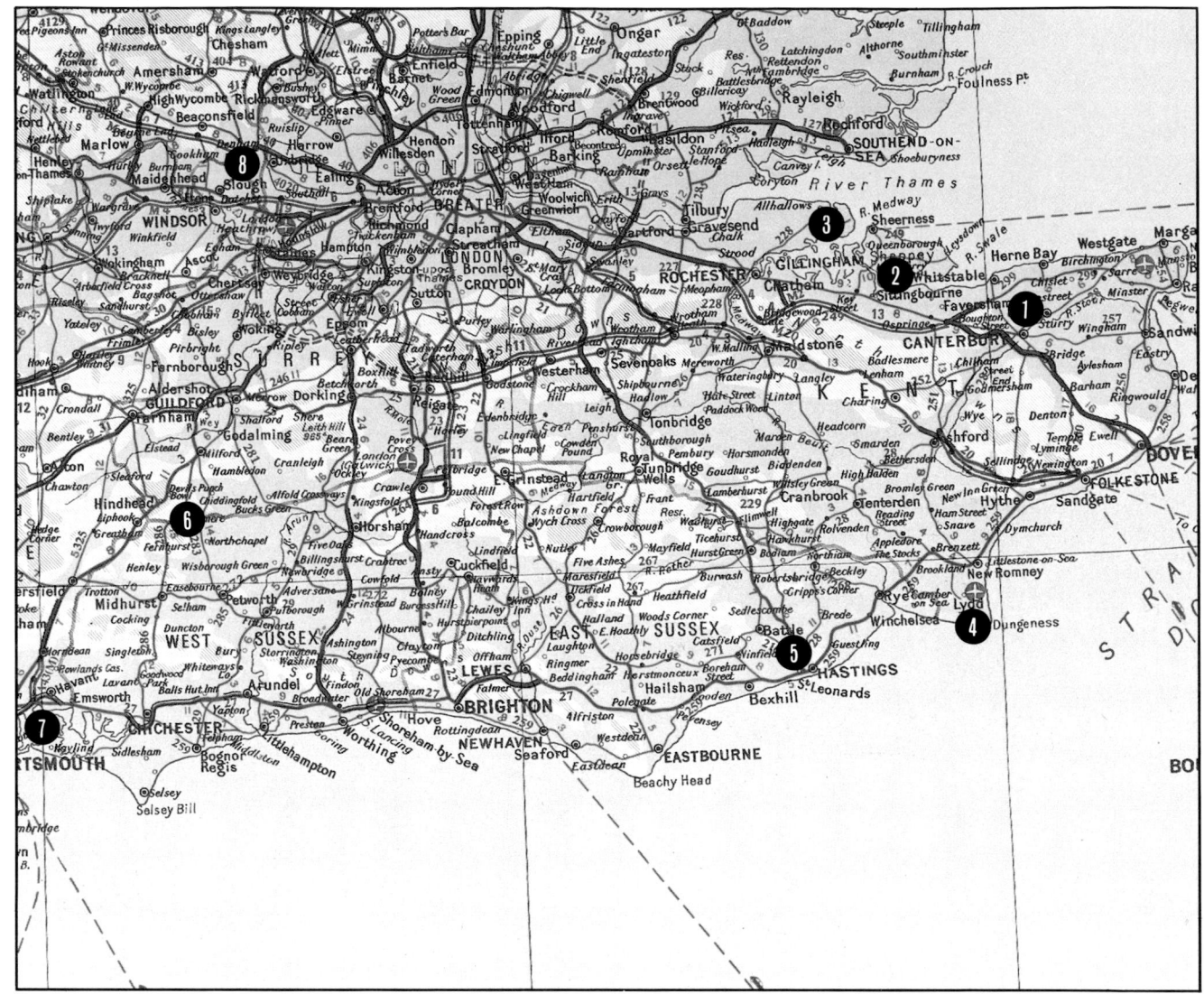

1. *Church Wood, Blean*
2. *Elmley*
3. *Northward Hill*
4. *Dungeness*
5. *Fore Wood*
6. *Barfold Copse*
7. *Langstone Harbour*
8. *Church Wood, Hedgerley*
9. *Snettisham*
10. *Titchwell*
11. *Strumpshaw Fen*
12. *Minsmere*
13. *North Warren*
14. *Havergate Island*
15. *Wolves Wood*
16. *Stour Wood*
17. *Fowlmere*
18. *The Lodge and Sutton Fen*
19. *Rye House Marsh*
20. *Ouse Washes*

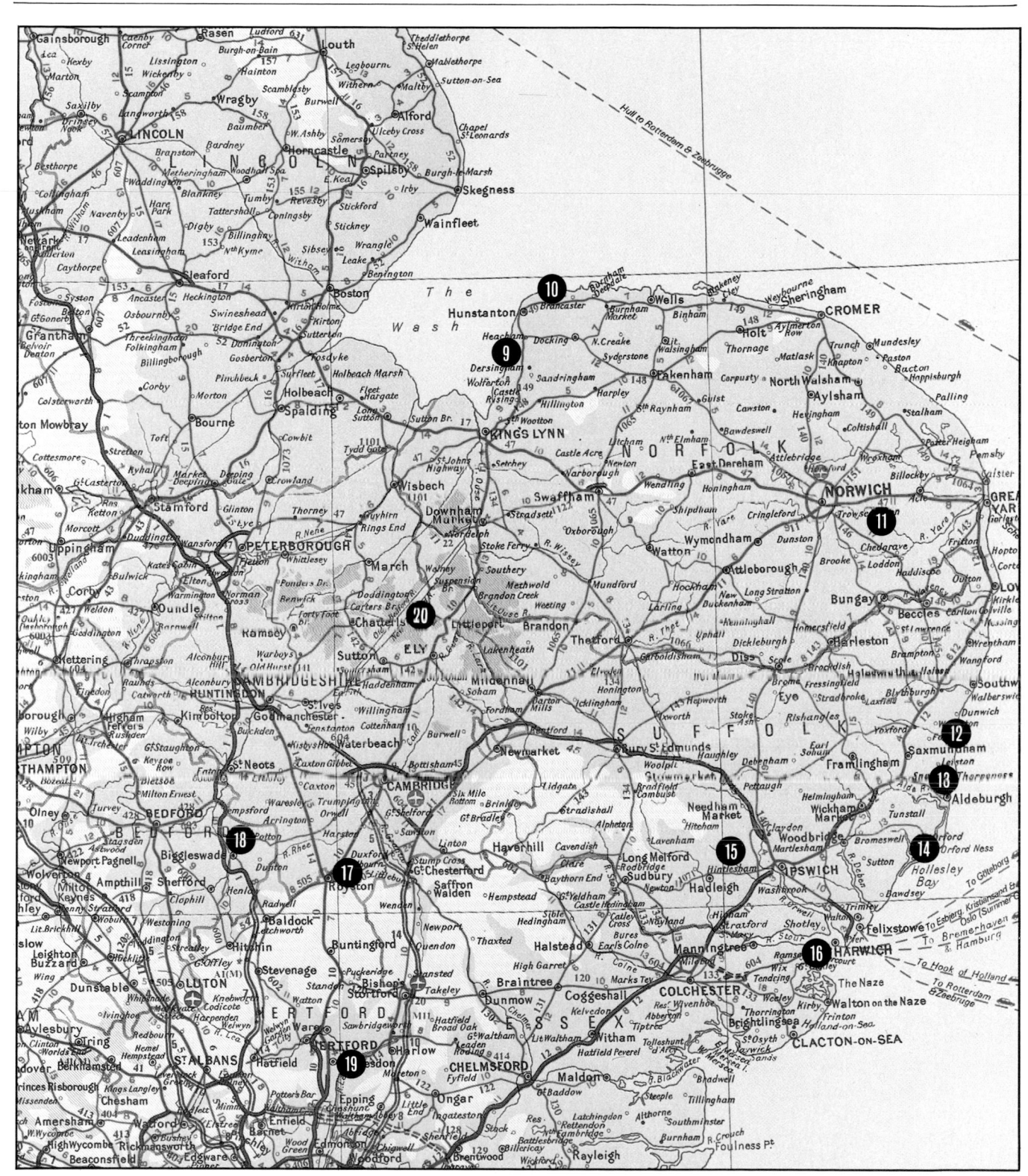

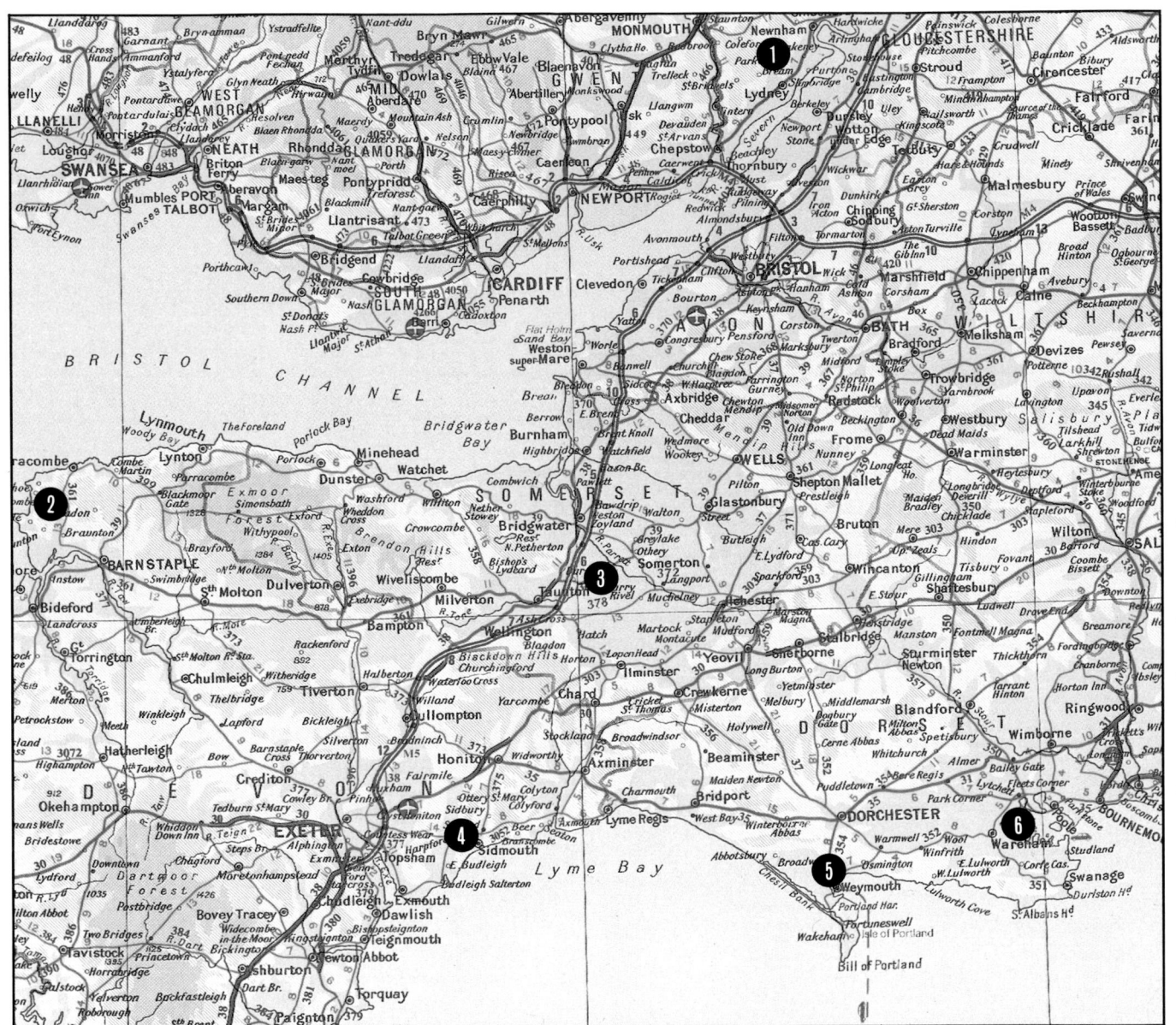

1. Nagshead
2. Chapel Wood
3. West Sedgemoor
4. Aylesbeare and Harpford Commons
5. Radipole
6. Arne

7. South Stack
8. Lake Vyrnwy
9. Ynys-hir
10. Gwenffrwd
11. Grassholm Island

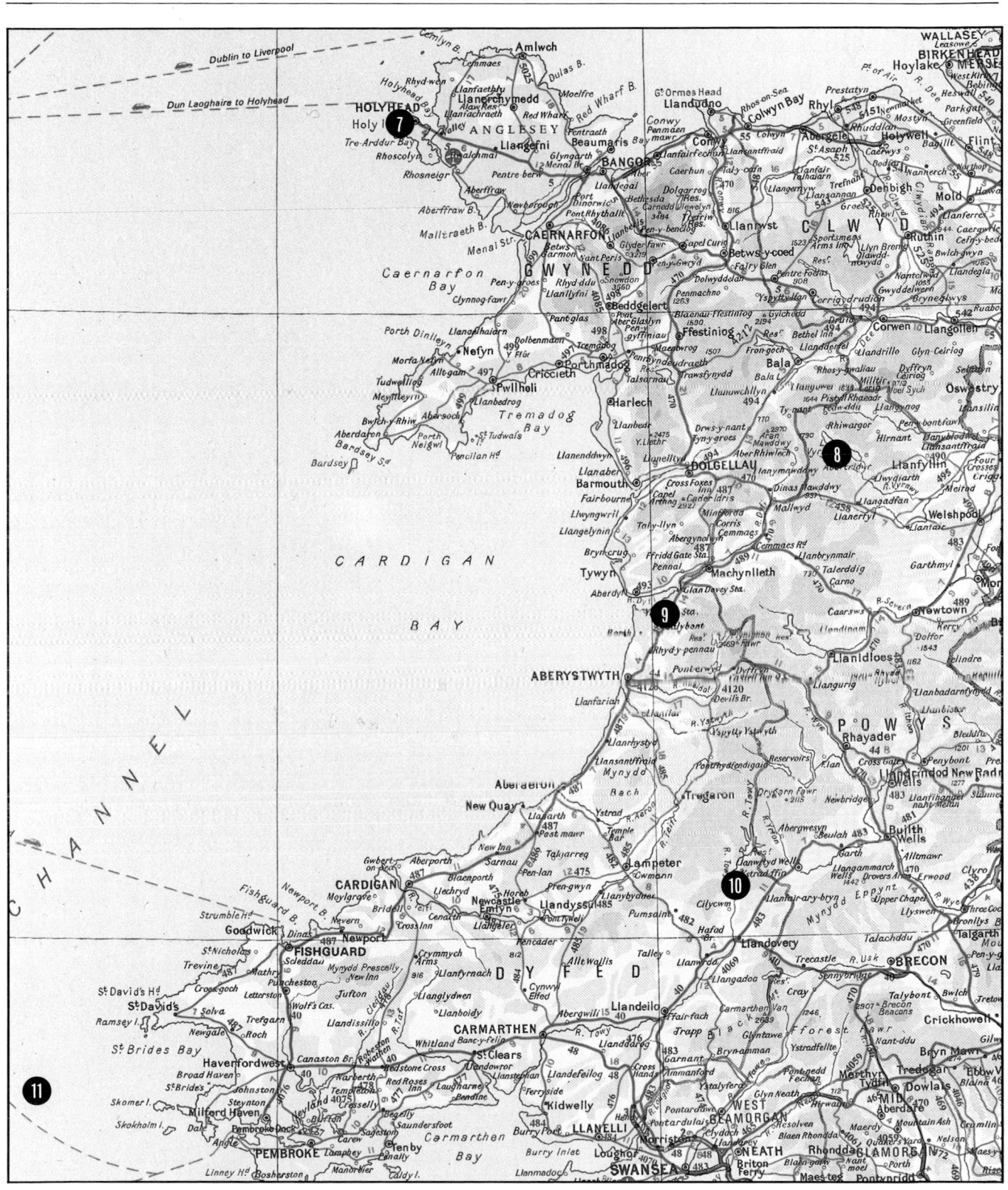

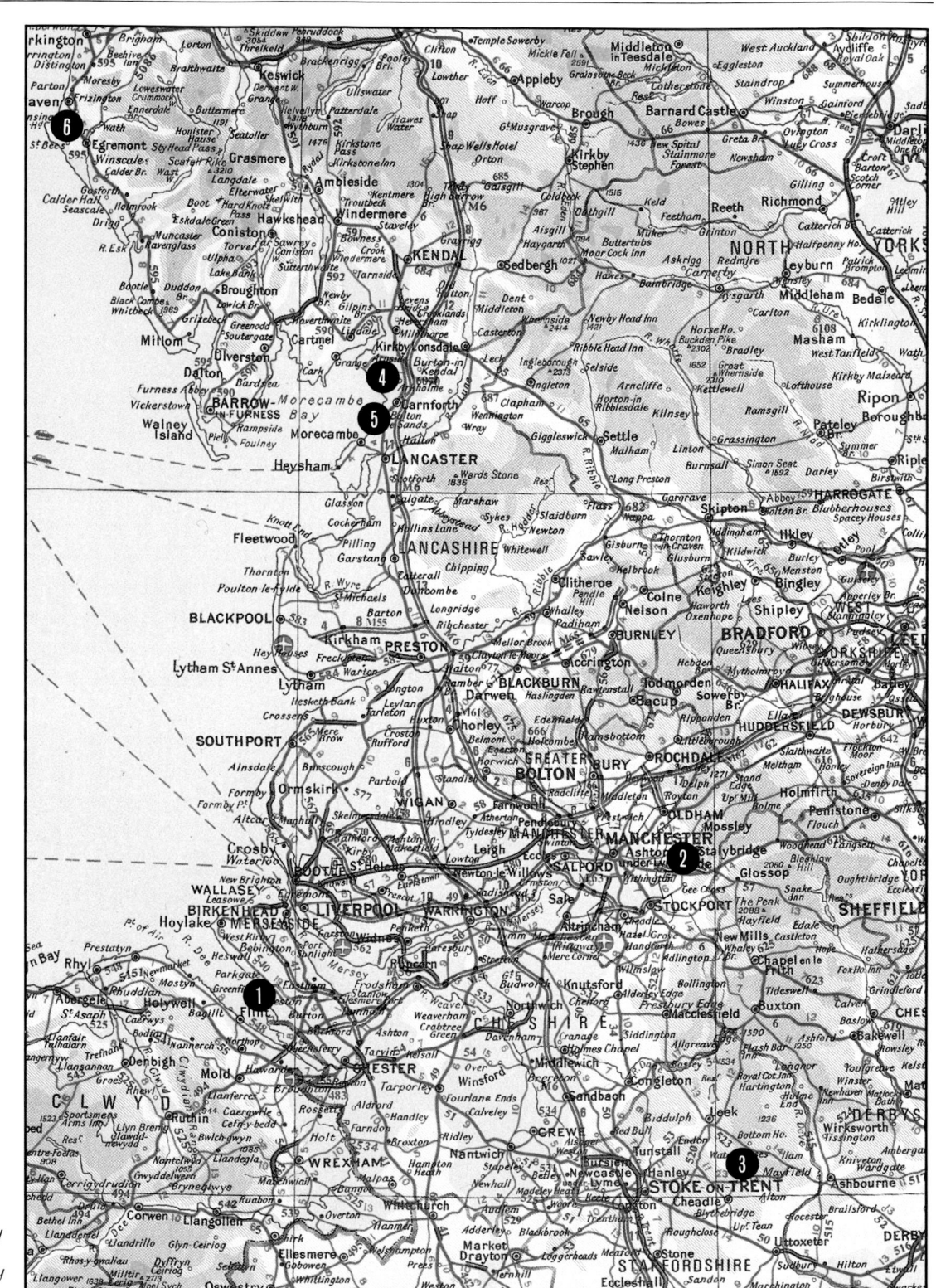

1. Gayton Sands
2. East Wood
3. Coombes Valley
4. Leighton Moss
5. Morecambe Bay
6. St Bees Head

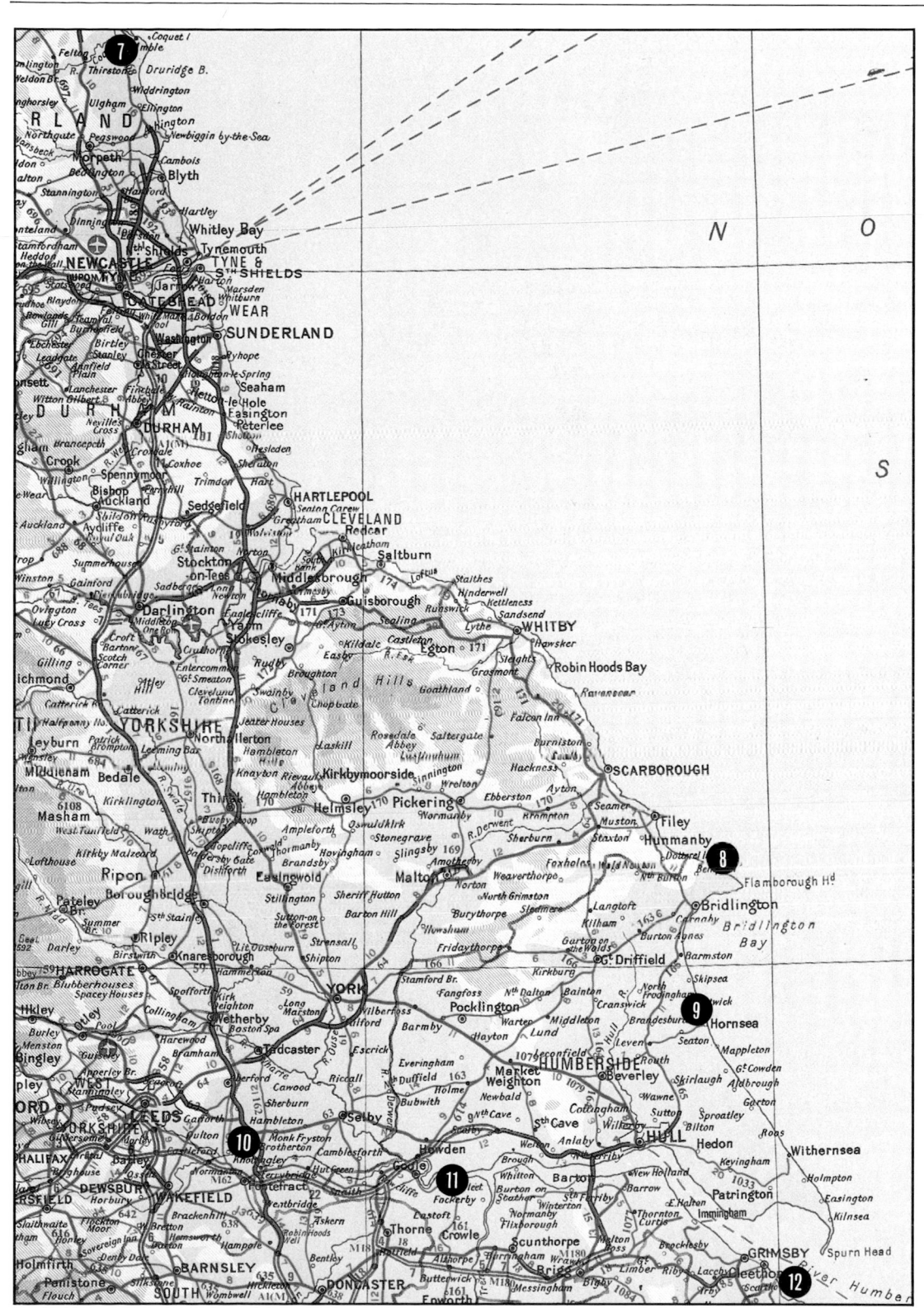

7. *Coquet Island*
8. *Bempton Cliffs*
9. *Hornsea Mere*
10. *Fairburn Ings*
11. *Blacktoft Sands*
12. *Tetney*

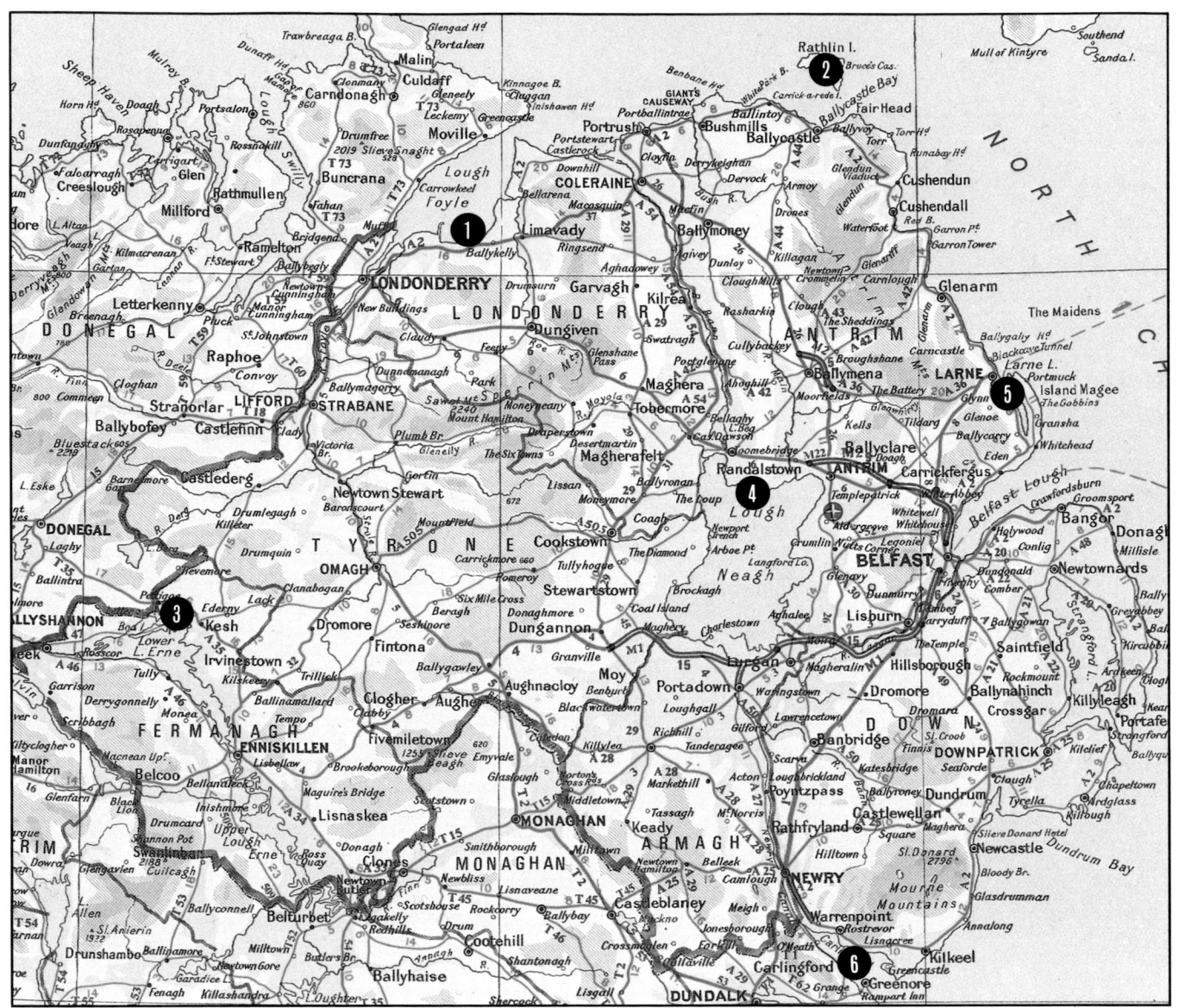

1. Lough Foyle
2. Rathlin Island Cliffs
3. Castlecaldwell
4. Shane's Castle
5. Swan Island
6. Green Island

7. Lochwinnoch
8. Horse Island
9. Loch Ken/River Dee
10. Mull of Galloway
11. Vane Farm
12. Skinflats
13. Forth Islands

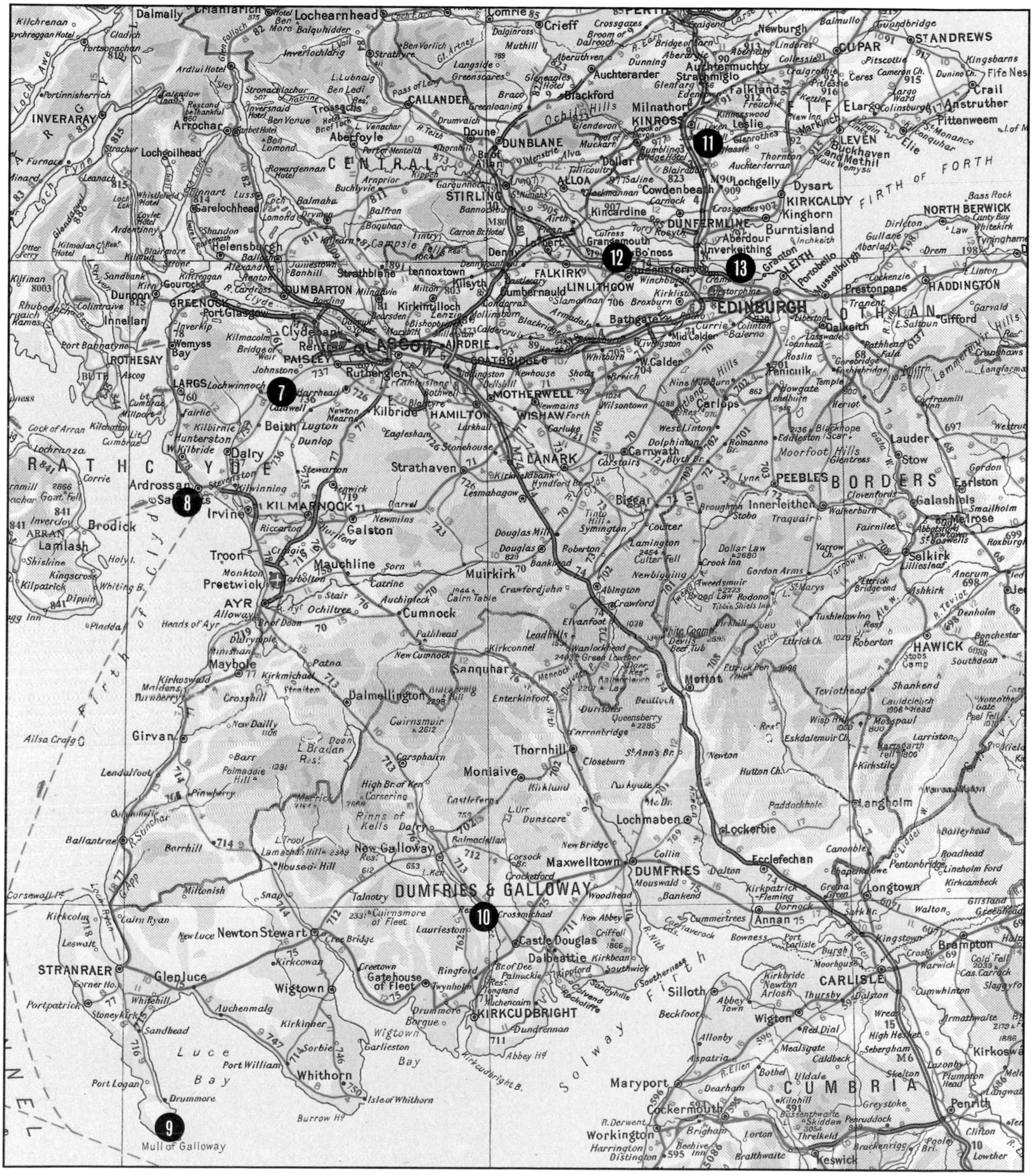
STRATHCLYDE
CENTRAL
DUMFRIES & GALLOWAY
BORDERS
CUMBRIA
FIFE
LOTHIAN
FIRTH OF FORTH
Firth of Clyde
Solway Firth
Luce Bay
Wigtown Bay
GLASGOW
EDINBURGH
STIRLING
DUMBARTON
PAISLEY
AYR
KILMARNOCK
DUMFRIES
CARLISLE
HAWICK
PEEBLES
LANARK
MOTHERWELL
HAMILTON
GREENOCK
ROTHESAY
INVERARAY
CALLANDER
DUNBLANE
KINROSS
CUPAR
ST ANDREWS
KIRKCALDY
DUNFERMLINE
LEITH
HADDINGTON
NORTH BERWICK
STRANRAER
KIRKCUDBRIGHT
Newton Stewart
Castle Douglas
Girvan
Maybole
Troon
Prestwick
Irvine
Ardrossan
Largs
Brodick
Lamlash
Dunoon
Helensburgh
Arrochar
Aberfoyle
Lochearnhead
Crieff
Falkirk
Linlithgow
Bo'ness
Queensferry
Grangemouth
Alloa
Cumnock
Sanquhar
Thornhill
Moffat
Lockerbie
Langholm
Annan
Gretna Green
Longtown
Brampton
Penrith
Keswick
Cockermouth
Workington
Maryport
Wigton
Whithorn
Mull of Galloway
Galashiels
Selkirk
Melrose
Lauder
Biggar
Strathaven
Muirkirk
Dalmellington
Moniaive
New Galloway
Gatehouse of Fleet
Wigtown
Glenluce
Portpatrick
Ailsa Craig
7
8
9
10
11
12
13

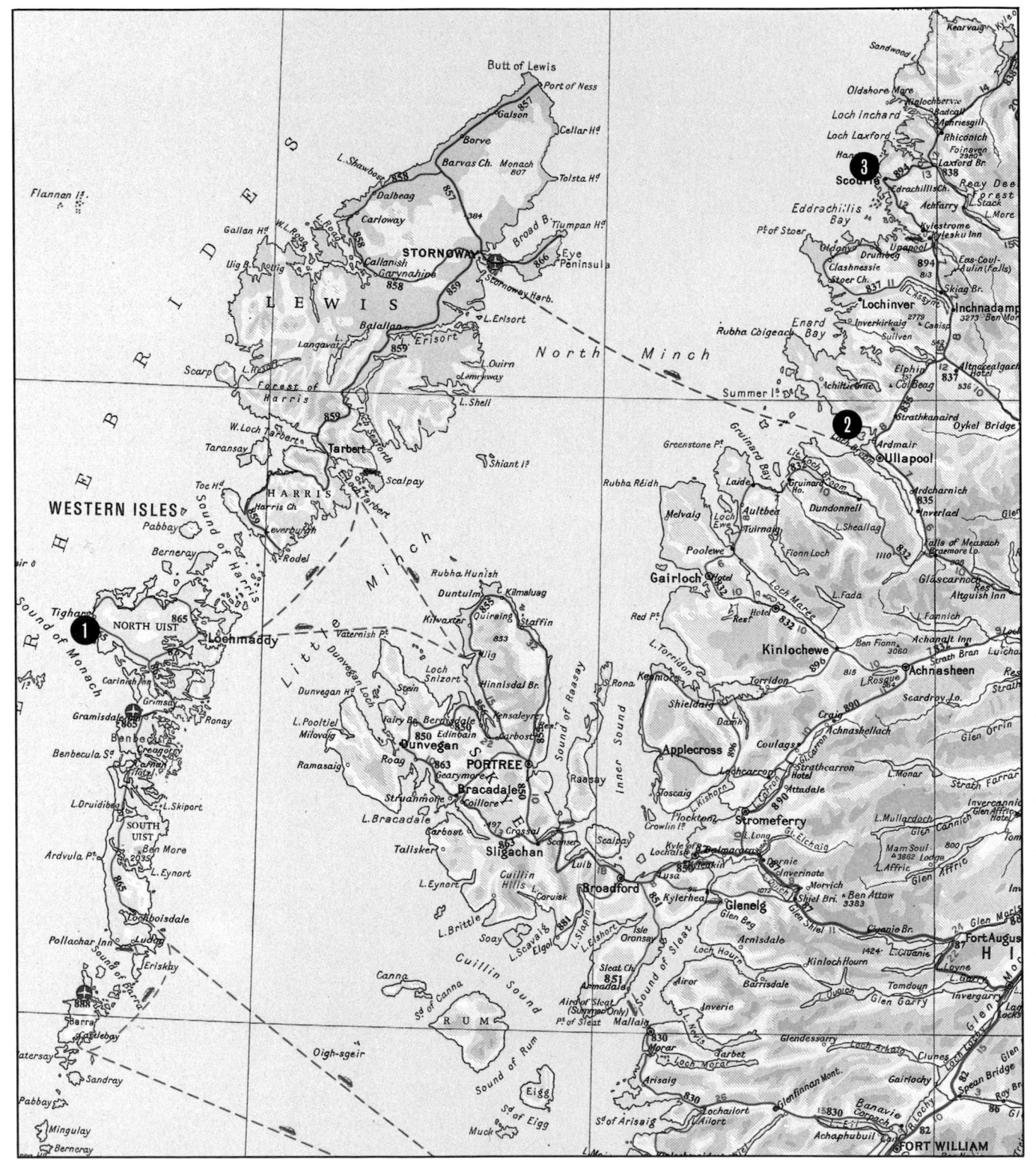

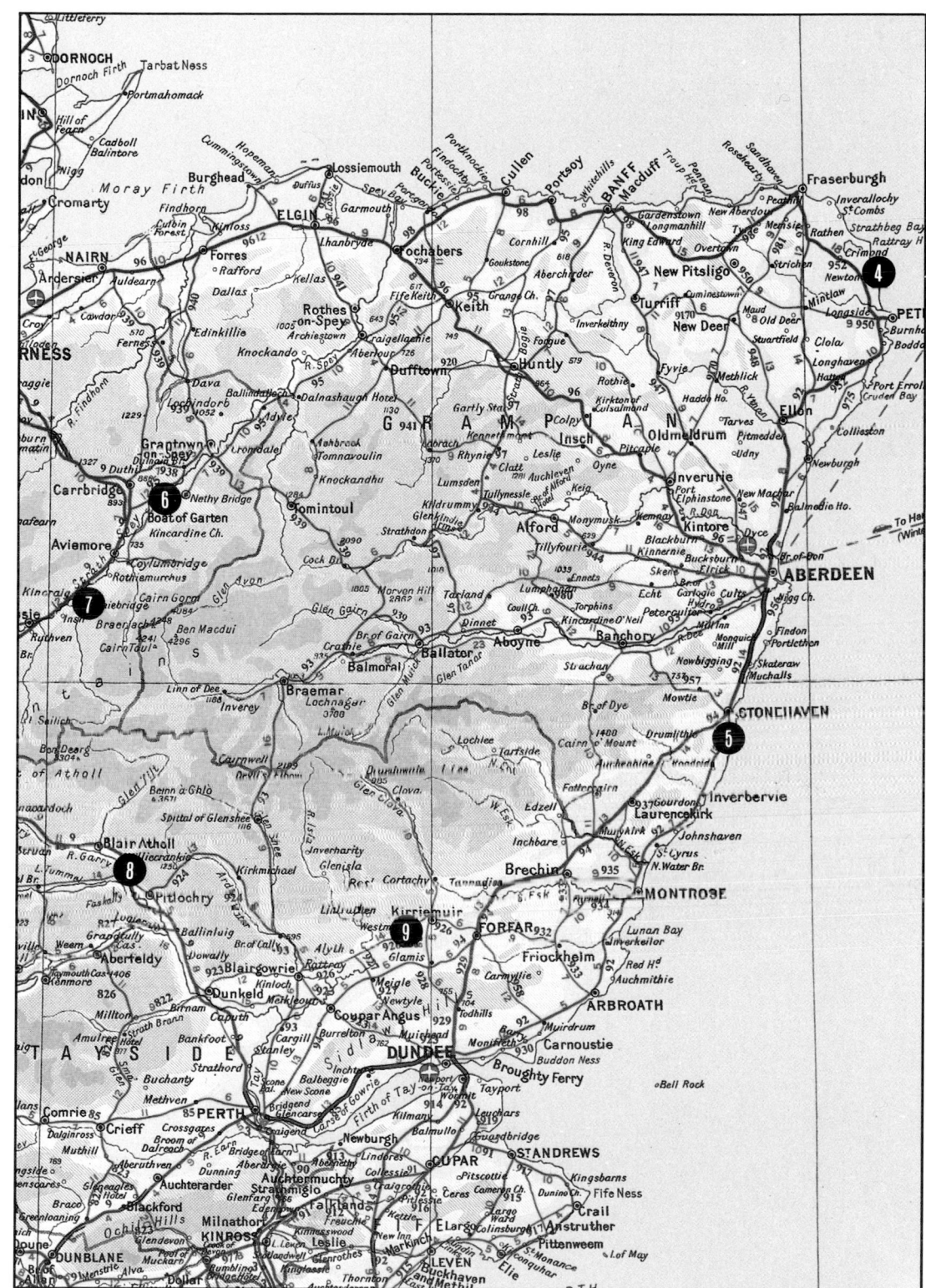

1. *Balranald*
2. *Isle Martin*
3. *Handa Island*
4. *Loch of Strathbeg*
5. *Fowlsheugh*
6. *Loch Garten*
7. *Insh Marshes*
8. *Killiecrankie*
9. *Loch of Kinnordy*

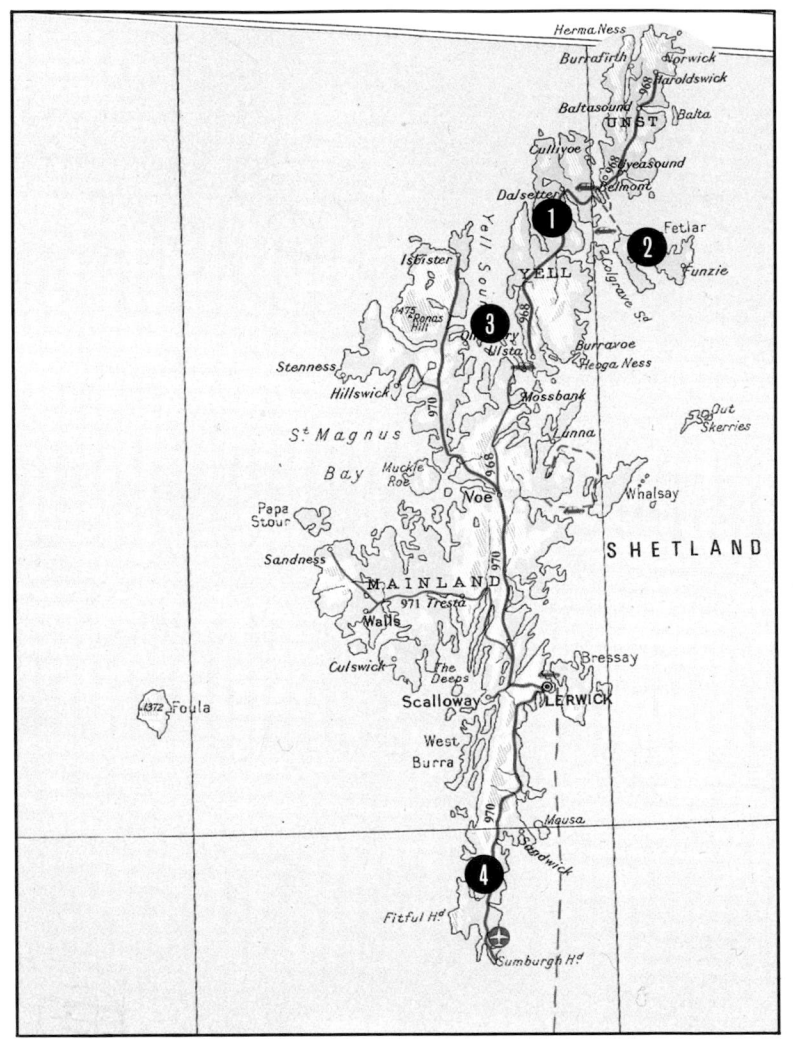

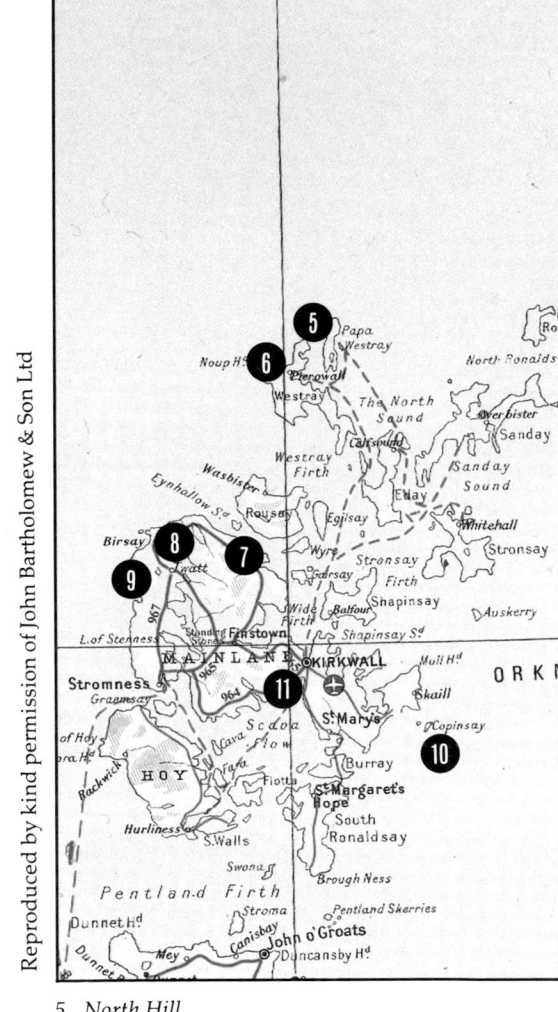

Reproduced by kind permission of John Bartholomew & Son Ltd

1. Lumbister
2. Fetlar
3. Yell Sound Islands
4. Loch of Spiggie
5. North Hill
6. Noup Cliffs
7. Birsay Moors
8. The Loons
9. Marwick Head
10. Copinsay
11. Hobbister

Arne, Dorset

SY972878 (Car park)   *1,200 acres*
SSSI, NCR1.* Mainly dry lowland heath, of great
importance for rare reptiles, dragonflies, plants
and birds such as the Dartford warbler. 3 miles
east of Wareham, approached from Stoborough off
the A351, Swanage-Wareham Road.

The Arne Peninsula protrudes into the north-west corner of Poole Harbour. The reserve holds a wide variety of habitats, of which undoubtedly the most important nationally is the extensive area of lowland heath. In addition, deciduous and coniferous woodlands, freshwater reedbeds and marsh, saltings leading to large expanses of mud-flats as the tide recedes in the harbour, together with its geographical location, give the Peninsula great biological diversity.

Lowland Heath The dominant vegetation of the heaths is ling, with other ericaceous species, which are liberally mixed with gorse. In places Scots pine and bracken are invaders into the system. In the wet valleys and bogs the star attraction is the Dorset heath, a species which away from the Purbeck heaths is a rarity. Other species present include bog cotton, bog myrtle, all three species of sundew, bog asphodel and in the wettest places carpets of *Sphagnum*.

Woodland Scattered areas of both coniferous (Scots pine with some maritime pine) and deciduous (sweet chestnut and silver birch) woodlands. In the damper valleys areas of carr (sallow and birch).

Marsh and Reed Swamp There are extensive areas of reedbeds, both fresh and brackish, with pools. A variety of marsh plants such as club-rushes, rushes and pondweeds are present.

Saltings These are dominated by *Spartina* grass, which only arrived in the harbour towards the end of last century. This grass now covers vast areas of what was once mud-flat. On the landward side of the saltings a mixed community of sea aster, sea lavender and sea milkwort is to be found. The sides of the creeks are bordered with sea purslane and English scurvy-grass.

Management The heaths need constant attention, if they are to retain their characteristic flora and fauna. To achieve this, it is necessary to burn rotationally or mow the heath, recycle gorse patches by cutting, control invading pine and cut and spray the encroaching bracken with selective herbicide. Because fire takes hold easily in heath-land, it is necessary to maintain a network of firebreaks.

Extensive work to improve and transform once tidal marshes to freshwater has been undertaken. A continuing programme of maintenance is needed to maintain the marshland habitat and improve further areas.

Birds The Dartford warbler is without question the most interesting species present on the heaths. Its numbers vary from year to year, becoming depleted especially after severe winters. Other inhabitants of the heathland are stonechat, yellowhammer, linnet and meadow pipit. Where there is a scattering of pines the summer evening sound is that of 'churring' nightjars. During the winter hen harriers are not infrequently seen quartering the heaths.

The woodlands provide habitat for five species of tits, chiffchaff, willow warbler, goldcrest, tree-creeper, etc., as well as sparrowhawk, kestrel and buzzard.

Reed warblers, reed buntings, moorhens, water rails, mallard and teal breed in the reedbeds and marshes. A notable recent species to breed in the marsh is the bearded tit.

The *Spartina* marshes have only redshank as a breeding species.

The mud flats hold a variety of waders and ducks, principally during passage times and the winter period. Of the waders the most numerous are redshank, curlew, dunlin and oystercatcher but there are at times large numbers of black-tailed godwit and spotted redshank, besides smaller numbers of several other species. During the winter teal, mallard, shelduck and wigeon are the most common but also good numbers of goldeneye and red-breasted merganser. On the harbour water great crested grebes are frequent and in the early part of the year both Slavonian and black-necked grebes may be encountered.

Mammals Twenty-five species have been recorded, including roe and Sika deer, badger and harvest mouse.

Reptiles All six species occur, the reserve being especially important for two nationally rare species of heathland, the sand lizard and smooth snake.

Insects Arne is an entomologists' paradise with many rare and local species present. They are too numerous to name but so far thirty-three species of butterfly, nearly 800 moths, fourteen grass-hoppers and their allies and twenty-two species of dragonfly have been recorded. Many other groups are still poorly recorded but doubtless will also produce impressive lists.

Spiders Well over 200 species have so far been identified.

Sparrowhawk

Aylesbeare Common, Devon

SY057898   *450 acres*
SSI, NCR1. Dry and wet heath with a rich flora.
A good site for characteristic insects and birds.
Part of Woodbury Common heathland complex,
east of Exeter, close to the village of Newton
Poppleford.

Woodbury Common was at one time a huge expanse of dry heathland, with patches of wet heath and bog, scrub and oak woodland. Many parts have been enclosed and ploughed, or planted with conifers, so the original heath is now broken up into many isolated fragments. Aylesbeare and Harpford Commons, which form the RSPB reserve, are the largest and ecologically most important of these fragments and have been graded as a site of national conservation importance.

The reserve consists mainly of a dry heath community, bell heather and ling mixed with the low-growing western gorse, producing in late summer a brilliant display of purple and gold. In some parts there are patches of the taller European gorse, and throughout the area are scattered pines, most of which are small and stunted.

The commons also contain a number of wet heath areas, characterised by the profusion of pale-pink cross-leaved heath. Within these wet flushes are small patches of *Sphagnum* moss, with bog cotton, tussocks of purple moor-grass and a variety of much rarer flowering plants such as pale butterwort, lesser butterfly orchid, sundew and saw-wort.

The valley bottoms have small, stony streams, along which are strips of woodland, with carpets of bluebells and primroses in spring.

Birds The reserve was, until recently, the Devon stronghold of the Dartford warbler, but unfortunately the severe winter of 1978 wiped out the entire population. However, there are still good numbers of other heathland species, such as nightjar, tree pipit and stonechat, while the surrounding woods have breeding buzzards and in summer hobbies sometimes visit the reserve in search of dragonflies.

Insects The insect life of the commons is very rich and varied, with at least sixteen species of dragonflies having been recorded, including the rare southern damselfly. The butterfly population is also very varied with thirty-seven species having been recorded since the reserve was established in 1977.

Management The first aim of management at Aylesbeare and Harpford Commons is maintenance of the heathland plants and animals. Problems include accidental fires, disturbance by

Cross-leaved heath

trespassers and the spread of pine from adjacent plantations. The streams and small pools also require careful attention to maintain their sensitive plant communities and gorse thicket is being encouraged in the hope that Dartford warblers will one day reappear. Volunteer work parties have the difficult and rather painful winter task of cutting the tall, leggy gorse clumps to encourage new bushy growth.

A nature trail and reserve guide is available for visitors. Due to the extreme fire risk, the trail goes around the perimeter of the reserve, mainly on wide firebreaks.

Balranald, Western Isles

NF707707   *1,625 acres*
SSI, NCR1. An area of calcareous machair with
lagoon, swamp and drier fringing marsh. Of great
importance for the density of breeding waders,
with many wildfowl and good numbers of
corncrake. West of the A865 between the
settlements of Tigharry and Paiblesgarry,
including the peninsula of Ard an Runail.

The reserve is predominantly grazing land, with some arable and hay-fields. There are a number of pools and marshes. The magnificent Atlantic beaches with sweeping white sands backed with dunes and large stretches of 'machair', level grassland with a great variety of wild flowers, provide a colourful sight in spring and summer.

Balranald is managed by the local crofters but, although much of the land is still worked on traditional lines, modern agricultural practices are unfortunately beginning to have a noticeable impact on the reserve. Pastureland is being converted to arable, the machair is being fragmented and changed from a patchwork of wild flowers to a monotonous sweep of green, while the marshes and pools are gradually being drained to extend the grazing land.

Birds Despite agricultural changes, the area still contains probably the densest population of wading birds in the whole of Britain. Large numbers of lapwing, redshank, curlew, oystercatcher, dunlin and snipe nest throughout the reserve. In spring their distinctive calls and spectacular display flights enliven the beaches and farmland. Arctic tern, little tern and at least eight species of duck also nest but the reserve's most important ornithological feature is probably its population of corncrakes. This secretive relative of the moorhen is now almost extinct on the British mainland, where modern agricultural practices, particularly the early cutting of grass-fields for silage, prevent the corncrake from nesting successfully. However, in the Western Isles, the traditional methods and the presence of marshes with extensive beds of iris and other lush vegetation have provided a more secure home. However, even here its future is by no means secure.

Flowers The flowering plants of Balranald are very varied, particularly on the machair, where the herb-rich turf contains frog orchid, wild thyme, eyebright, field gentian, fairy flax, milkwort and many others, in addition to many grasses.

The marshes are equally colourful in spring and summer, with iris, northern marsh and early marsh orchids, ragged robin, cotton grass and bogbean.

Insects Its northerly and exposed situation makes the reserve less than ideal for butterflies and other large flying insects, but good numbers of common blue, meadow brown, the northern species of large heath, and migrants such as red admiral and painted lady, can all be seen in good numbers.

Barfold Copse, Surrey

SU928318   *13 acres*
South-west of Haslemere, near the Sussex/Surrey border.

This reserve is an oak woodland with an understorey of unmanaged hazel, set among a much larger area of woodland with some permanent pasture adjacent.

Management There is no warden, but management is carried out by several local members' groups and some individual members. The work is largely restoration of bridges and paths, provision of nestboxes and cutting of neglected hazel to promote vigorous growth.

Birds Although the bird life of the wood has not been studied closely, it is unlikely that any unusual species are present. Many characteristic woodland birds such as tits, robins and nuthatches may be seen.

Plants Because of the rather acid soil the most obvious plants are holly and foxglove. There are relatively few flowering plants compared with woods on more basic soils. There are, however, many ferns, largely associated with the stream, and exotic species, such as rhododendron and western hemlock.

Bempton Cliffs, Humberside

TA197741   *60 acres*
SSSI, NCR1.* The only large breeding colony of seabirds on chalk in Britain and the largest colony in England. North-west of Flamborough Head, the reserve is best approached from Bempton Village by driving up Cliff Lane. The footpath from Filey

to Flamborough Head runs along the entire length of the reserve.

Bempton Cliffs reserve runs for five miles southward from Speeton, where the low clay cliffs of Filey Bay give way to a chalk outcrop, rising sharply to 445 feet and continuing past Flamborough Head to beyond Bridlington. This chalk has eroded to provide ledges and cracks for seabird nest-sites. To the landward side of the footpath are intensively cultivated fields and the landscape is open, with no trees except isolated crab apples and hawthorns.

Birds Bempton Cliffs is part of England's largest seabird colony with eight species breeding here. Commonest is the kittiwake, with more than 80,000 pairs on the whole of the Flamborough headland. Amongst the kittiwakes on the cliff-faces, it can be difficult to pick out the 400 pairs of nesting fulmars, but they can often be seen gliding on updraughts of wind along the cliff-face. Despite there being no more than 1,000 pairs of herring gulls, their raucous cries leave little doubt about their presence. The auks are well represented with 14,000 adult guillemots, 3,000 razorbills and 4,000 puffins. Bempton is famous as the only English gannet colony and the only one on the British mainland, but it was not until the 1920s that gannets first nested here. From one or two pairs it increased to 109 in 1976 and to 312 in 1981. The eighth seabird species is the shag, about 20 pairs of which nest in the sea caves at the foot of the cliffs.

Seabirds at Bempton were for many years subject to large-scale egg-taking for trade and kittiwakes, particularly, were killed for their feathers, popular as hat decoration in the 19th century. Indeed it was to protect seabirds here that the first British legislation to protect birds, other than for sporting purposes, was passed in 1869.

Its prominent position on the east coast attracts passing migrants and in autumn almost any species might turn up. Ring ouzels, redstarts and both pied and spotted flycatchers pass through regularly and among the more uncommon migrants recorded here are Alpine swift, bluethroat and greenish warbler. Especially in autumn, when shearwaters, terns and skuas pass, sea-watching can be rewarding.

Flowers In the narrow strip of vegetation between the fields and cliffs on this very narrow reserve over 220 species of flowering plants have been recorded. One of the most conspicuous in early summer is red campion, which has a variety of colour shades from white to deep red. Typical chalkland plants here include common scurvy grass, field mouse-ear, yellow oat and rough hawkbit.

Gannet

Insects Of the fifteen species of butterfly here, the most easily seen are the whites, large, small and green-veined, and small tortoiseshell. Two migrants, the painted lady and red admiral, are regulars from midsummer on.

For visitors There is a small information centre and a leaflet about the reserve. Viewing places have been provided with safety barriers.

Birsay Moors and Cottasgarth, Mainland, Orkney

HY368197   *3,883 acres*
These reserves cover a very large area of moorland. The grid reference given is for the entrance to the Cottasgarth reserve which lies about 5 miles north of Finstown.

Over much of the reserve area peat has been cut for centuries and is still cut today using traditional methods.

The Birsay Moors and Cottasgarth are basically areas of heather moorland but, within that blanket description, habitat varies from dry heath totally dominated by heather, to wet heaths with, in addition, cross-leaved heath, cotton grass, deer grass and bog asphodel, and to various marsh and fen communities in which rushes or iris are often dominant. Several burns run through the moors, one of the most interesting being the Burn of Hillside, which flows through the raised mire of Glim's Moss and the calcareous valley mire known as the Dee of Dirkadale. The latter is dominated by a species-rich sedge-bryophyte community while in places there are low clumps of willow scrub and a reed bed. Several small hill-top lochans exist, in some of which bogbean is abundant.

Management Parts of this extensive moorland area are owned by the Society while others are leased and the major benefit which has accrued is the prevention of the reclamation of the moors to which large areas of Orkney have been subjected. Present policy is to allow heather to follow a natural cycle of growth and regeneration without the pressures of grazing and burning. Planting of native trees and shrubs, such as willow and rowan, which at one time must have been common in these areas, is planned, especially in the sheltered valleys of the burns.

Birds The commonest moorland birds are skylark and meadow pipit but smaller numbers of wrens, wheatears, stonechats, twites and reed buntings are also present, while there are considerable colonies of ground-nesting starlings. The Dee of Dirkadale holds, in addition, several pairs of sedge warblers, Orkney's only regularly breeding warbler. These small bird populations

Hen harriers

support the presence of several pairs of merlins while Orkney voles and rabbits provide the diet for short-eared owls, kestrels (again ground-nesting) and hen harriers. The latter, an Orkney speciality, is a polygamous breeder, males usually having two or three, and on occasions up to seven females.

Large colonies of gulls are also to be found on the moors as are small numbers of great and arctic skuas. Eight species of waders nest including dunlin and golden plover and outstandingly large numbers of curlew. Teal, wigeon and red-breasted merganser are among the breeding ducks while the tiny hill lochans are also the home of several pairs of red-throated divers, the latter being especially vulnerable to human disturbance.

Mammals Among the mammals the Orkney vole is of perhaps the greatest interest. This sub-species of the common vole of continental Europe is found, in Britain, only in Orkney and Guernsey. Orkney voles are now believed to have been introduced to the islands but perhaps as early as Neolithic times. Otters occur sparingly along the burns.

Flowers In Dale of Cottasgarth may be found bog whortleberry and lesser twayblade but the Dee of Dirkadale is by far the richest area for the botanist. The summer showing of heath spotted orchids, northern marsh orchid and early marsh orchid is especially spectacular and some fifteen species of sedges are to be found.

Blacktoft Sands, Humberside

SE843232   *460 acres*
SSSI, NCR1.* An extensive reedbed holding typical breeding birds such as reed warblers and, in some years, marsh harrier. Newly created lagoons attract waders and duck. Situated on the south bank of the Humber, east of Ouse Fleet.

Reedbed One of the largest tracts of continuous reedbed in the country, though largely tidal. The reed attains heights of nine or ten feet and shades out most other plants, except for halbert-leaved orache which manages to grow in areas of poor reed growth.

Rough Grass and Saltmarsh Couch grass forms dense swards in isolated higher areas where reeds do not grow, whilst close to the rivers are edges of saltmarsh where the influence of the Humber tides encourages sea clubrush, sea aster and sea purslane to grow.

Mudflats Low-lying mudflats have formed behind the stone training walls at the junction of the Rivers Trent and Ouse, because the daily inundations by the Humber tides prevent any plant growth other than algae.

Lagoons Lagoons have been created with heavy machinery in couch grass areas near the western end of the reserve. Here water levels are manipulated to provide feeding and nesting areas for birds.

Scrub Willow bushes have been transplanted to form screening to the lagoons with smaller numbers of alder and elder, and as they grow will form areas of scrub attractive to many small birds.

Management The main aim is to maintain the extensive reedbed system with its associated nesting and wintering species. The reedswamp is largely self-sustaining at the present time, but a noticeable feature is the lack of open, standing, permanent water. Such areas have been provided by bulldozing shallow scrapes where water levels can be manipulated to give the right conditions for nesting and wintering birds. Islands within these new lagoons are managed to provide nesting habitats for wildfowl and waders.

To break down and reduce growth of the dense swards of couch grass it is grazed by cattle. The resulting short grass with clumps of thicker vegetation is more attractive to nesting wildfowl and waders.

Tidal influence prevents the natural establishment of willow bushes because the salt kills the seeds. Willows with well-developed root systems have therefore been transplanted. These are now growing well and providing an additional habitat.

Birds Among typical reedbed nesting species are up to 100 pairs of bearded tits, about 10 per cent of the British population. About 400 pairs of reed warblers which nest here are near their northern limit in Britain. Small numbers of water rails breed and occasionally marsh harriers nest. Many shelduck nest under the dense reedbed litter, taking their young down to the estuary on the day they hatch.

Where the edge of the reedbed gives way to rough grass, sedge and grasshopper warblers, as well as large numbers of reed buntings, nest. The grassy areas support few species, but one to three pairs of short-eared owls do breed each year.

Mallard, teal and gadwall nest on islands in the new lagoons, with lapwing, snipe, redshank, and little ringed plover on the islands and around the edges. The planted willow bushes are now attracting goldfinches, linnets and redpolls to breed, and even without bushes, song thrush, blackbird and several other species normally associated with trees nest on the ground here.

The water levels on the lagoons are lowered in the autumn to provide the wet mud and shallow water attractive to passage waders. An interesting variety occurs at this time of the year and has included avocet, spotted redshank, greenshank, wood sandpiper, little stint and curlew sandpiper. In recent years ruff have been seen in large numbers through the autumn, and small parties stay to the end of the year.

Some species of duck, notably teal, also like the conditions found on the lagoons and sometimes large numbers, up to 1,000, flight in at high tide to roost until the tide drops, before flying back out to the Humber. Likewise, up to 2,000 waders also roost over spring tide periods, mainly redshank and dunlin.

The mudflats at the confluence support good numbers of wintering mallard and teal, whilst out on the Humber up to 600 pinkfeet can be seen.

Hen harriers arrive in the late autumn to stay over the winter, up to seven roosting by night in the reedbeds. Merlins are regularly seen and up to ten short-eared owls also winter. Large numbers of bearded tits also stay through the winter months after the autumn irruptions when some leave to winter elsewhere, though severe winter weather reduces the population and is the major cause of mortality with this species.

Insects Several species of wainscot moths associated with reed and grasses include the rare fen, silky, and obscure wainscots, and also crescent striped. Many other species of moths are at their northern limit here and are consequently of local interest.

Dromius longiceps, a fenland beetle, occurs at Blacktoft Sands in large numbers, but at only a handful of other sites in eastern England. Several coastal species of beetles and bugs are found here, no doubt only occurring so far inland because of the closeness of the Humber estuary.

From late June plum reed aphids swarm on to the reed after over-wintering on plum trees, but weather factors seem to dictate whether huge numbers are involved or just moderate numbers.

The new lagoons harbour a range of invertebrates and small numbers of eels and sticklebacks, which form an important part of the food chain for waders and wildfowl.

Castlecaldwell Forest, Co Fermanagh

H007603   *591 acres*

Five miles east of Belleek on the main Belleek-Kesh road in West Fermanagh. It is signposted from both Belleek and Kesh.

This is one of the oldest State forests in Ireland, dating from 1913. Owned by the Northern Ireland Forest Service it became a nature reserve in 1969 following an agreement between RSPB and the Forest Service.

Shoveler

The reserve is essentially a commercial forest, but as a result of severe windblows in 1957, 1959 and 1961 the age structure is very uneven and this variation in tree height has resulted in a richness of habitat within the conifer plantations. In addition the indented shoreline and narrow peninsula mean that the plantations are comparatively small. During the past 100 years the water level of Lower Lough Erne has been lowered twice and this has produced an accreted foreshore which has been colonised by a variety of natural scrub. This in turn adds diversity of habitat. In addition to this many of the old hardwoods have been preserved.

Management This consists mainly of making clearings in the dense scrub that covers most of the shore and islands to improve habitat for nesting species, especially common scoter.

Birds The reserve is at its best for birds in spring and early summer and is without doubt one of the best places in Northern Ireland where a wide selection of breeding birds can be seen. A walk around Rossergole trail should reveal such singing warblers as blackcap, garden, willow, chiffchaff, sedge and grasshopper as well as siskins and the commoner woodland birds. Sparrowhawk, kestrel and long-eared owl all breed on the reserve and calling corncrake can be heard during May and June in the adjoining grassland. On the lake displaying great crested grebe, little grebe, red-breasted merganser, tufted duck, teal, mallard and the comparatively uncommon common scoter can be found. This latter species uses Lower Lough Erne as its main breeding ground in the British Isles with 100-120 breeding pairs.

In addition to Castlecaldwell Reserve with its twenty islands the RSPB owns or manages thirteen other islands scattered over the northern half of Lower Lough Erne. These hold breeding Sandwich terns, arctic terns, five species of duck including common scoter, several colonies of black-headed and lesser black-backed gulls and the largest, Innishmeely, has a heronry and rookery.

For Visitors An educational emphasis has been put on the reserve. Beside the car park an extensive educational display has been set up in the old stable building and a room equipped as a lecture room. A trail leaflet has been written especially for children of primary school age.

Chapel Wood, Devon
SS483415   *14 acres*
Near the village of Georgeham, between
Barnstaple and Ilfracombe.
The wood gets its name from the chapel, now in ruins, which was built in the wood during the

Common scoter

13th century. Further archaeological interest is provided by the remains of a hill-top fort. Originally oak woodland, Chapel Wood was extensively replanted in the last century with Douglas fir, beech and a variety of other species. More recent planting of exotic tree species such as copper beech, southern beech, horse chestnut, red oak, Norway spruce and western hemlock, gives the wood the appearance of an arboretum. **Management** is on a small scale with footpath maintenance, fence repair and similar estate work being the chief tasks.

Birds For such a small area, Chapel Wood has an impressive variety of birds. Buzzards and sparrowhawks breed regularly and ravens were also regular until their nest-tree blew down in a storm. Pied flycatchers are a recent addition to the list of breeding birds, which also includes nuthatch and all three species of woodpecker.

The reserve is surrounded by farmland and woodland, and on the higher fields flocks of thrushes and waders such as curlew and lapwing are seen in the winter months.

Flowers The soils of Chapel Wood are rather acidic, and as a result there is not a great variety of wild flowers, although bluebells, primroses and foxgloves provide a splash of colour in spring. Scattered amongst them are plants which almost certainly 'escaped' from gardens or were deliberately planted, such as star-of-Bethlehem and Solomon's seal.

Church Wood, Blean, Kent
TR123593   *350 acres*
SSSI, NCR1. Blean Woods forms an extensive area of woodland, of which Church Wood is an important part, with its stands of mature oak in addition to a variety of other woodland types. Part of a large complex of oak woodland to the north-west of Canterbury, near Rough Common.

The ancient woodland of Blean is one of a handful of large old oakwoods left in southern England, and for that reason is graded as a nationally important site for wildlife conservation. The RSPB reserve, acquired in 1982, has a wide variety of woodland types, growing on gravel and London clay soils. This variety is due not only to the mixture of soil types, but also to the different types of management which have taken place in the past. About half the area is covered by blocks of oak high forest, the finest having been planted around 1840, while the remainder is mixed woodland — hazel and chestnut coppice with a few patches of conifer plantation.

Birds Church Wood is rich in birds, with over one per cent of the British nightingale population breeding in the area, and high densities of all three woodpeckers, nuthatches and tree pipits. All the common forest and scrub warblers breed there — blackcaps, chiffchaffs and garden warblers in the woodland; lesser whitethroats, whitethroats and a few grasshopper warblers in the scrub, and even sedge warblers in some damp areas. Redstarts and wood warblers, scarce birds in south-eastern England, still breed here. Irregular breeders include stonechats and siskins. In the clearings nightjars churr on still summer evenings, sparrowhawks dash down the grassy rides and in some years hobbies pursue swallows and martins along the wood edge.

Insects   Blean is famous for its insect life, and since the last century entomologists have come to the area in search of the many rare insects. As long ago as 1915, Blean was included on a list of nationally important sites worthy of nature reserve status. Then, as now, one of the main attractions was the rare and threatened heath fritillary butterfly.

Plants   The woodland floor, dotted here and there with the nest-mounds of the wood ant, provides the right conditions for many plants including heather and a good variety of trees and shrubs. Trees include wild cherry, hornbeam, ash and wild service, while the understorey is composed largely of hazel with spindle, dogwood and guelder rose, and sallows and alders along the stream bank. But the oaks are the reserve's chief glory. Many of them have now grown into fine timber trees with a high commercial value. With competing forestry interests, the Society has had to pay a high price to safeguard their future, but with careful management Church Wood should provide a secure haven for wildlife for generations to come.

Church Wood, Hedgerley, Buckinghamshire

SU973873   *34 acres*
In the village of Hedgerley, near Beaconsfield.
The habitats at Church Wood are a mixture of woodland types, with some fine mature beeches, areas of oak and ash and a quantity of dense birch thicket. In addition, there is alder and hazel coppice and an area of scrubby pasture.

Management   Because there is no warden here, management is undertaken by the local members' group. Paths are cleared, hazel plots are coppiced and birch is thinned. The aim is to improve the wood for all forms of wildlife, by providing a variety of habitats.

Birds   There are no outstanding bird species, but many characteristic woodland birds are present including woodcock, nuthatch and six species of tits.

Other Animals and Plants   Many species of butterfly have been recorded; of particular interest are white admiral, purple hairstreak and grizzled skipper. The mammal list includes stoat, weasel, wood mouse and dormouse. The wood is fairly rich in plants, with more than 200 recorded species, including bugle, butcher's broom and green hellebore.

Coombes Valley, Staffordshire

SK005530   *370 acres*
Part SSSI. Lies to the south of the A523 Leek-Ashbourne road about one mile along the minor road signposted to Apesford.
The narrow, steep-sided, mostly wooded valley of the Coombes Brook, gouged out at the end of the last ice age, contains a number of interesting habitats. The most important of these is the old oak woodland but only a few patches of this now remain and much of our management is designed to increase and safeguard this. Young developing woodland or open bracken slopes cover much of the remaining area, although there is a relatively small area of grassland. Much of the beauty and character of the reserve is due to the Coombes Brook which winds its way through the whole length of the reserve. Together with its side streams it forms a rich unpolluted habitat which is the perfect complement for the woodland.

Management   Since much of the valley has been greatly affected by man's activities, such as charcoal burning, timber extraction and estate development, a number of problems were inherited when the land was obtained. Most of these have a greatly detrimental effect on the wildlife of the area and so a top priority is to put things right. The worst problem was deforestation which, together with burning, had created large open areas dominated by bracken. As a close second came the problem of introduced plant species, worst of which were sycamore, introduced and cultivated for the production of charcoal, and rhododendron, planted for its attractive flowers and for cover for game.

All three of these combined to reduce greatly the potential of the site for wildlife and to threaten the existence of the old oak woodland. Hence some action had to be taken. Already we have removed all the rhododendron, about 35 acres, growing on the reserve and considerable progress has been made in reducing the bracken-dominated areas. Replanting and natural regeneration of our typical native species, such as oak, ash, holly, birch and rowan, together with a few wych elm

Badger

and small leaved lime has followed. The sycamore is present both as a scattered species, becoming slowly dominant in the better sections of woodland, and as the dominant species in specially coppiced areas. The scattered sycamores are being removed slowly so as not to create too big a hole in the canopy, the existing woodland then being encouraged to fill in the gap. Replanting may be necessary in a few cases but generally the existing canopy simply expands. In the coppiced areas, wholesale clearance has to be carried out followed by replanting of native species. An interesting management exercise is being carried out on some of the grassland. Here the land is still farmed, but the wildlife potential is being improved by the planting of hedgerows and, in some fields, by the planting of trees eventually to create a parkland type of woodland that is still grazed.

Birds The bird community in the woodlands is typical of old oakwoods of the Southern Pennines with large numbers of tits, redstarts, tree pipits, wood warblers, nuthatch and all three woodpeckers. With so much young developing woodland it is hardly surprising that the willow warbler is the most common species though the chiffchaff is scarce. Two small colonies of pied flycatchers are now established in older patches of woodland and this species could very well become numerous as the habitat improves, so long as we continue to provide lots of nesting sites by way of nestboxes. Tits, chaffinches and other small species form a large part of the diet of the sparrowhawks which breed. Some species are present in quite reasonable numbers but difficult to see, but the visitor may be rewarded with a quick glimpse in the early summer or late autumn of the odd tawny or long-eared owl or a woodcock.

The stream, of course, has its own species and grey wagtail, dipper and kingfisher are prominent amongst these. The heron is also often seen here fishing for the many brown trout which can be seen from the bridges.

Reptiles and Amphibians The valley is an extremely important site for most other branches of natural history, not least of which is that of reptiles and amphibians. A pool, dug in 1971 to diversify the habitat a little, now supports large populations of breeding frogs, toads and newts. Grass snakes, which can often be seen there, breed throughout the length of the valley. Slow worms and viviparous lizards are to be found only in the drier parts of the reserve and the viper is a very scarce species.

Mammals are present in quite large numbers. Small mammals in particular figure largely in the diet of the owls, but large mammals, such as the red deer, are present in only very small numbers.

Kittiwake

Bats are common in the woodland but can only be seen in the evening as can the badgers which are present in large numbers.

Insects Insects abound and many butterflies can be seen around the nature trail which takes the visitor through the whole range of habitats in the valley. Some species, such as holly blue, green hairstreak, grizzled skipper and high brown fritillary, which may be scarce elsewhere, are quite common here. The stream attracts large numbers of insects and in early June swarms of mayflies may be seen above the many small pools. Dragonflies and damselflies can be seen chasing other insects both here and oh the pool while alder, caddis and stone flies infest the waterside vegetation. Longhorn beetles, the larvae of which live in dead wood, can be seen sitting on the hogweed flowers while the iridescent green alder beetle occurs on most of the alders. The large snake fly, a good indicator of old oak woodland, is quite common and may be found sitting on vegetation in a sunny spot in the woodland or on flowers.

Plants Just as large numbers of insects are required to support a large healthy bird population, so a wide variety of plants are necessary to hold and feed the insect population as well as directly feeding the birds. With such a diversity of habitats in the reserve there is obviously a wide range of plants involved, flowering over a long period from March until the first severe frosts usually in November. The woodland plants generally tend to be early flowerers so these are at their best in May and June, when carpets of bluebells, wood anemones and red campions may be seen. Primroses are fairly common at the woodland edge together with dog violet and moschatel whilst out in the pastures the spring is enlivened by carpets of lousewort and the small adder's-tongue fern. As the summer progresses so the bird's-foot trefoil and tormentil appear in the fields and foxgloves flower along the hedgerows and in woodland clearings. The bird cherry and guelder rose shrubs are now in flower. Later the common spotted orchid will appear and this will be followed by betony, scabious, knapweed and greater butterfly orchid.

Copinsay, Orkney

HY608016   *375 acres*
Copinsay lies about 2½ miles off the East Mainland of Orkney. It is reached by boat from either Newark Bay (HY567039) or Skaill (HY589064).

Copinsay has a manned lighthouse and an old farmhouse which may be used as somewhat spartan accommodation by reserve visitors. One room of the house has been converted into an information and display centre. The farmhouse once held the farmer, his wife, and their fourteen children; a school existed on the island purely for this one family.

Copinsay is one of the localities within Orkney where seabirds and their eggs were collected in large quantities up until the early part of this century. Today's nature reserve was bought as a memorial to James Fisher, ornithologist, author, broadcaster and staunch supporter of the RSPB.

The reserve, in fact, consists of five islands. The main island is attached at low tide to Ward Holm, Corn Holm and Black Holm, while less than a mile away to the north-east lies the Horse of Copinsay. The main island is grass-covered and slopes upwards to the south-east facing cliffs which are just under a mile in length and between 200 and 250 feet high. The other islands are also grass-covered and have low cliff coastlines; the exception is Black Holm which has a dense cover of scentless mayweed.

Management Copinsay was formerly heavily grazed by sheep but in 1976 all the sheep were removed and the island has since remained ungrazed. The effects of this policy are being studied and a decision as to whether grazing is necessarily disadvantageous will be made in the near future. It is planned to attempt some planting of bushes and trees to provide shelter for migrants.

Birds The reserve has a very important seabird colony, census work in 1979 suggesting totals of 30,000 individual guillemots, 1,000 razorbills, 1,300 fulmars and some 10,000 apparently occupied kittiwake nests. In addition small numbers of shags, puffins and black guillemots also nest and there is a small cormorant colony on the Horse. A few hundred pairs of the larger gulls are present and there is a small colony of arctic terns with a few pairs of common terns. Other breeding species include oystercatcher, ringed plover, eider, twite, rock dove and raven while corncrakes are believed to have nested in recent years.

Apart from its breeding birds, Copinsay is also famed for its migrants. Situated as it is off the east side of Orkney, it attracts many migrant species of Continental origin during periods of easterly winds. Birds such as black redstart, bluethroat, barred warbler, red-backed shrike, scarlet rosefinch and ortolan bunting are of almost annual occurrence while Richard's pipit and rustic bunting have also been seen.

Mammals Otters have been recorded from the island while cetaceans are seen offshore from time to time.

Plants Among the plants to be found, the fine colony of oyster plant and the luxuriant growth of sea aster are both worthy of mention.

Coquet Island, Northumberland

NU294046   *16 acres*
SSSI, NCR2. The most southerly eider colony on the east coast, with breeding puffins and a substantial tern colony. Off the Northumberland coast near the village of Amble. There is no visiting.

Coquet is a low, flat-topped island, its most obvious feature being the lighthouse. Around the edges of the island are low cliffs and shingle beaches, while the centre is mainly covered by short grass and extensive nettle-beds.

Management The nettles are a result of enrichment of the soil by bird-droppings. If they were allowed to spread they would take over areas where terns nest and they are, therefore, controlled by spraying. The remainder of the vegetation is kept short by a mixture of salt-spray, strong winds and rabbit-grazing.

Birds The main wildlife interest of Coquet Island is its colonies of breeding seabirds, most notable of which is the rare roseate tern, which nests in clumps of vegetation or hollows, such as the entrances of disused rabbit burrows. Common, arctic and Sandwich terns also nest here in considerable numbers, favouring more open nest-sites. The nettle-beds provide a good hiding-place for the tern chicks to escape predation by gulls. The ground is scarred by a profusion of puffin burrows, since a healthy population of these attractive birds nest below the surface of the island. Another common breeding species is the eider; the males forming noisy flocks at the water's edge, leaving the well-camouflaged females to incubate the eggs and care for the ducklings.

Coquet is of limited wildlife interest apart from its birdlife, with few flowering plants or butterflies, but seals can often be seen and other sea mammals are occasionally spotted.

Dinas, Dyfed

SN788470   *129 acres*
See Gwenffrwd for reserve status. North of Llandovery to the west of the road from Rhandirmwyn to Llyn Brianne reservoir.

The main habitat is hanging oakwood with smaller areas of alder carr and marsh. The reserve is bordered on one side by a gorge through which the Doethie runs.

Management The oakwoods have been subject to no management during the last 100 years apart from occasional felling and there has been little regeneration. However, birch has come into some places where trees have been felled and it shows signs of colonising most bare areas. Sheep grazing

Common tern

has reduced the shrub layer and in many places trees grow from a bare, grassy floor or from bracken.

Birds During winter foraging tits are found in the woods with nuthatches, tree creepers and both green and great spotted woodpeckers. In spring and early summer pied flycatchers, wood warblers and redstarts breed. A variety of birds of prey can be seen from the reserve: in addition to buzzards and sparrowhawks, both of which breed, red kites, peregrines and occasionally kestrels are in the sky. In the adjoining alder carr blackcaps and long-tailed tits breed in bramble and blackthorn. In the calmer upper reaches of the river gorge, dippers and in summer common sandpipers can be seen searching for food. Goosanders, which have only recently started to breed in the area, can be seen flying from one feeding area to another.

Flowers In woodland glades where bracken has not yet taken over, it is possible to find such plants as ivy-leaved bellflowers, but generally sheep grazing means that few plants of any size are to be seen. Among the rocks, beyond the reach of the most agile Welsh mountain sheep, plants such as pennywort and wood sage can grow unmolested. In the marsh below the alder carr, water forget-me-not and marsh marigold grow.

Dungeness, Kent

TR063196   *1193 acres*
SSSI, NCR1.* Perhaps the largest shingle ridge in Europe. Rich and varied flora and a variety of breeding seabirds. At the tip of the shingle promontory, south-east of Lydd.

Open Shingle Although much disturbed during the recent past when Dungeness was used as a military training area, the RSPB reserve contains some of the finest examples of sea-deposited shingle ridges in Europe. The exposed nature of the area and the lack of soil restricts plant growth to the hollows and the sheltered sides of the larger ridges. A surprising number of flowering plants live a meagre existence in this hostile environment. Foxglove, viper's bugloss, wood sage, sea campion, and the nationally rare Nottingham catchfly are common. Broom abounds and has developed its own local prostrate variety and many large gorse clumps are present. Air pollution is at a very low level and the lichen flora is particularly rich.

Shingle/grassland interface On the landward side of the reserve where the shingle abuts the alluvial soils of the Romney Marsh, fingers of grassland with many clumps of gorse extend into

the shingle. The shingle here contains much silt and there are areas of stunted prostrate blackthorn, the older bushes acting as host to mixed colonies of epiphytic lichens.

The heavily rabbit-grazed turf bordering the shingle contains many ephemeral spring flowers such as early forget-me-not, lesser chickweed, spring vetch and wall speedwell. In the spring the area provides nesting cover for yellowhammers, reed buntings, whitethroats, red-legged and common partridges and many pairs of linnets.

The Fossil Pits began as seawater lagoons formed at an early stage in the development of Dungeness. With the build-up of shingle these lagoons became isolated from the shore and the water changed from salt to fresh. Three pits can be seen from the visitors' path. They are now filled with peat and almost completely overgrown with sallows, but some small areas of fen vegetation remain. Several uncommon plants are present such as marsh cinquefoil, hop sedge, saw sedge, jointed rush and marsh fern. The two larger pits, the Open Pits, both contain areas of open water and are thought to be the only areas of natural fresh water in a shingle formation in the world.

These islands of vegetation provide feeding and resting cover for large numbers of migrant birds in spring and autumn. In spring they provide nesting cover for reed warblers, sedge warblers, reed buntings, little grebes and gadwall, and safety for broods of tufted duck and occasionally shoveler.

The Burrowes Pit was excavated in the 1970s to a laid-down plan with the co-operation of a gravel company, and named in memory of Robert Burrowes, who gave the reserve to the RSPB in 1930 and so established the Society's first reserve. Its many islands in spring and summer now support increasing colonies of terns and gulls, including Sandwich tern, roseate tern and common gull. The shallow margins provide feeding areas for a wide variety of migrant waders.

In winter the pit is a safe day-time refuge for many hundreds of wildfowl which at night feed on the Romney Marsh. Large numbers of diving duck are present, the most numerous being tufted duck and pochard but smew, goldeneye and goosander are present in small numbers.

Management With all the main natural habitats of the reserve being of great scientific interest due to the unique nature of the area, physical management work is restricted to the Burrowes Pit. Work here is directed towards producing a wide variety of island surfaces, varying from bare shingle for terns to partly and densely vegetated surfaces for gulls and wildfowl.

Future management will include gravel excava-

Nottingham catchfly

tion in an area of currently little value to wildlife, to produce artificially a number of shallow pools with marginal vegetation and areas of scrub similar in character to the fossil pits.

Birds After almost dying out at their original breeding site on the open shingle in the early 1960s, the few descendants of the once large colonies of terns and gulls re-established themselves in the early 1970s on the islands in the Burrowes Pit. The colony now consists of common terns, Sandwich terns and a small number of roseate terns, over 1,000 pairs of black-headed and a small number of herring and common gulls. Mediterranean gulls are recorded each spring and two pairs bred in 1981.

In winter large numbers of surface ducks are present, consisting mostly of mallard, teal and shoveler with occasionally wigeon, gadwall and pintail. Wintering diving ducks include tufted, pochard, goldeneye, goosander and smew. Red-necked, black-necked and Slavonian grebes are seen each autumn and up to three merlins are present in winter. Dungeness has long been famous as a landfall for migrant birds and many unusual birds are recorded each year.

Reptiles and Amphibians The grass snake, viviparous lizard, marsh frog, toad and smooth newt are all present in small numbers.

Mammals All of the commoner small mammals are present, including pygmy shrew, water shrew and water vole. Small populations of harvest mice are present in some of the fossil pits. The fox, stoat, weasel and hedgehog are all seen regularly. The badger is a rare visitor.

Insects A wide variety of migrant butterflies occur with occasionally large numbers of peacocks, red admirals and painted ladies, and the clouded yellow is recorded annually. Many unusual migrant moths are recorded in late summer and autumn.

Plants The area is of special interest to botanists with several unusual plants, such as marsh cinquefoil, bulbous meadow-grass, sheep's bit, upright chickweed, Nottingham catchfly and the nationally rare yellow vetch.

East Wood, Stalybridge, Cheshire

SJ972977   *12 acres*
Lies within the municipally owned Cheetham Park, Stalybridge. Entry from Mottram Road or Park Street but no vehicles permitted in park.

East Wood occupies part of a small, wooded valley, known locally as a clough. Lancashire cotton towns stretch north and westwards while Pennine moorland rises steeply to the east.

Almost completely enveloped by industrial suburbs of Greater Manchester, the tiny reserve with its pools and stream has a quiet charm which is quite unexpected by most visitors. "Can Stalybridge really lie just down the road?" is a question they not infrequently ask themselves.

Management Aimed at balancing the educational and conservation interests of a woodland habitat which is now a very scarce commodity locally. Above all, it seeks to provide a natural environment that will quicken the curiosity, and stimulate the imagination, of the young.

Birds The wood comprises nearly 1,000 mature deciduous trees which are complemented by those of the parkland beyond. Breeding birds include tawny owl, treecreeper, great spotted woodpecker and nuthatch, and grey wagtail and kingfisher often visit the water areas. Wood warblers occur regularly in summer and bramblings and sparrowhawks may appear in the winter months.

Fossils are sometimes found in the Coal Measures shale while mammals, fish, amphibians and plants, both flowering and otherwise, are sufficiently varied to attract any naturalist.

Curlew

Elmley Marshes, Kent

TQ938679   *3,300 acres*
SSSI, NCR1. Part of the large Swale SSSI.
Formerly rough grazing of very little natural history interest, but thanks to management is now nationally important for breeding and wintering wildfowl. Access via A249 across Kingsferry Bridge onto the Isle of Sheppey.

Situated in the south-west corner of the Isle of Sheppey and comprising a large area of grazing marsh, tidal mudflats, saltings and some arable farmland. The grazing marsh, unploughed rough pasture reclaimed from the sea by construction of sea walls over the centuries, is rich in wildlife. The wide fleets and ditches, marking the former tidal creeks, provide sites for wetland birds to nest and feed and are home for a variety of plants and insects. Much of the North Kent marshland has been converted in recent years to arable farmland, with a great loss of flora and fauna being the result.

Management On the 680 acres of Spitend Marsh, the RSPB manages the area specifically for the wildlife. A long-term project of dam building and water manipulation is providing a habitat for wildfowl and waders of outstanding numbers and variety. The livestock are also managed to produce a variety of sward lengths to attract the maximum diversity of wildlife. Hides overlook the flood lagoons.

Pennywort

In winter on the flood lagoons there may be up to 10,000 wigeon, thousands of mallard and teal, hundreds of shoveler, pintail and many pochard, tufted duck and gadwall. A large winter wader roost of grey plover, dunlin, knot, curlew, ringed plover and redshank can be seen at high tide. Up to 2,000 white-fronted geese sometimes roost overnight. Wintering raptors, hen harrier, merlin, and short-eared owl are frequent and occasionally rough-legged buzzard and peregrine are to be seen.

In spring there are large concentrations of breeding redshank, lapwing, mallard, shoveler and pochard plus some gadwall, tufted duck, ringed plover, oystercatcher and yellow wagtail and occasionally garganey and ruff. Migrant spring waders also occur.

Marsh harriers are commonly seen during summer and autumn. Migrant waders start arriving in June and continue through to November, often with some rarities. Duck numbers begin to build up from August.

The mudflats of the Swale are some of the finest wader feeding habitat in the country, being plentiful in marine invertebrate life. Large numbers of grey plover, curlew and dunlin can be seen when the tide is out. Small numbers of brent geese can occasionally be seen and cormorants, red-breasted mergansers and several species of grebe exploit the fish of this estuary.

The saltings scattered around the sea wall are some of the finest examples of their kind, having a wide variety of halophytic plants able to withstand regular inundation by salt water. The zonation of the plants, depending on how frequently they are covered by salt water, can be clearly seen. On some of the larger saltmarsh islands, thousands of black-headed gulls and some common terns nest. One such island, Flanders Mare, is overlooked by a hide at Spitend Point.

Amphibians and Reptiles In May the large, abundant marsh frogs croak noisily. Viviparous lizards and grass snakes may be glimpsed as they slip away from human approach.

Mammals The young of the plentiful hares and rabbits are the main prey of the reserve's stoat and weasel population, while water voles can be seen swimming or feeding on the edges of the fleets.

Insects The constant buzz of Roesel's bush cricket is a noticeable sound of the reserve in summer. Common species of butterflies are plentiful and large numbers of dragonflies and damselflies occur here. A rare moth, the ground lackey, lives on the saltings where it lays its eggs

Whooper swan

which, like the caterpillars, are tolerant of flooding and high salt concentration.

Plants Most of the botanical interest is in the saltings or near the sea walls. The maritime sea and strawberry clover are frequent and sea clubrush is the most abundant aquatic plant in the fleets. Several rare grasses, among them beard grass, grow on the reserve.

Fairburn Ings, West Yorkshire
SE450275   *680 acres*
West of the A1, 2 miles north of Ferrybridge.

On the edge of the industrialised section of the Aire valley, with collieries, a power station and Castleford and its environs to the south and rolling farmland to the north, the reserve is situated in unpromising surroundings.

From Fairburn village, the reserve can be seen stretching away for 2½ miles to the west — open water and deciduous woodland immediately below the village, arable and grazed farmland with shallow pools to the west, and slag heaps and slurry ponds to the south.

From Cut Lane, a footpath runs down to the river between Fairburn Cut and the water area of Village and Main Bays. The Cut is an old canal which connected a railway under the village, from limestone quarries to the north, with the river to the south. The trees along the Cut provide nesting areas for many small birds, whilst the hawthorns are popular with wintering fieldfare and redwing both for feeding and roosting.

The water areas have formed since the middle of the century, as the result of mining subsidence, a process which is continuing, particularly at the western end.

The reserve is important for its wildfowl, all the commoner species being present throughout the year. Goldeneye and goosander are numerous from November to March. During spring and autumn passage, common, arctic and black terns and little gulls are regular after easterly winds. A pair of the latter attempted to breed amongst the black-headed gull colony in 1978. A roost of thousands of swallows is a feature of most autumns, though numbers are decreasing due to the loss of waterside vegetation, as the result of continuing subsidence.

At the end of the Cut, the path leads onto a section of reclaimed slag bank. The dominant species is silver birch, which grows readily on the bare slag. Besides the planted trees foxglove, coltsfoot and willowherb are natural colonists, the latter providing food for elephant hawk moth larvae. This area is the stronghold of willow warblers and as a denser understorey develops, helped by thinning the birches and removing sycamore, blackcap, garden warbler and lesser whitethroat are moving in. In winter large flocks of redpoll, with a few siskin, feed on the birch and alder seeds.

The western end of the reserve is under agricultural tenancy and consists of arable and rough grazing, together with several shallow subsidence pools, known locally as flashes, which formed in 1976. Further subsidence is predicted for this area. The dense cover provides nesting areas for the common water birds and, occasionally, garganey. Snipe, lapwing and redshank are resident and most of the commoner waders are recorded on passage. A herd of whooper swans is regular each winter, the birds roosting on the reserve and feeding on nearby farmland.

This end of the reserve is designated as a washland to prevent flooding of towns upstream. Winter floods are spectacular and attractive to wildfowl, but spring flooding can mean heavy losses for nesting birds.

Several pairs of reed warblers, nearing their northern limit at Fairburn, nest in the small reedbeds, so efforts are being made to encourage reeds to spread. Additional habitat is being provided by coppicing willows.

The remainder of the reserve consists of slag heaps and slurry ponds, at present still being worked by the National Coal Board, and although rather lacking in wildlife (and aesthetic charm) they provide nesting sites for a few pairs of little ringed plover. In winter large flocks of gulls roost on the slurry ponds, and glaucous gulls are regular. Once NCB operations have ceased, this area will be reclaimed which will greatly increase its value to wildlife.

Fetlar, Shetland

HU69   *1,700 acres*
SSSI, NCR1. Important for its breeding birds, mainly seabirds, such as arctic skua and puffin, but also corncrake and twite. The flora is interesting, having developed on base-rich serpentine rock at sub-Arctic latitude.

Fetlar is the smallest of the three inhabited north isles of the Shetland archipelago, lying to the east of Yell and south of Unst.

About one-sixth of the 10,000-acre island has reserve status. This area encompasses the summits of Vord Hill and Stackaberg, with their surrounding slopes and the coastline from the 350-foot cliffs of the East Neap westward to the

stony peninsula of Urie Ness. However, ecologically, the island has to be considered as a whole unit.

Today, the human population is about 100, the bulk of their livelihoods based on crofting and small-scale farming. In the 19th century the population reached 900 and evidence of the former townships and land boundaries can still be seen. The extensive areas of arable ground and ley pastures form one of the island's six main habitats. Much of the western side of the island is peat moorland dominated by heather, with patches of blanket bog on the lower ground.

The third habitat is serpentine moorland which covers about one-quarter of the island and, in Britain, only appears here and on neighbouring Unst. This is broken terrain with much exposed rock and a fascinating, if rather stunted, ground flora, extending over Stackaberg, Vord Hill and Busta Hill northwards to the cliffs, southwards to the lower pastures and eastward to rather fragmented areas of Aith and Funzie.

The numerous wet marshes, some of which were dug for peat, are an important breeding habitat for birds. The fifth habitat is freshwater lochs and pools, most of which are very shallow, but without substantial vegetation.

Finally, there is the coastline, which is regular and, with its many wicks and geos, has a length of over forty miles. There are long stretches of high, broken cliffs, a few short lengths of precipitous cliffs and many sections of low, sandy, stony and boulder beaches.

Birds   Fetlar has some interesting and important birds breeding. The degraded pastures provide cover for nesting waders such as lapwings, redshanks, curlews and snipe, while the improved pastures and crops are invaluable feeding areas for both breeding birds and passage migrants. The peat moorland has large colonies of bonxies (great skuas), arctic skuas and many waders, notably golden plovers and dunlins. There are several sizeable colonies of arctic terns. The serpentine moorland, too, has some interesting populations. From 1967 to 1975, a pair of snowy owls nested among the rocky outcrops of Stackaberg, but it is for populations of whimbrels, Arctic skuas and Arctic terns that these moors are nationally important. In addition, eight more species of wader nest here.

In the wetter areas, two-thirds of the British population of red-necked phalaropes breeds, and there is a management programme aimed at improving or maintaining several marshes in optimum conditions for the phalaropes. Many of the breeding birds use the waters of the lochs and pools for feeding and display, and it is here that

Red-necked phalarope

the phalaropes can be seen searching for invertebrate food among the margins of the stony pools. Each year at least one pair of red-throated divers attempt to breed.

The varied coastline provides breeding habitat for a variety of seabirds. Most abundant are fulmars, followed by puffins and the nocturnal storm petrels. There are smaller numbers of shags, Manx shearwaters, kittiwakes, common terns, razorbills, guillemots, black guillemots, great black-backed gulls, lesser black-backed gulls and herring gulls. Other birds to be seen here include ravens, hooded crows, rock pipits and Shetland wrens.

Mammals Only five species of mammal are to be found on Fetlar, and two of these, rabbit and hedgehog, were introduced. The others are house mouse, field mouse and otter, a healthy population of which is to be found around the coast. There are a great many common seals to be seen in the waters of Fetlar and a large colony of grey seals produce as many as 100 pups each year.

Fore Wood, East Sussex

TQ756126   *135 acres*
SSSI. Deciduous woodland with typical bird population. Beside the village of Crowhurst, off the A2100 Battle-Hastings road.

When bought in 1976, the whole wood was a neglected coppice which, like many others in southern England, had not been systematically managed for over thirty years. The coppice, or underwood, consists principally of sweet chestnut and hornbeam in roughly equal proportions, the chestnut occurring on the sandy slopes whilst the hornbeam is confined to heavy clay soils on the plateau. Oaks occur throughout the wood, in places abundantly enough to form dense oakwood, but elsewhere widely scattered, towering head-and-shoulders above the coppice.

The two steep-sided ravines, or ghylls, are fed by springs which usually dry up in the summer, but conditions are damp enough for the growth of alders.

Management The ancient practice of coppicing has been revived and eventually about 25 acres of hornbeam will be managed on a rotation of around twelve years, giving a whole range of habitats from the bare ground of newly-felled coppice, through the bushy phase much loved by warblers, to the 'pole stage' when the growth becomes tall and spindly and less attractive to birds; then the coppice will be felled and the cycle repeated.

Sweet chestnut is a native of the Mediterranean area but in recent centuries it has been extensively planted in Kent and Sussex for its straight stems

Guillemot

which make excellent hop poles and fencing material; unfortunately, the coppice is of very little value to wildlife and is here being gradually cleared out; oaks and other native trees are planted in its place.

Areas of hornbeam not managed as coppice are being heavily thinned so that the remaining trees can thicken up and spread their branches, yet still allow sufficient light to penetrate the canopy for an understorey of bramble and bushes to develop.

Other habitats already created include a pond, a glade and wide, grassy rides with shrubby borders.

Birds All the typical birds of a southern wood breed here: these include six species of tits, greater and lesser spotted woodpeckers, woodcock, tawny owl, treecreeper and nuthatch. Each year a pair of sparrowhawks and at least one pair of hawfinches nest. Summer visitors such as cuckoo, blackcap, garden warbler, willow warbler and chiffchaff are all attracted to the young coppice. The pond has breeding moorhen and mallard, whilst in autumn and winter it may be visited by kingfisher, grey wagtail, teal and green sandpiper.

Mammals There is a long-established badger sett; lucky visitors sometimes have close views of foxes.

Amphibians Palmate newts and common frogs breed in the pond.

Insects Butterflies are common in the managed areas and include the white admiral, a species confined to southern woods; they are on the wing in July and early August. White-letter hairstreaks were seen for the first time in 1981.

Flowers In early spring wood anemones carpet the clay soil, followed a few weeks later by acres of bluebells on sandy soil. There are several vigorous colonies of early purple orchids; later-flowering orchids found here are common spotted, broad-leaved helleborine, common twayblade and bird's-nest, this last species being scarce in East Sussex.

The ghylls provide damp, cool conditions ideal for a variety of plants, including hay-scented buckler fern, great woodrush and a rare moss *Fissidens rivularis.*

Forth Islands, Lothian

Inchmickery NT207805, The Lamb 535866, Fidra 512869, Eyebroughty 495863   *9 acres*
A collection of small islands in the Forth Estuary. The main interest of these islands is their colonies of seabirds, particularly several species of tern. Inchmickery, for example, offshore from Cramond, has around 500 pairs of Sandwich terns,

400 pairs of common terns and a small number of roseate terns. Other breeding species include cormorant, shag, eider and herring and black-headed gulls. The vegetation of Inchmickery, the largest of these islands, is rather poor, consisting largely of nettles, since much of the island is covered with ruined buildings.

The other islands, situated at the mouth of the Forth near North Berwick are much smaller than Inchmickery, and have a more limited bird population.

Fowlmere, Cambridgeshire

TL407461   *66 acres*
SSSI. Disused cress-beds, now an extensive reedbed, forming an 'oasis' for wildlife in an intensive arable landscape. South of the village of Fowlmere, off the Fowlmere-Melbourne road.

Once part of the southernmost arm of the Cambridgeshire Fens, this area has, like the rest of the Fens, been drained and converted to agriculture. Pure springs welling up from the chalk rock led to the development of a watercress farm at Fowlmere at the end of the last century, but most of this is now disused. The reedbed which sprang up on the site is now the RSPB Fowlmere Reserve.

Management As with all reedswamps on our reserves, the main management task is prevention of the swamp drying out and being succeeded by scrub. Paths and hides for visitors have been provided.

Birds The reserve was purchased in 1977 from funds raised by the Young Ornithologists' Club and is a haven for birds in an area of intensive arable agriculture. The reedswamp in summer is alive with reed and sedge warblers, while the ditches and open water have little grebes, moorhens, water rails and, on occasions, tufted duck and mallard. Amongst the reedbeds are clumps of hawthorn scrub and trees such as alder and willow. These attract summer migrants such as turtle dove, blackcap and both lesser and common whitethroats. In winter, flocks of redwings and fieldfares are attracted to the abundant crop of berries, while corn buntings and pied wagtails roost in the reeds and tits, redpolls and siskins search for food among the trees.

Plants The plant life of the reserve is very varied, particularly on the outcrops of chalk found throughout the reserve. Bee orchids and cowslips are amongst the more spectacular of these, but many others can be seen, including adder's-tongue fern and the highly poisonous deadly nightshade.

Mammals Fowlmere has a variety of mammals, including water shrews as well as the commoner pygmy and common shrews.

Amphibians and reptiles Frogs and toads spawn in the ditches and open water, where grass snakes may also hunt. Viviparous lizards are found in the drier parts.

For visitors There is a nature trail around the reserve and a large thatched observation hide gives good views out over the reedbed.

Fowlsheugh, Grampian

NO880798   *27 acres*
SSSI, NCR1.* One of the largest seabird colonies in the country with very large numbers of kittiwakes, razorbills and guillemots. Over a mile of cliffs to the south of Stonehaven.

Birds The cliffs of Fowlsheugh are over 200 feet high, and their ledges are crammed in summer with thousands of seabirds — 30,000 pairs of guillemots, 30,000 pairs of kittiwakes, 5,000 pairs of razorbills with smaller numbers of shags, puffins and herring gulls. Near sea level there are several pairs of eider. These totals make Fowlsheugh one of the biggest seabird colonies in Britain. During the breeding season this spectacular sight can easily be viewed by visitors to the cliff-top.

Botanically this reserve is of little interest — the reserve boundary is only a few feet from the cliff edge, and the vegetation consists mainly of rough grass.

This is another of the reserves purchased with funds collected by members of the Young Ornithologists' Club.

Gayton Sands, Cheshire

SJ274786   *5,040 acres*
SSSI, NCR1.* One of Britain's most important sites for wintering waders and wildfowl. Near Neston on the northern shore of the estuary of the River Dee.

Almost half the reserve is saltmarsh dissected by numerous creeks. In recent years the expansion of the marsh has been accelerated by the growth of cord grass or *Spartina*, which is colonising the mudflats and is now dominant over much of the lower marsh. Beyond the saltmarsh lie the extensive sandbanks and mudflats that comprise the rest of the reserve.

Management Although it is planned that most of the reserve will remain in its semi-natural state, management of the upper shore by creation of bunded freshwater pools and scrapes will add brackish and fresh water to the reserve and add to the variety of birds.

Birds The invertebrates in the mud and the vast quantity of seed produced by the saltmarsh plants

Grey plover

are food for the thousands of waders and wildfowl that winter on the reserve. Large flocks of curlew, redshank, oystercatcher, knot, dunlin and grey plover feed on the mudflats and at high tide flight to roost on the saltmarsh. The reserve is especially important for shelduck, with peak numbers in autumn, and for overwintering pintail. Mallard, wigeon and teal also overwinter in large numbers. In spring and autumn the reserve is a staging post for many waders which pause to feed and then continue their migration: sanderling, dunlin, ringed and grey plovers on passage feed on the inner mudflats while greenshank, spotted redshank and ruff visit the upper saltmarsh pools.

Saltmarsh seeds are an important source of food for numerous finches and buntings. Chaffinches, greenfinches, linnets and reed buntings are regular winter visitors, often joined by large flocks of bramblings. Usually a small flock of twites spend the winter on the reserve.

Water rails, heard but seldom seen, inhabit the dense *Spartina*. Birds of prey hunt over the saltmarsh: sparrowhawks and kestrels from the neighbouring farmland are recorded throughout the year and hen harriers, peregrines, merlins and short-eared owls are winter visitors.

Breeding birds of the saltmarsh include redshank, oystercatcher, skylark, meadow pipit and reed bunting. In Neston reedbed reed, sedge and grasshopper warblers breed.

Plants In addition to the *Spartina* on the pioneer saltmarsh zone are glasswort and annual sea blite. Higher up the shore the middle marsh includes large patches of saltmarsh plants, including the purple- and yellow-flowered sea aster. In the spring many of the higher creeks have edges white with the blossom of scurvy grass, contrasting with the grey-green foliage of the sea purslane. Because parts of the inner saltmarsh have been grazed for many years by cattle and sheep, the number of flowering plants has been reduced and grass is the dominant vegetation.

Where freshwater seeps on to the marsh there are stands of clubrush and a series of springs issuing on the shore below Moorside has encouraged the common reed, which now forms the Neston reedbed. Other freshwater marsh plants here are reed-mace, great hairy willow herb and great water dock.

Mammals There is a surprisingly high population of small mammals, which provide food for foxes and weasels as well as short-eared owls and kestrels. Among the mammals recorded are wood mouse and water shrew.

Marsh samphire

Grassholm, Dyfed

SM599093 23 acres
SSSI, NCR1.* Internationally important for its large breeding population of gannets. Lies off the western tip of Dyfed, beyond the islands of Skomer and Skokholm and is inaccessible except in very calm weather.

Birds The main ornithological interest of Grassholm is its colony of gannets, which is now the second largest in Britain and the third largest in the world. This gannetry has expanded dramatically over the last hundred years; only twenty pairs nested in 1860 but by 1924 there were 2,000 pairs, by 1951 8,000 and by 1980 over 20,000 pairs. By contrast, the puffin colony has crashed from at least 100,000 pairs at the turn of the century to just 130 pairs by 1934 and only one or two pairs today. It appears likely that the chief reason for this decline is the collapse of the puffins' extensive network of breeding burrows, caused simply by the high density of birds in the fragile peaty soil. At the same time the colony of gannets has expanded greatly over the island, occupying formerly suitable habitat for the puffins.

Other breeding birds include small numbers of kittiwake, razorbill, guillemot, shag, herring gull and great black-backed gull, and also of interest are the parties of grey seals which can often be seen bobbing offshore or hauled out on the shingle beaches.

Archaeology Grassholm is of some archaeological interest, since a small collection of artefacts in the National Museum of Wales, said to have been found on Grassholm, includes pottery of Iron Age type, flint flakes and 'fragmentary pot-boilers'. The remains of a settlement on the island have recently been excavated, but its date of construction is still unknown. Other apparent hut-sites have now been identified as bomb craters dating from the Second World War!

No management is at present undertaken on Grassholm, and due to its inaccessibility there are few visitors to the island. Fortunately the gannets are faring very well without any human intervention, but the future of the colony is more assured now that the island is protected as a nature reserve.

Green Island, Blockhouse Island and Greencastle Point, Co Down

241111, 255098 and 240116 resp. 2½ acres
Can be viewed from Greencastle Pier. There is no access.

Birds This group of islands constitutes one of Britain's most important tern colonies due to the large number of roseate terns nesting here, around

150 pairs in most years. Most of the terns of all species nest on Green Island itself, with an over-spill population building up in recent years on the point. Greencastle Point will probably have to play a more major role in the coming years as Green Island is being eroded at a phenomenal rate; thirty years ago it was large enough to support a flock of sheep for the summer, all that remains now is a raised shingle spit about 160 feet long and 50 feet wide. Unbelievably it still holds around 300 pairs of Sandwich, 430 pairs of common and 60 pairs of arctic terns!

The only islands which are covered with any amount of vegetation are those off The Point. Blockhouse is, as the name implies, dominated by a ruined building, only two walls of which remain, providing breeding sites for cormorants and great black-backed gulls. Hopefully if the demise of Green Island continues we may, by careful management, be able to re-establish the tern colony on this island.

Gwenffrwd, Dyfed

SN749460   *6,799 acres*
SSSI, NCR1. A complex of habitats — oakwoods, grassland and heath — characteristic of the 'slate' hill country of South Central Wales. The reserve comprises four main habitats: moorland, hanging oak woodlands, farmland and wooded river valleys, lying north of Llandovery beyond the village of Cilycwm.

Moorland is extensively grazed by sheep and the heather is managed by patch-burning when conditions permit. It supports small numbers of red grouse, wheatears and whinchats. Buzzards, ravens, kites and sometimes merlins can be seen here when conditions are good. In the boggy areas sundew and butterwort are common.

The hanging **oak woodlands** have not been managed for nearly 100 years and persistent sheep-grazing has removed all trace of any shrub layer or regenerating trees, leaving mature oaks on a mossy or grassy sward. Pied flycatchers, wood warblers and redstarts are common in spring and early summer and nesting birds of prey include buzzard, sparrowhawk and tawny owl. Kites have nested on the reserve in the past. A revival of the old woodland management scheme is being considered to supplement the existing woodland planting schemes. Purple hairstreak butterflies can sometimes be seen on sunny summer days in the woods.

Around the **farmland,** hedges provide some of the most valuable wildlife areas with many scrub-loving birds like blackcaps and occasional whitethroats to be seen in the spring and summer.

Under the roadside hedges can be found the biggest variety of plants anywhere on the reserve with violets and primroses common in spring, plants such as golden saxifrage on damp banks and in summer occasional broad-leaved helleborines. Around farm buildings one can usually find at least one pair of swallows, spotted flycatchers and pied wagtails and some interesting plants like rusty-backed fern can be found growing on walls.

The **river valleys** vary from steep-sided torrents where grey wagtails nest and ferns grow well in the damp atmosphere, to well-wooded valleys alongside gently flowing waters. Pied flycatchers and wood warblers mix with a good variety of not uncommon woodland species especially tits (including marsh and willow) and dippers and common sandpipers can be found on the rivers. The trees in the valleys are very unevenly aged, due to these woods' history of supplying firewood in quantity until fairly recently and this, coupled with the diversity of species (oak, ash, wych elm and alder), means that these woods are much more productive than the oak woods on the valley sides. In some of the open glades and pastures in summer the golden-ringed dragonfly and the beautiful blue-winged damselfly may be seen.

Handa, Highland

NC140480   *766 acres*
SSSI, NCR2. Large colonies of cliff-nesting seabirds, particularly kittiwakes, razorbills and guillemots. Offshore near the village of Scourie, and reached by boat from Tarbet.

The island of Handa is formed from Torridonian Sandstone, a soft rock whose weathered cliff-ledges form the nesting sites of over 100,000 seabirds. The cliffs rise to over 400 feet in places on the north side, but elsewhere on the island there are sandy bays and dunes. The centre of the island is mostly rough sheep pasture and peat bog, with six small lochans, some drained by streams. A narrow belt of richer grassland and machair skirts the pasture in some places, and there is a recently established plantation of young trees.

Until 1848, seven families lived on Handa. Their food consisted mainly of fish, seabirds and potatoes and after the potato famine they emigrated to America. The remains of their fields can still be seen. Near the RSPB visitors' shelter there is a graveyard, to which bodies were brought at one time from the mainland for burial, to save them from scavenging wolves.

Birds The chief ornithological importance of the island is its breeding seabirds. There are over 25,000 pairs of guillemot, 10,000 pairs of kittiwake,

Gannet

9,000 pairs of razorbill, 3,500 pairs of fulmar, 300-400 pairs of puffin, 300 pairs of shag, and a few pairs of black guillemot. Few gulls breed, but there are increasing numbers of arctic and great skuas, both of which are recent colonists.

Other wildlife In common with most islands, the variety of mammals, reptiles and amphibians is small. Rabbits are plentiful, and both grey seals and otters sometimes appear on the island.

Plants The plant life of Handa includes a number of uncommon species such as pale butterwort, royal fern and the much rarer limestone bugle, but the majority of the island is dominated by deer grass with some heather and purple moor grass. This rather poor wildlife habitat is the result of a long history of sheep-grazing and extensive burning, but present management is intended to encourage the growth of moorland vegetation and to provide tree cover in due course.

Havergate Island, Suffolk

TM425496   *267 acres*
SSSI, NNR, NCR1. The muddy lagoons hold a variety of breeding, wintering and passage birds, including Britain's largest avocet colony. In the River Alde near the village of Orford.

Six shallow lagoons with small islands are the main habitat on the island. There is also a considerable area of couch grass and some patches of gorse. Much of the island is bordered with saltmarsh.

Management Before the Second World War the island was sheep pasture, but a stray shell from a nearby range damaged a sluice and the island was inundated with seawater. Since the island first became an RSPB reserve in 1948, the main aim of management has been to create lagoons and to control the level and salinity of the water in them. Help with this came from the Royal Engineers. Wells have been bored to supply freshwater, which is necessary to provide the conditions in which the invertebrate food of avocets flourishes. For control of the water it is vital to maintain the network of sluices and ditches. The other major task is to keep the small nesting islands free from vegetation.

Birds Avocets must take pride of place, because this reserve has one of the two main British colonies. After an absence as British breeding birds for more than 150 years, a few pairs of avocets returned to Havergate at some time during World War II. Now between 95 and 100 pairs nest here.

A significant number of Sandwich terns nest on the islands in the lagoons. The colony is usually in the region of 150 to 200 pairs, but it fluctuates and

Merlin

was as low as 75 pairs in 1981. The small islands usually have 25 to 30 pairs of common tern and there are usually two or three pairs of arctic terns, of special interest because they are nesting so far south. Occasionally short-eared owls nest on the island, but they are always to be seen hunting over the grassland areas.

Although few duck nest, mallard, wigeon, teal, pintail, shoveler and gadwall all winter on the island.

The spring and autumn passages of waders can be very interesting with a variety of birds passing through. Regulars include black-tailed and bar-tailed godwits, spotted redshank, greenshank, whimbrel, common and curlew sandpipers, turnstone, ruff and little stint.

Each year, however, other less common species are recorded.

Mammals Hares are the most obvious of the island's mammals, especially in March when they display. Stoats and weasels are present and are occasionally seen. Coypus sometimes come down the river, but have to be controlled because of the damage their large holes cause in the banks. The most common smaller mammals are water and field voles, and common and water shrews.

Insects Commonest among the seventeen recorded butterfly species are Essex and small skippers, meadow and wall browns and the four common species of Vanessid.

Plants There is a surprising variety of plants on the island. The large communities of sea lavender, thrift and sea purslane bring colour to the saltmarsh when they flower. On the shingle ridge are herb Robert, English stonecrop, biting stonecrop, yellow vetch (one of the largest communities on the Suffolk coast) and sea pea. Sea wormwood flourishes throughout the island. Among the clovers on the island are the rare subterranean and suffocated clovers. Another rarity is slender hare's-ear. Two exotic species introduced before the island became a reserve, Duke of Argyll's tea-tree and tamarisk, give good cover for passerines, and in recent years elder and hawthorn have been planted for this purpose.

Hobbister, Mainland, Orkney

HY381068   *1,875 acres*
The main entrance to Hobbister lies some 5 miles south-west of Kirkwall on the A964.

The area is leased from Highland Park Distillery and the cutting of peat, for use in the distillery, is carried out in the southern part of the reserve.

Hobbister has a similar range of habitats to the Birsay Moors. Primarily an area of heather moorland, waterlogging produces bog and fen-type habitats in certain areas. The Swartaback Burn runs through the northern part of the reserve into the Loch of Kirbister, part of the stony shoreline of which is also included in the reserve. The southern boundary of Hobbister is composed of a cliff-line reaching a maximum of 30 metres in height and, to the west, the tidal sandflats of Waulkmill Bay backed by the small saltmarsh of Skaith.

Management As with the Birsay Moors the main advantage of creating a moorland reserve in Orkney is to prevent further reclamation and conversion to permanent pasture. Burning and grazing are prevented so as to allow heather to pass through a natural cycle of growth, deterioration and regeneration. Planting of native trees and shrubs in the sheltered valley of the Burn of Swartaback is planned.

Birds The Hobbister moorland has remained virtually unburned and ungrazed for a considerable period and, consequently, holds one of the best moorland bird communities remaining in Orkney. Censuses in 1980 revealed about 100 pairs of meadow pipits, forty-two of wrens, thirty-five of skylarks and seventeen of twites while stonechats are probably commoner here than anywhere else on Mainland Orkney. The wader population is dominated by curlews, almost 100 pairs breeding on the reserve, while the loch shore is one of the few places in Orkney where common sandpipers nest. Some 300 pairs of the larger gulls breed on the higher moor and about 200 pairs of common gulls can be found in the lower zone. Five pairs of short-eared owls, three pairs of kestrels and a pair of merlins utilise the abundant prey while up to seven hen harrier nests are found in most years. The cliffs do not hold huge seabird colonies but almost 300 pairs of fulmars and a dozen pairs of black guillemots breed, as well as a pair of ravens.

The saltmarsh and shore of Waulkmill Bay attract passage waders and, in the bay itself, great northern divers are regular in winter, while black-throated divers (a rare bird in Orkney) and Slavonian grebes have been seen quite frequently in recent years.

Mammals Otters breed on the Hobbister reserve and Orkney voles are common; offshore, porpoises occur regularly while both species of seal may be seen.

Plants Apart from the moorland plant communities which are basically similar to those of the Birsay Moors (see page 124) the saltmarsh area within the reserve is of interest to the botanist containing as it does long-bracted sedge and narrow blysmus.

Hornsea Mere, North Humberside

TA188471   *580 acres*
SSSI, NCR1. A nutrient-rich lake with a variety of insects and plants. Important wintering area for wildfowl. South of Bridlington, beside the B1242 in the village of Hornsea.

Most obvious of the habitats is the open water of the mere itself, two miles long by three-quarters of a mile wide. The mere is shallow, being no more than twelve feet at its deepest and four feet at the eastern end while at the more silted western end it is only two feet deep. Along the northern and western shores are woods — mainly deciduous trees with alder and willow in the wetter areas and a mixture including oak, ash and sycamore. There is no public access to the wood, which contains old, silted-up ditches that are dangerous obstacles. The farmland, a mixture of pasture and arable, between the public footpath and the waterside is included in the reserve. The other main habitat is reedswamps, which are most extensive at the western end of the mere.

Birds In winter the mere attracts large numbers of wildfowl — mallard, teal, wigeon, pochard, tufted duck and goldeneye are recorded in hundreds with smaller numbers of shoveler and gadwall with occasional pintail and goosander. The spring gathering of goldeneye and the late summer flock of moulting mute swans are both dramatic annual events. In severe weather over 1,000 coots visit the reserve. Hard weather also brings divers, grebes and sea-duck. Another winter feature is the roost of fifty or more cormorants. In addition to mallard, small numbers of pochard, tufted duck, shoveler and gadwall sometimes nest, but their low breeding success is thought to be due to predation by foxes and pike.

The reedswamp is generally drier than is ideal for birds, but there is a population of reed warblers, making the reserve the most northerly population of this species on the east side of the country.

In addition there are nesting sedge warblers and reed buntings and in winter many water rails, small numbers of bearded tits and the occasional bittern seek cover in the reeds.

While there is no longer a heronry at the western end of the reserve, there has been the recent gain of sparrowhawk as a breeding species. This is most often seen in winter or visiting the late summer and autumn starling roosts around the mere. Other woodland birds include great spotted woodpecker, treecreeper, tawny owl and jay. Woodcock are sometimes numerous in hard winters. There is only one

Avocet

rookery on the reserve, but there are two more just beyond the boundary.

There is not a day in the year that a visit to Hornsea Mere may be without its surprises, because its variety of habitat combined with its position, only half-a-mile from the coast, brings a wide range of birds. Small migrants such as wheatears and whinchats, such waders as ruff, greenshank and spotted redshank and all the commoner terns as well as black terns are recorded annually.

Of particular interest are the large numbers of little gulls, at times as many as fifty, that visit the reserve in late summer.

Plants   A rich flora is assured by the variety of habitats. Among several hundred species recorded, amphibious bistort, yellow flag, lady's smock, ragged robin, cowslip, bird's foot trefoil, lady's bedstraw, agrimony, red campion, herb bennet and enchanter's nightshade, are typical of the flowers that may be seen from the footpath round the mere as it goes from the water's edge through the fields and along the side of the wood.

Mammals   Foxes are quite common and are often seen in daylight, but much more elusive and unlikely to be seen is the tiny harvest mouse, nests of which have been found in the rough grass.

Insects   Visitors during the summer may find mosquitoes to be the most conspicuous insect, but butterflies too are quite numerous with ringlet, orange tip and small skipper among the fifteen regular species.

Horse Island, Strathclyde

NW212428   *5 acres*

Horse Island is a small, low-lying island half-a-mile offshore from Ardrossan Harbour on the Ayrshire Coast.

It is to a large extent a rocky island, although the central areas of the 'mainland' and small offshore islets produce luxurious growths of grasses, nettles and bluebells during the summer. The intertidal zone between these islets and Horse Island is sandy and shingle beaches have developed along the southern and south-eastern edges of the island, and also an eastern islet.

Birds   Terns have for many years been the main attraction of the island and the breeding colony is an important one in the Clyde area. Up to four species have been recorded breeding on the island over the years, but only common and arctic terns occur regularly, in numbers which fluctuate annually. Sandwich terns and the occasional roseate also breed irregularly.

Gulls are by far the most numerous birds on the

Little gull

island: between 600 and 800 pairs of lesser black-backed and herring gulls breed every year, together with small numbers of greater black-backed gulls and a small colony of black-headed gulls. The latter was a once numerous breeding bird of the island. These noisy birds tend to dominate the island during the summer and one might be forgiven for thinking that they were the only breeding birds present. A closer examination will soon show this is not the case.

A healthy population of about fifty pairs of eider duck nest regularly, their nests often framed by tufts of thrift or beds of bluebells. During the past four years, mallard and shelduck have established themselves as breeding birds, the latter using old rabbit burrows as nesting sites. Breeding waders include oystercatcher and ringed plover, although redshank, dunlin, turnstone and curlew use the island regularly as a roosting and feeding site.

Horse Island is only really accessible during the summer when sea and weather conditions are most favourable, and therefore knowledge of birds using the island in winter is limited. During the harsh winter of 1979 over 2,000 greylag geese roosted on the island after being forced from the mainland by the severe weather. Small numbers of wigeon, teal and snipe have been recorded flighting out from time to time. The waters around the island support a range of seabirds, such as auks, kittiwakes, cormorants and shags, whilst gannets from nearby Ailsa Craig often feed offshore.

High tides inundate up to 60 per cent of the island during winter months, often drowning out many of the active rabbit burrows. However, a few animals manage to survive each year to continue the breeding cycle. These high tides also deposit a great deal of flotsam on the island, and the early spring visits to record the year's nest sites always produce some interesting finds.

Insh Marshes, Highland

NH775998   *1,238 acres*

SSSI, NCR1*. Part of the most important tract of flood-plain mire in Northern Britain with a distinctive flora and fauna. Also of importance for its breeding and wintering wildfowl.

Nestling between the Monadhiath mountains to the west and the vast wilderness of the Cairngorms to the east, the Insh Marshes are part of the flood-plain of the Spey. Elevated stopping places on the perimeter road give uninterrupted views across the valley including much of the reserve.

By far the most extensive of the variety of habitats on the reserve is the sedge fen. Found in all the wetter parts of the reserve it gives way to reeds in the areas of shallow standing water. In drier areas there is rough pasture. Invading willow carr has formed large patches of scrub and beside the river are large stands of willow, with bird cherry and alder. As well as in the river, water occurs in a series of large pools or lochans and many relict drainage ditches.

On the higher ground on either side of the valley, the marsh gives way to birch woodland, often with considerable juniper understorey. There are a number of wet flushes throughout the wood.

Management Improvement of the conditions for wintering whooper swans and for breeding wildfowl and waders, at the same time maintaining the very high botanical interest of the area, is the main aim of management. Among the wide range of techniques employed are the creation of new areas of standing water, reintroduction of cattle into the sedge fen to graze areas suitable for nesting wildfowl and waders, and the maintenance of the comprehensive ditch system. Woodland areas are diversified by planting typical native trees and natural regeneration of the birchwoods is being encouraged by control of grazing. Encroaching bracken, which supports few insects, is controlled in favour of a more insect-rich grassland.

Birds Of international importance for wintering whooper swans, the Insh Marshes has at times over one per cent of the north west European population — about 200 birds. Unlike many other British whooper swan haunts, where the bulk of the swans' winter feeding is in stubble or other crops, Insh provides a largely natural diet.

Winter flooding is a regular feature and may put the low ground under six feet of water at times. Greylags are common, particularly on spring and autumn passage. Most numerous of the wintering duck are mallard, but teal, wigeon, tufted duck and goldeneye are also frequent. Many of these stay to breed and there are also occasional pairs of shoveler, a rare species so far north. Both goosander and red-breasted merganser are present in small numbers.

In late February and early March, lapwings and oystercatchers gather on the banks of the Spey, spreading into the marshes as they dry out. They are followed by curlews and black-headed gulls. Later in spring common sandpipers can be found and one of Britain's rarest breeding waders, the wood sandpiper, nests nearby. Although it does frequently feed in the sedge beds on the reserve, it is seldom seen.

Many meadow pipits and reed buntings breed in the damp fen areas and where there is scrub there are sedge and willow warblers. A few pairs of grasshopper warblers are present in most years.

The woodlands support many breeding chaffinches and willow warblers as well as treecreepers and the common species of tit. Small numbers of redstarts and an odd pair of pied flycatchers, which are infrequent in Scotland, breed. Redpolls and tree pipits are present in good numbers.

Birds of prey are a feature of this reserve and although buzzards are the only species to breed regularly, others regularly hunt the marshland edge and woods. Hen harriers, sparrowhawks, peregrines and ospreys are often recorded. In some summers marsh harriers are seen and it is hoped that they will one day stay to breed.

Plants Botanically the reserve is of considerable interest with nationally important sedge communities, including extensive tracts of the uncommon northern sedge. Among the wide range of aquatic plants are the least yellow waterlily and the greater bladderwort, both local species in Britain. Parts of the fen are rich with species such as valerian, angelica and cowbane. The grassy flood-prevention banks close to the Spey have a wide variety of plants, including mountain pansy, melancholy thistle and wood cranesbill.

Insects Although only partly studied, the invertebrate fauna of the reserve is clearly rich with rare spiders, beetles and flies all having been recorded. Several very local moths are found. Among them are three splendidly named species, all associated with woodland — Rannoch sprawler, Kentish glory and cousin german.

Isle Martin, Highland

NH095994   *375 acres*
Situated at the seaward end of Loch Broom, and accessible by boat from Ullapool.

Isle Martin's main interest lies in its varied and attractive seaboard and, for this reason, is perhaps best appreciated from a boat. Passing under the high north cliffs of the island one is threatened not only by their dark, sunless face but also by the impressive grey ridge of Ben Mor Coigach, the presence of which seems to loom over the whole landscape. On these cliffs are fair numbers of nesting fulmars and shags and occasionally a peregrine may be seen hunting in their vicinity. There are also small numbers of rock dove and hooded crow and, of special interest, a heronry of

Eider

about half a dozen nests at a place where the cliff is less steep. Also from a boat on this north side one can see the main regions of tree growth, including a small aspen copse. The most abundant tree is rowan with some birch but owing to the past heavy burning and sheep-grazing regime, the tree cover is exceedingly small.

As one moves around the west tip of the island, the cliff falls off greatly in height, though there are still drops of about 100 feet on the south-west facing cliff which holds nesting black guillemot, herring gull and buzzard as well as more fulmar and shag. Clinging to this cliff are more growths of young aspen and holly and just four tiny patches of juniper, as well as scattered rowan and birch, willow and rose. The cliffs hold many of the more interesting plants of the reserve including roseroot and royal fern and, at their base or where the cliff turns to steep bank, carpets of primrose show boldly in the spring.

Completing the tour around the island the east beach offers small colonies of both arctic tern and common gull while the more scattered nests of oystercatcher and ringed plover are also concentrated in this habitat. From the low rocky shores on this side otters come and go, following their conspicuous trails which criss-cross one corner of the reserve. In this same corner a few rocks just offshore afford a laying-up point for the occasional common seal and both this species and the grey seal can be seen in the water anywhere around the island.

The interior of the island is fairly typical north-west Highland heather moor, eroded and bleak with no tree cover and a short list of plant species. Nevertheless, as the flowering season progresses, a number of plants add their colour successively to the dark moor. Heath spotted orchid and bog asphodel are particularly conspicuous and widespread whilst in the wetter areas, where bog cotton predominates, sundew and two species of butterwort lie in wait for their insect prey.

A few twite and stonechat feed amongst the taller heather stands and, near the coast, the occasional nest of red-breasted merganser and eider is to be found.

In the area of former meadow on the lower east side of the reserve, and amongst the ruins of an old crofting village, wheatear abound and a few other songbirds can be seen. Some of this area is dotted with bluebells in the spring and, a little later, English stonecrop is conspicuous in rocky areas, particularly near the shore.

Although sheep were removed in about 1969, cattle roved all parts of the island more or less until the inception of the reserve some eleven years later. This grazing pressure, along with that

Black guillemot

exerted by a healthy rabbit population, has effectively eliminated tree regeneration and it will now be very interesting to observe the natural spread of trees outwards from their tenuous cliff refuges. It is hoped to be able to aid this natural recovery of the degraded habitat by some tree planting and by protecting from the rabbits some areas of natural regeneration. Over the years it may be that profound changes occur in the vegetation of the reserve, leading to a diversification and enrichment of habitat that will be reflected, not least, in its birdlife.

Killiecrankie, Tayside

NN910620   *555 acres*
SSI, part NCR1. A mixture of woodland types, forming perhaps the best lowland woodland in the area. West of A9, 4 miles north of Pitlochry.

The reserve is situated on the west side of the River Garry overlooking the famous Pass of Killiecrankie. A small by-road winds its way through the middle of it from Tenandry to Killiecrankie, giving excellent views of the surrounding reserve and countryside. A variety of habitats are present, the main types being oak woodland, farmland, birch-clad crags and moorland with wet lime-rich areas.

The deciduous woodland covering the slopes above the River Garry is the finest example of its kind in the region. Sessile oak is the dominant species, but there is also plenty of birch, ash and wych elm. Hazel is in abundance as the understorey.

Management   In the past, many exotic trees were planted around the estate house. Some of these, like rhododendron and sycamore, have to be controlled to stop them from spreading into the natural woodland. Hazel coppicing is being carried out by the wardens, using traditional methods.

Birds   Spring is the best time to visit the woodland, when the trees are alive with birdsong and the floor is carpeted with early flowers. Redstarts and wood warblers are the reserve specialities. Other breeding birds are garden warbler, tree pipit, treecreeper, great spotted woodpecker, tawny owl and woodcock. Along the river banks grey wagtails, dippers and common sandpipers nest.

The crags consist of steep wooded slopes with some areas of scree below the rocky outcrops. This is a good area to watch for the reserve's birds of prey: two or three pairs of kestrels and one pair of buzzards nest regularly. Occasionally peregrines and ravens can be seen.

At the top of the crags, the heather moorland reaches its highest point at 1,300 feet. It then stretches away west to Tulloch Hill. On the higher ground, scattered larch can be seen with birch scrub on the lower slopes. Some good wet flushes are situated near the northern boundary. Breeding birds include red and black grouse, snipe, curlew, wheatear, whinchat and meadow pipit.

Plants While the farmland is not particularly good for birds, it does have some boggy areas that are excellent for flowers, which include globe flower, grass of Parnassus, northern marsh orchid and marsh lousewort. Among the crags grow the rare sticky catchfly and both the scarce shining and bloody cranesbills. Among the heather on the moorland there are lesser twayblade, and intermediate wintergreen. In the boggier areas are Scottish asphodel, yellow mountain saxifrage and several rare sedges and rushes.

Lake Vyrnwy, Powys

SH985215   *16,000 acres*
Situated at the south-west end of the Berwyn Mountains, some 23 miles west of Oswestry, the reserve is most easily reached through the small towns of Llansantffraid-ym-Mechain and Llanfyllin or via the narrow mountain road from Bala, about 10 miles to the north.

The reserve supports an interesting and important variety of bird, mammal and plant life, as it encompasses a wide range of habitats, from the lake itself with its fringe of scrub woodland at about 750 feet above sea level, through small meadows, pockets of deciduous woodland, conifer forest and heather moorland up to 900 feet above sea level.

The moorland at Vyrnwy covers some 8,150 acres of this total, just over 3,000 is heather, the remainder is made up of grass moorland and mire. The whole of the area is grazed by between 7,000-12,000 Welsh mountain sheep and over several hundred years has been burnt as part of moorland management for them.

There are less than 250 acres of deciduous woodland, mainly consisting of sessile oak, beech and mountain ash. Reputedly more than twice as much existed before the construction of the dam. Much of the management that is being undertaken is restoring and extending many of the remaining oak woodlands by excluding grazing animals and planting young trees.

The afforestation at Vyrnwy commenced in 1896, and some stands of these first plantings, mainly Douglas fir, may still be seen in several areas around the perimeter of the lake. In 1914 the Liverpool Corporation (the water authority subsequently taken over by the Severn-Trent Water Authority) entered into a joint management agreement with the Forestry Commission, by which time the forests extended to 920 acres mainly of Douglas fir, Sitka spruce and Japanese larch. Today the forest covers more than 450 acres and there are no plans for expansion.

The lake is over 1,100 acres in extent and in places up to 70 feet deep. Due to its steep-sided nature, the invertebrate fauna around the margins is sparse.

The mountain streams and rivers are among the most interesting habitats on the reserve, holding several species of specialised plants, ferns and birds. It is hoped that in the future the edges of many of the streams that run through the dark, impoverished forest areas will not be planted up once they have been clear-felled, so as to increase this valuable and specialised habitat that is so important to many species of flora and fauna.

Birds Because of the regime of burning and despite grazing the moorland, there is still a fairly healthy population of red grouse and large numbers of breeding curlew and whinchats. Less common are golden plover, hen harrier, merlin and stonechat.

In the mixed woodland around much of the lake and in the smaller scrub woodland areas there are large numbers of garden and willow warblers, blackcaps and chiffchaffs. In the sessile oakwoods the specialities are pied flycatchers, redstarts and wood warblers, whose frequent bursts of song in spring call attention to their presence. Among the other birds in the woodland are jays, nuthatches, willow tits, treecreepers and both blue and great tits. The young plantations have a high density of breeding birds. The commonest are tree pipit, willow warbler and chaffinch. Less frequently seen are whitethroats and blackcock. In the high forest, there is an impoverished shrub layer, but many pairs of siskins and goldcrests breed in the canopy, with smaller numbers of crossbills and sparrowhawks. Buzzards are much in evidence here and on summer days may be seen soaring in the thermals above the valley sides, with ravens whose deep-throated calls echo against the high ridges. Tawny owls fill the air of late winter and early spring nights with their calls.

On the lake itself there are several pairs of great crested grebes, but more important is the population of goosanders which is increasing · in numbers at the north end of the lake. Common sandpipers, mallard and teal all breed by the lake. Several species of wader have been recorded on the muddy area at the north end of the lake and they include oystercatcher, redshank, spotted

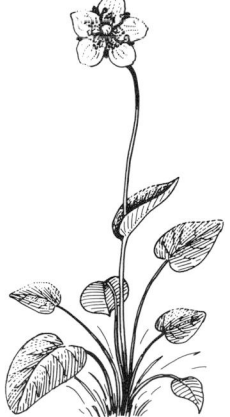

Grass of Parnassus

redshank and greenshank. Grey wagtails and dippers are common on the mountain streams and rivers and there is a pair of kingfishers.

Mammals In the shrubby wooded areas there is a large badger population, whose well-trodden paths bear evidence of many generations' use. Polecat and red squirrel are widespread throughout the younger forest areas, but the commonest species is the field vole, an important source of food for birds of prey. The fox is common throughout the forests.

Amphibians Where there are small, still pools on the mountain streams, both common newts and frogs breed.

Insects Notable among the butterflies to be found in the shrubby areas are speckled wood, ringlet, green hairstreak, orange-tip, peacock and several species of fritillary.

Plants In the damper moorland among the heather and sphagnum moss, lesser twayblade and cranberry grow. There is a far richer flora in boggy places in the lower valley. In early summer the graceful, long-stemmed violet flowers of butterwort may be seen and another insectivorous plant, sundew, is abundant. Red rattle, bog pimpernel, New Zealand willow herb and the starry yellow spikes of bog asphodel follow as the season progresses.

In spring the young plantations are carpeted with wood sorrel, and later there are the rambling stands of climbing corydalis and patches of enchanter's nightshade. Starry saxifrage and the tiny blue ivy-leaved bellflower are among the more interesting plants that grow by the streams. Large areas of ferns such as oak fern and beech fern grow along the shaded banks and mountain fern grows in the more open grass areas.

Fish Brown trout and chub are native to the lake with brook and rainbow trout introduced.

Langstone Harbour, Hampshire

SU720045   *1,370 acres*
SSSI, NCR1*. A very important wintering site for waders and wildfowl, the most notable being dunlins, curlews, grey plovers, shelduck and brent geese. Breeding birds include little and common terns.

The reserve occupies the major part of Langstone Harbour, including the low islands.

Birds Langstone Harbour is unusual among RSPB reserves in that almost all of the reserve is submerged at high tide. It was acquired by the Society primarily in order to safeguard the huge population of wintering waders and wildfowl which feed on the plants and animals of the intertidal mudflats. Among waders are large numbers

Marsh harrier

of dunlin, oystercatcher, grey plover, curlew, redshank, and both black-tailed and bar-tailed godwits. It is, however, the brent geese which are the most obvious feature of the reserve in winter, with peak counts of well over 8,000. At times they can be remarkably tame, and spend the high tide period bobbing near the water's edge in compact flocks. At low tide, they spread out over the mud, feeding on the beds of eel-grass which grow in the harbour and which form the staple food of the geese when they first arrive. In most winters the eel-grass is soon finished so that the geese are forced to find other sources of food — saltmarsh vegetation, fields of grass and even young winter wheat.

In spring and summer the bird population of Langstone Harbour is greatly reduced, because there are few suitable nesting sites available. The small islands in the harbour do hold a variety of breeding birds including ringed plover, oyster-catcher, redshank, common tern and, most important, little tern. Unfortunately, these are vulnerable to disturbance by trespassers and many nests are also lost due to flooding by high spring tides.

Plants The only really visible plants of the inter-tidal mud are eel-grass and various species of algae. However, the islands support a number of flowering plants, saltmarsh species such as sea lavender, thrift, sea wormwood and golden samphire, shingle plants like sea campion and biting stonecrop and, in the highest parts, even patches of scrub consisting mainly of blackthorn, gorse and small oak trees.

Insects The amount of available habitat and suitable food-plants limits the insect life of the reserve, but brimstone, red admiral and large and small skippers are among the butterflies seen.

Mammals Surprisingly, a number of mammals have been recorded on the islands, including bats, common shrew, short-tailed vole, fox, grey seal and even a small deer (probably roe).

Leighton Moss, Lancashire

SD478751   *321 acres*
SSSI, NCR1. A flood-plain mire colonised mainly by reedbeds, which provide habitat for species such as bittern and reed warbler, which are rare so far north in England.

Leighton Moss occupies the floor of a small, unspoilt and attractively wooded valley that was once an arm of Morecambe Bay. Cut off from the sea by an embankment and tidal sluice, it is now a freshwater marsh, fed by several streams that drain from the limestone hills. Although the area looks natural now, for eighty years until 1917 it was drained and farmed. Once drainage was stopped marshland vegetation soon took over, but the old drainage dykes still exist, as do the stone gateposts which marked the field entrances.

The habitats on the reserve are open water, reedswamp, fen edge, woodland and scrub. The water is only about three-and-a-half feet deep and is therefore ideal for the growth of aquatic plants. The meres are among 200 acres of reedswamp which gives way in the drier parts to a fen edge of rush and tussock grass with large numbers of willows. On the limestone slopes there is hawthorn, blackthorn and ash scrub, giving way to typical limestone woodland with ash, oak and yew dominant.

Management The area of open water has been increased by excavating ponds within reedbeds, embanking some areas and controlling reed and willow. More reed edge is created by cleaning out dykes. Alder, elder, buckthorn and guelder rose have been planted in the fen edge to increase the available cover. Small islands have been made in the meres by floating out large clumps of flag and anchoring them.

Birds Black-headed gulls, several species of duck, coots, moorhens and lapwings breed on the islands, which in winter are loafing areas for large numbers of wildfowl, of which mallard, teal, shoveler, pintail and wigeon are the most numerous. With suitable water levels in spring and autumn waders such as greenshank, common and spotted redshanks are recorded. Snipe and lapwing are present throughout the year. Herons hunt for the abundant eels and, in summer, swallows, martins and swifts hawk for insects over the water.

The most important species of the reedswamp are bitterns and bearded tits, both of which have increased in recent years. Reed and sedge warblers, water rails and reed buntings are plentiful. Marsh harriers are regular spring visitors, but have not bred. Large numbers of starlings and pied wagtails roost in the reeds for much of the year, and in spring and autumn swallows and sand martins have roosts here. Such an evening abundance of food attracts regular sparrowhawks and the occasional peregrine, merlin or hobby. Willow coppicing has increased the number of grasshopper warblers and the spread of bramble has brought blackcaps and garden warblers. Wrens, willow warblers, sedge warblers, reed buntings and whitethroats are all common in the fen edge.

In the woodland the resident thrushes, robins, wrens and tits are joined by several species of warblers. Tawny owls and jays are abundant and woodpeckers are heard regularly.

Insects In the fen edge many species of moth have been recorded including the elephant, eyed and poplar hawks. Butterflies include many peacocks, tortoiseshells, green-veined whites and brimstones.

The oaks in the wood hold a good population of purple hairstreaks, while on the limestone outcrops and grassy slopes there are pearl-bordered, small pearl-bordered and high brown fritillaries, meadow and wall browns and brown argus.

Mammals A breeding pair of otters has been on the reserve for many years. They may often be seen in the mornings and evenings and even sometimes during the day. Mink are a recent and unwelcome recent arrival. Among the small mammals, water shrews may be seen crossing the paths through the reedbed and their high-pitched squeaks can be heard. A small herd of red deer regularly lies up in the reeds. Roe deer have been attracted by the increased cover that has been planted.

Fish Eels, rudd and sticklebacks are among the numerous fish that have been recorded.

Plants While much of the reedswamp is dense reed, there are small areas of yellow flags and reedmace, with many scattered willows. Annual reed cutting has encouraged a diversity of plants with purple loosestrife, bur-reed, bur marigold, great water dock and many sedges. The best area for flowering plants is the fen edge with a succession of colours throughout the growing season — cowslip, meadowsweet, valerian, hemp agrimony, meadow rue and knapweed. In the wetter parts of the willow scrub the herb layer is dominated by marshland plants, especially iris and great water dock.

For Visitors There is an information centre at Myers Farm and a public causeway across the reserve. Hides have been provided on the reserve.

Loch Garten, Highland

HN977185   *1,518 acres*
SSSI, NCR1*. Part of a remnant of Caledonian pine forest with its characteristic plants and animals. Famous for its ospreys, but important for other species, especially the Scottish crossbill. Scots pine woodland and moorland around Lochs Garten and Mallachie, on a minor road mid-way between the villages of Boat of Garten and Nethybridge.

The reserve forms part of the larger Abernethy Forest. With five main distinct habitats, namely Scots pine woodland, moorland, peatland and bog, loch and farmland, it is the most diverse area, biologically, within the forest. The main features of the reserve were formed some 10,000

Sand martins

years ago during the last Ice Age, and are hollows filled with water and peat, and moraines of sand and gravel — a hummock and hollow terrain created by the finer particles of glacial debris. Following denudation by the ice, vegetation slowly recolonised the landscape, and about 8,000 years ago Scots pine established itself as the dominant tree species throughout a large area of Scotland. The resulting forest became known as the Forest of Caledon. Though part of the reserve area has had a history of felling and planting in the last couple of centuries, some of the woodland and many scattered trees are direct descendants of this ancient forest. Exploitation of Abernethy Forest took place from the 17th century onwards, with much timber being floated down the River Spey to sawmills on the coast for shipbuilding. Other trees were bored out at mills within the forest and transported south to provide water and sewage pipes for some of our major cities.

Management   The main aims of management of this diverse area are to maintain and preserve its distinctive features, but where possible to improve habitats to the benefit of the flora and fauna. In the woodland this will mean some management aimed at creating diversity of age and structure in the denser stands, and allowing for natural regeneration of managed and bare areas.

On the moorland, whilst some established woodland will be retained, encroaching birch and pine will be cleared from the open ground, and a programme of rotational burning of heather plots will create a variety of habitat for several moorland breeding species. Creation of small areas of open water within the large peatland area will help retain a rich and varied insect fauna.

Birds   The area of the reserve has long been known to be ornithologically rich, with good resident populations of the commoner woodland species like coal tit, treecreeper, goldcrest, wren and chaffinch. In summer, migrant visitors such as redstart, willow warbler, spotted flycatcher and siskin add greatly to the diversity to create a varied breeding population covering fifty to sixty species. Apart from the now famous pair of ospreys which arrive to breed each April, the reserve holds important populations of other local species. A healthy population of crested tits exists, one of five tit species on the reserve and the rarest in Britain. In most years small flocks of Scottish crossbills are to be seen and heard as they feed noisily on the pine cones. Capercaillie are resident mainly in the woods, and black grouse lek and breed on the moor.

In spring the lochs attract a good variety of passage wildfowl and a roost of up to 3,000 black-headed gulls, and though breeding wildfowl are restricted usually to mallard, teal, tufted duck and occasional wigeon, activity again increases in autumn with many birds roosting and feeding. As the south-bound pink-footed and greylag geese pass overhead, a flock of about 1,000 of the latter stay on and feed in the area, roosting each evening on Loch Garten.

The lochs are also regular feeding areas for the ospreys, and in August, Loch Garten is a favoured area for the young ospreys to visit whilst learning to fish for themselves.

Mammals   Roe deer and squirrels are the commonest large mammals, with foxes, rabbits and hares also present. Badgers and occasionally wildcats visit the area, and in winter small numbers of red deer visit the woods from the nearby hills. Otters have been recorded and in some years they breed by Loch Mallachie.

Plants   Because of the long history of Scots pine woodland, many interesting and local species of plants occur. Out of six species of orchid, lesser twayblade and creeping lady's tresses are specialities of the area, and a single clump of twinflower is expanding. Three of the wintergreen species occur, common, intermediate and serrated, and in the lochs the local water lobelia and intermediate bladderwort occur. The current total is about 240 plant species, including nineteen sedges.

Insects and Spiders   The rarest of our ten species of dragonfly is the northern coenagrion. Other dragonflies include the common blue and large red damselfly, and later in the year the black sympetrum should easily be seen.

With nineteen species of butterfly and over 260 species of moth recorded the reserve has a very rich lepidoptera fauna, and recent work on the spider population has located only the third British site for the water-associated *Dolomedes fimbriatus*. Preliminary work on the beetle population has produced 420 species, five per cent of which are strongly associated with old native pinewood areas, some of them very rare in a British context.

Loch Ken/River Dee Marshes, Dumfries and Galloway

NX638765 and NX695694   *390 acres*
SSSI, NCR1. A wide range of plant communities within the base-poor marsh group and also of importance for its large population of wintering wildfowl.

The marshes created by flooding behind the South of Scotland Electricity Board dam have long been of importance to breeding waders and waterfowl, but they are even more important as

Wood warbler

wintering places for wildfowl. The surrounding farmland, rough hill grazing, moorland, conifer forests and smaller areas of broad-leaved woodland all help to provide both a variety of habitats and fine scenery.

The farmland is mostly under grass for hay, silage and grazing with barley as the main cereal crop. The woodland has some fine oaks with ash, alder and rowan and some hazel scrub.

Management Most work is carried out on the wetland areas. It is aimed at providing less vegetated marshes with controlled water levels and islands on which wildfowl can loaf and breed. In addition the drier areas are to be grazed to allow space for breeding waders and grazing wildfowl. The provision of feeding and roosting space for Greenland whitefronts is of international importance.

It is also important to allow the regeneration of the prime oak woodland. The emphasis here is on maintenance of open woodland with native trees and shrubs. The alders and hazels are to be coppiced rotationally to keep an open aspect, in which the ground layer of plants can receive essential sunlight.

Birds During winter the farmland is grazed by greylags and Greenland whitefronts and small flocks of wigeon and whooper swans. The winter flocks of chaffinches and thrushes attract hunting sparrowhawks and occasional merlins. Wintering duck — mallard, teal, shoveler and pintail — seek refuge on the marshes, while diving duck, such as tufted duck, pochard, goldeneye and goosanders are seen on the river. The occasional hen harrier or peregrine is seen over the marshes and hunting barn owls are a common sight.

In spring buzzards display above the wood and at dusk there are roding woodcock and the loud calls of tawny owls. Willow, garden and wood warblers, tree pipits, blackcaps, redstarts and a few pied flycatchers are the summer migrants that breed here. There is a healthy population of willow tits, a local speciality, in the wetter areas of birch and alder.

In the marshes there are breeding mallard, teal, shoveler, quite large numbers of sedge warblers and reed buntings and a few pairs of grasshopper warblers. In the numerous bays of the river broods of tufted duck and goosander can be seen and great crested grebes manage to find anchorage for their nests. Common sandpipers nest along the shore, despite disturbance by angling, water-skiing and boating on some parts of the river. Herons and, less frequently, kingfishers are seen by the river and in the marshes. Linnets and yellowhammers breed in the drier, uncultivable farmland and in the wetter areas there are breeding snipe, curlew, redshank, lapwing and oystercatchers.

Mammals Red squirrels are still found in the woods, particularly where there is hazel. Otters, however, are declining. Mink are quite numerous despite control by fishing and game interests. Roe deer with plenty of feeding opportunities are often seen.

Insects Of the more obvious insects in the woodlands are Scotch argus butterflies to be seen sunning themselves along woodland edges and in glades during August. Large dragonflies, such as the common aeshna, hawk for other insects along the rides. The marshes are ideal for breeding caddis-flies and mayflies, but the most obvious insects are common blue damselflies and the large golden-ringed dragonflies.

Plants In spring the woodland is carpeted by bluebells and greater stitchwort. In the marshes, in parts overgrown with reed-grass, sedges and rushes, flowering bogbean and marsh cinquefoil cover large areas of the more open parts. There is a wealth of summer colour with meadowsweet, valerian, both yellow and purple loosestrife, marsh woundwort and in one small, raised area three rare plants — spignel, upright vetch and saw-wort.

Loch of Kinnordy, Tayside

NO361539   *200 acres*
SSSI, NCR2. An interesting fen community with many breeding wildfowl and the open water is also important for wintering wildfowl.

About 1½ miles north-west of Kirriemuir, the reserve consists of 200 acres of marsh, floating bog and open water with a thin strip of woodland along the southern edge.

Birds The lochans are frequented by large numbers of duck, principally mallard, teal, shoveler and tufted duck with lesser numbers of wigeon, gadwall and pochard. Almost all breed on the reserve as do mute swans and one or two pairs of little grebes. Great crested grebes are present in spring and summer and occasionally rear young on the reserve. Scotland's first breeding ruddy ducks were recorded here. Unfortunately the ducklings all seem to have fallen prey to pike.

The loch supports a black-headed gullery of about 6,000 pairs, many of which breed in the bogbean in front of the west hide. Moorhen and coot also breed here and the elusive water rail may often be seen from the hides in July and August.

The marshland supports breeding redshank, snipe, reed bunting and almost 100 pairs of sedge warblers.

Roe deer

In the woodland most of the common woodland species breed. The most numerous are willow warblers. Sparrowhawks are sometimes seen dashing along the woodland edges and woodcock can be seen roding on summer evenings. On one of the Scots pine-covered islands a pair of long-eared owls breed.

In autumn lapwings gather on the exposed mud and a variety of passage waders occur in varying numbers each year. Common sandpiper, ruff, redshank and curlew are regular with greenshank, green sandpiper, whimbrel, dunlin and Temminck's stint more occasional. At this time of year peregrines are seen fairly regularly. Winter brings grey geese to the loch and its surrounds. Most of them are greylags.

Management Work here has only recently started, but it is planned to install a sluice to control water levels, so that sufficiently high levels can be maintained in spring for young duck to feed in pike-free shallows.

Mammals Roe deer and stoats are frequently seen in the marshy areas. Pipistrelles are seen in summer evenings.

Plants A large variety of waterplants grow at Kinnordy. Most obvious is the bogbean which covers large areas of the main lochan in floating islands. Further spread may have to be prevented in order to maintain areas of open water. Other marsh plants include rushes and sedges of several species, reed, cowbane, marsh cinquefoil and yellow water-lily. All round the edge of the marsh are water forget-me-nots and northern marsh orchids.

The woodland, which is mainly on the southern edge of the reserve is very varied in its make-up. Norway spruce, sycamore, Norway and field maple, silver and downy birch, various willows and sallows are to be found. Both common and red-berried elder grow beneath the dense canopy of spruces at the reserve entrance. The ground flora of the woodland is typical — but the particularly fine clumps of red campion deserve mention. In the more open area between the hides there are large stands of rosebay willowherb along the edge of which can be found valerian, yellow meadow vetchling and in the more shaded areas twayblade.

The remainder of the reserve is rough grassland, covered with meadowsweet, thistles and a variety of 'open-country' plants.

Peregrine

Loch of Spiggie, Shetland

HU370170   *284 acres*
SSSI, NCR2. A wintering wildfowl site, of particular importance for its whooper swans. Situated in the south mainland of Shetland one kilometre south-west of Scousburgh.

The Loch of Spiggie is one of the Society's most recent acquisitions. It is the largest eutrophic loch in south Shetland, and is also one of the richest in animal and plant life. The loch, famous for its trout fishing, is situated four miles north of Sumburgh where the main airport for Shetland is sited. It was an arm of the sea at one time, before being cut off by the formation of a barrier which is now Scousburgh beach and dunes.

The Society owns the water area only. The surrounding land is used for sheep and cattle grazing and, to a much lesser extent, for the growing of crops to feed these animals during the long dark winters. A few potatoes are also grown in this strip cultivation method of farming.

In the north-west, north-east and south-west corners as well as between the loch itself and the neighbouring loch, the Loch of Brow, are marshlands.

Birds Red-necked phalaropes breed in some years, and ducks on migration such as garganey, gadwall, goosander and pintail seek food and refuge on the marshes. In winter, flights of whooper swans gather, sometimes building up to as many as 300 birds, and readily feed at the shallow north end. The Loch of Spiggie is the most important site for wintering wildfowl in Shetland with up to 240 tufted duck, 180 wigeon and pochard, and seventy-five goldeneye being seen on it and neighbouring Loch of Brow, of which the Society owns a part. Up to eighty long-tailed ducks moult on the loch during the spring.

Other Animals Occasional frogs can be seen or heard in the drainage ditches, and otter spraints provide proof of this mammal's presence. Water crickets, water spiders, horse leeches and freshwater shrimps abound around the edge of the loch.

Plants Bogbean and marsh marigold carpet these marshes, and the marestail *Hippuris vulgaris*, very rare in Shetland, has a foothold.

Tufted duck

Loch of Strathbeg, Grampian

NK073590   *2,327 acres*
*SSI, NCR1. The largest dune slack pool in
Britain, of international importance for wintering
wildfowl. Lies between Peterhead and
Fraserburgh, between the A952 and the sea close to
Rattray Head.*

At its widest the reserve stretches from high water
mark some four miles inland and covers a
diversity of habitat including open loch, sand
dunes, fen woodland and freshwater marsh.
Control of shooting rights over neighbouring
farmland allows wildfowl areas where they can be
sure of peaceful feeding and resting.

Extremely shallow and rich with much of its
floor covered in stonewort and pondweeds, it is
an ideal staging post and wintering place for
migrant wildfowl. The annual rise and fall
between winter and summer levels is less than 30
inches. This is, however, sufficient to flood the
marshes and some of the low-lying farmland to
the west of the loch. The exposed nature helps to
prevent the rapid encroachment of aquatic
vegetation.

The freshwater marsh is most extensive at the
western end of the loch and, in the vicinity of the
Savoch burn mouth, there are large beds of reed-
grass, and most of the small reedbeds. On the
west side there is willow scrub, which increases
in density, forming an attractive area of fen
woodland in the south-west corner.

Management   The loch, with its surrounding
marshes, dunes and gravel bar, is a Grade 1 Site of
Special Scientific Interest and forms a comparatively undisturbed 'natural' area. Therefore, major
management is unnecessary and probably un-
desirable. However, on a small scale, pools are
being excavated on the edge of the marshland and
a small permanent island is being built. The pools
are already in use by wildfowl for feeding and
resting. The island was occupied by a tern colony
the first season after its completion and it is also
used by roosting goosanders and whooper swans.
An area of tall grass has been mowed to provide
an additional rough weather roost for some of the
reserve's greylags.

Birds   Because of its size, geographical position
and the lack of any nearby freshwater bodies,
Strathbeg is an internationally important staging
post and wintering area for migrant wildfowl.
Large numbers of ducks, geese and swans winter
on the loch and even greater numbers pass
through on autumn and spring migration. The
species in greatest number are tufted duck and
pochard. Large coot flocks also occur. In summer
about 300 mute swans come to the reserve to moult.

In addition to the wildfowl, other birds are
attracted to the reserve. Among the rarities
recorded are Caspian tern, red-footed falcon and
great white egret.

Mammals   Roe deer, including does and two or
sometimes three kids are frequently seen here.
There is a badger sett and signs of badgers
digging for bumble bee nests can sometimes be
seen from the path. Among the mammals, pride
of place must go to the otters, whose infrequent
daylight appearances always delight visitors.

Plants   With its variety of habitats the reserve
has a diversity of plant species. In the dunes
notable species are Scots lovage, grass of
Parnassus, field gentian and autumn gentian. The
loch has a number of pondweeds and around its
margins there are common spikerush and the
extremely localised buttercup *Ranunculus reptans*.
Among the marsh plants great hairy willowherb
is of note.

Lochwinnoch, Strathclyde

NS355583   *388 acres*
*SSI. In the valley stretching from Kilbirnie to
Lochwinnoch are four shallow lochs, Kilbirnie
Loch, Barr Loch, Aird Meadow and Castle Semple
Loch.*

The RSPB Reserve includes the Barr Loch and
Aird Meadow, together with their surrounding
marshland and three small areas of deciduous
woodland. The adjacent Castle Semple Water
Park, part of the Clyde Muirshiel Regional Park,
is run by the Strathclyde Regional Council as a
water recreation area.

The shallow water and marshy fringes of the
extensive Barr Loch and smaller Aird Meadow
form the reserve's major habitat. Like so many
wetlands, these lochs have a history of
manipulation by man. Originally a shallow loch,
Barr Loch was drained by an elaborate system of
ditches and pumps in 1814 and farmed for many
years. During the 1950s the system fell into
disrepair and the area gradually reflooded,
producing a fine marsh for a time before reverting
to the original shallow loch.

Birds   The lochs are a major feeding and roosting
area for wildfowl, especially in winter, when up
to 5,000 wildfowl, mostly mallard, tufted duck,
pochard and coot with smaller numbers of teal,
shoveler, wigeon and goldeneye are present.
Peak numbers are during autumn migration
when up to 1,000 each of tufted duck, pochard
and coot occur. A wintering flock of up to 500
greylag geese roost on Barr Loch and a few
whooper swans winter here. Small numbers of
mallard, tufted duck, pochard and shoveler
remain to breed. The lochs are the breeding

Whooper swan

ground of several pairs of great crested grebes, one of the larger colonies in Scotland.

Occasional dry spells lower water levels and expose mud on Barr Loch attracting migrant waders. Management work is directed to controlling and lowering water levels, developing muddy fringes and the growth of aquatic and marsh vegetation to attract more wildfowl and waders. Islands have been made as roosting and nesting sites for gulls and duck. The marshes around the loch teem with nesting sedge warblers. There are also reed buntings, and a few pairs of grasshopper warblers and water rail. A few hundred pairs of black-headed gulls nest on Aird Meadow.

The mixed deciduous woodland supports populations of warblers, finches, thrushes and treecreepers. Great spotted woodpeckers are sometimes seen and sparrowhawks nest. There is a small rookery.

Plants   The lochs are surrounded by marshes of reed sweet grass, reed canary grass and mountain water sedge, and in summer are decorated with meadowsweet, valerian, bogbean, flag and purple loosestrife. Interesting plants include bird's-nest and butterfly orchids.

For Visitors   A most attractive Nature Centre of Norwegian design was opened in 1978 and houses regularly changing displays, lecture room, RSPB gift shop and an observation tower with telescopes. These facilities are widely used by school parties and the general public. A nature trail leading to two observation hides offers easy study of the reserve's wildlife.

Situated only a few miles from Glasgow and other centres of population, the reserve's wealth of wildlife makes it ideal as a study centre.

Sparrowhawk

The Lodge, Bedfordshire

TL188478   *104 acres*
SSSI. Ornamental woodland, together with relics of Greensand heath, supporting a typical range of woodland species. 1½ miles to the east of Sandy on the B1042 Cambridge road.

The Lodge, the headquarters of the RSPB since 1961, stands in 104 acres of woodland and heath on part of an outcrop of the Lower Greensand known as Sandy Warren. The major habitats are of mixed open oak and pine woodland with denser areas of birch. The heathland is particularly important, being one of the last remnants of Lower Greensand heath north of the Thames. The influence of the gardens and that of the many artificial ponds extends onto the reserve to produce an area of diverse habitat.

Curlew

Management   Efforts are directed at creating stability in these different habitats, and especially in the creation and maintenance of mature woodland. This involves the control of such species as sycamore and rhododendron that threaten to overwhelm the regenerating species such as oak, beech and birch. Recently a birch coppice has been initiated to rejuvenate areas of dense and unproductive birch scrub in order to provide suitable nesting habitat for a number of species of birds. The heath has been seriously affected by the invasion of pine and birch. Work has recently been carried out to extend the heather area by felling some of the invading birch woodland. Problems also exist with only limited natural regeneration of the heather, which a programme of planting should help to eliminate. The conifer plantations are to be gradually thinned and regenerating hardwoods will be encouraged in an effort to diversify these rather dense and unproductive areas.

Birds   The commoner woodland breeding species are represented on the reserve with willow warblers, chiffchaffs, blackcaps and garden warblers arriving in the spring to join the resident nuthatches, treecreepers, great and lesser spotted woodpeckers and tawny owls. Goldcrests and coal tits are particularly common in the areas of pine, while stock doves and jackdaws nest in the quarry. Turtle doves arrive in May and nest in the more open wooded areas while tree pipits breed in small numbers on the areas of open grassland and around the heath. Spotted flycatchers can be seen hawking for flies in the garden in the summer. Winter brings vast flocks of wood pigeons to their evening roosts in the surrounding woodland and crossbills and bramblings are regular. Sparrowhawks are becoming increasingly common although this species does not nest on the reserve.

Plants   Although the reserve is not noted for its flora, it does have an impressive list of fungi, with stinkhorn abundant in late summer and fly agaric common in autumn.

Insects   The Lodge is one of the few sites in the area where pine hawk moths breed. Emperor moths and the rarer rosy footman occur on the heath. Among the regular butterflies is the holly blue, whose broods of caterpillars feed alternately on holly and ivy.

Mammals   Foxes, stoats and weasels are often seen. Among the small mammals is the yellow-necked mouse, some of which have been seen in the offices at the Lodge. Muntjac deer, whose ancestors escaped from Woburn, are frequently seen and their tracks may be seen in the snow.

Reptiles and Amphibians   The only reptile

recorded is the common lizard, but common frogs, toads and newts are all common. Of particular interest is the colony of natterjack toads which were reintroduced to the heath in 1980 in an attempt to re-establish a breeding population of this very rare amphibian.

The Loons, Mainland, Orkney

HY253243   *89 acres*
The Loons lies some 11 miles north of Stromness and 3¼ miles north-west of Dounby. The area includes old peat-cuttings which have not been utilised for over thirty years.

The Loons is a basin mire enclosed to the north and south by low hills of Old Red Sandstone and separated from the Loch of Isbister, immediately to the south, by low ridges of glacial till. Large sections of the marsh become completely inundated in winter and, even in summer, the area remains extremely wet. The old peat-cuttings, now barely recognisable as such, help to add further diversity to the already very complex pattern of vegetation communities.

Management Grazing of the marshland is not detrimental to either the botanical or the ornithological interest and the grazing is let to local farmers. Management of the reserve will be aimed at maintaining its present high water-table.

Birds The Loons is, without doubt, the best wetland site to have survived the widespread drainage schemes that have robbed Orkney of so much prime marshland habitat. The area supports a high density of breeding ducks and waders. Census work during 1981 has shown that eight species of ducks nested including five pairs of wigeon and six pairs of pintail. Amongst the waders some fifty pairs of lapwing, thirty-five of curlew, eighteen of redshank, fifteen of snipe, ten of oystercatcher, seven of ringed plover and seven of dunlin all find room to breed while, in addition, there are colonies of 175 pairs of common gulls, ninety pairs of black-headed gulls and 250 pairs of arctic terns. An evening visit in summer also offers the chance of hearing, and perhaps even catching a glimpse of that increasingly elusive species, the corncrake.

Mammals Orkney voles are fairly common on the reserve while otters also occur from time to time.

Plants To date eighty-six species of higher plants and twenty-six bryophytes have been recorded. Of note are bog pimpernel, northern marsh orchid, early marsh orchid and heath spotted orchid, grass of Parnassus, knotted pearlwort, small bladderwort and alpine meadow rue.

Amphibians Orkney has no reptiles and only one amphibian, the toad; the Loons is one of the sites where the latter may be seen.

Lough Foyle, Co. Derry

C546224   *3,300 acres*
Numerous access points from the Limavady to Londonderry Road. The best areas are Longfield Point and Ballykelly. Faughanvale is also worth a look in from October to December. The Roe Estuary can be reached via minor roads from Limavady and is best visited on a rising tide (as are most open foreshore stretches).

Birds The eight-and-a-half miles of shoreline under RSPB control is the most important stretch of the Foyle for both wildfowl and waders, and provides the figures which make the lough a site of national and international importance for certain species.

Due to its geographical position the Foyle acts as a catchment area for wildfowl coming from the north and the stretch of foreshore between the old reclamation sites at Donnybrewer and Myroe provides a rich feeding ground, the mussel and mud banks being covered in eel grass. In mid to late October the visitor can be rewarded with the spectacular sight of over 25,000 wigeon (best viewed from the road through Greysteel or Longfield Point). Lost among this huge flock are smaller numbers of the other dabbling ducks and upwards of 500 pale-bellied brent geese. As the winter progresses these numbers fall away quite dramatically as the flock disperses elsewhere in Ireland, leaving behind a small wintering population. The arable land at Myroe and Donnybrewer provides the perfect habitat for the 650+ wild swans which use the area throughout the winter; the vast majority are whoopers but a careful look will reveal upwards of thirty Bewick's. Once an important area for geese, numbers have declined over the last fifty years, leaving small but regular flocks of greylags and Greenland whitefronts which frequent Myroe and Donnybrewer, while individual pink-feet and barnacles can also be seen from time to time.

At low tide it is virtually impossible to assess the numbers of waders scattered over the exposed acres of mud and mussel banks, but a check on the principal high tide roosts at the Roe, Ballykelly, and Longfield will reveal the true picture; over 3,000 curlew, 1,000+ redshank, 1,200 bar-tailed godwits, 1,000 golden plover and nationally significant populations of other species. Careful observation in the autumn will also reveal small numbers of less common passage waders such as curlew sandpipers, little stints, black-tailed

Common frog

godwits, ruff and even the odd American visitor.

The Foyle is also used by various birds of prey, notably peregrine, merlin and hen harrier, attracted by the wealth of waders and large flocks of finches and larks in the surrounding fields.

Finally it is worth noting that the true potential of this understudied area has not yet been fully appreciated and its importance may well increase with our increased observation.

Lumbister, Shetland

HU485967   *4,200 acres*
North and west of A968, 1 mile north-west of Mid Yell.

From the Hill of Colvister a fine view of the reserve, to the west, can be obtained. A series of large lochs extends to the north-west, surrounded by rolling heather moorland interspersed with many small pools. These acidic pools, which occur in the hollows in the thick layer of peat that forms a blanket over the reserve, are particularly numerous in the low-lying boggy areas. South of the Loch of Lumbister, the largest loch, is a group of ruined crofthouses surrounded by an area of grassland. Similar areas occur further to the south. All were vacated in 1868 when the area was turned over to sheep grazing which continues to the present day. Further west the Burn of Lumbister runs via a waterfall through a gorge to the steep-sided sea gully known as the Daal. Rugged sea cliffs to the north with caves, arches and stacks face the Atlantic. To the south the moorland dips more gently to meet a long sheltered bay called Whale Firth.

Birds   On the lochs and Whale Firth red-throated divers, eider and red-breasted mergansers can be seen during the summer, whilst both great and arctic skuas come to the lochs to bathe. Both skuas nest on the surrounding moorland along with golden plover, dunlin, curlew and snipe. Merlins often hunt along the heather slopes looking for skylarks, meadow pipits or the wheatears which nest in the peat banks. The fulmar is the most numerous cliff-nesting species with puffins, black guillemots, shags, rock doves, rock pipits and ravens also breeding on the cliffs. Colonies of common, herring and great black-backed gulls and a colony of arctic terns occur near the coast and the Shetland wren nests along the shore of Whale Firth.

Mammals   From the distribution of spraints, otters are clearly active over much of the reserve and several holts are present. They are most often seen along Whale Firth but also benefit from the presence of brown trout in several of the larger lochs.

Seabird cliff

Plants   Flowers indicative of acid conditions thrive, for example, butterwort, sundews and heath spotted orchid. Lesser twayblade can sometimes be found amongst the heather and water lobelia grows in two of the lochs. On the cliffs moss campion, roseroot and lovage are frequent whilst in the Daal primroses, honey-suckle and the dwarf form of juniper grow out of reach of the sheep.

Marwick Head, Mainland, Orkney

HY229242   *46 acres*
SSSI, NCR1. Marwick Head lies in the north-western corner of Mainland Orkney, some 15 miles north of Stromness and 7 miles north-west of Dounby.

The Kitchener Memorial stands within the reserve. The memorial was erected to the memory of Lord Kitchener of Khartoum who was killed when his ship, *HMS Hampshire*, struck a mine and sank, off Birsay, in 1916.

The major habitat at Marwick consists of almost a mile of cliff up to 280 feet high. Also included within the reserve boundary are the northern part of the rocky bay known as Mar Wick and some wet meadowland immediately inland from the bay.

Management   No management of habitat, apart from stockproof fencing, has been undertaken. NCC have seabird monitoring points on the cliff, counts being made during the summer months to try and assess population fluctuations.

Birds   The reserve has huge colonies of seabirds and a 1979 census revealed totals of 35,035 individual guillemots, 718 razorbills and 1,062 fulmars while, in addition, there were 9,710 apparently occupied kittiwake nests. Wheatears, rock pipits and rock doves also nest as does a pair of ravens, while the occasional peregrine may also be seen. The wet meadows inland from Mar Wick hold several pairs of breeding waders including redshank, curlew, snipe, lapwing and oystercatcher.

Mammals   Grey and common seals can often be seen in Mar Wick while signs of otters are also occasionally found in the bay, although the animals themselves are rarely encountered.

Plants   In late spring there is a spectacular showing of thrift and sea campion, as well as spring squill.

Orkney vole

Minsmere, Suffolk

TM473672   *1,500 acres*
SSSI, NCR1*. Reedbed, muddy lagoons, woodland and heath with rich variety of breeding, passage and wintering birds. Mainly in the parish of Westleton, 4 miles north of Leiston and 6 miles north-east of Saxmundham.

Management Invasion of the open heath by trees is controlled by selective thinning-out of Scots pine and birch. The woodland's natural regeneration is retarded by rabbits and therefore long-term maintenance must include planting young trees. Oak, beech and hawthorn are planted and sycamore, bracken and rhododendron are removed to improve the structure by opening the canopy to allow improved growth of the herb and shrub layers. The small area of pasture is maintained by licensed grazing and haymaking for the benefit of the flora and breeding snipe.

The reedswamp that is such a feature of the reserve has to be controlled. The reed must be prevented from invading the open meres and ditches, and trees must be prevented from invading the reedbeds. This is the most intensive, regular management carried out on the reserve.

One habitat, the Scrape, is man-made. It is a combination of shallow water, wet mud and small islands of varied surfaces — shingle, moss or grasses. It was created using heavy plant and a large amount of back-breaking human effort. To retain the open wet mud, so important to waders, management must be intensive, because it is a fertile area for plants. Care must also be taken over the control of water levels and their salinities, so that optimum conditions for wader feeding can be maintained. Vegetation on the islands has to be managed to remain suitable for breeding terns, avocets and other waders.

Birds Over 300 species have been recorded and about 100 breed each year. Between the middle of May and the end of July is an excellent time for an evening walk along the public footpaths on the heath to enjoy the churring nightjars, roding woodcock, owls and smaller birds such as the tree pipit and stonechat. It is in spring, before the leaves become too dense, that there are the best views of nuthatch, the three woodpeckers, nightingale, redstart and most of the other song-birds to be expected in southern England. Where the woodland meets the wetland edge, Cetti's warblers can be heard singing.

The 400 acres of reedbeds are wonderful for birds throughout the year. Bittern, marsh harrier, bearded tit and water rail are regularly seen. From the tree and island mere hides there are good views of warblers and wildfowl. Occasionally a spoonbill or a purple heron might be seen on the edge of the reeds and kingfishers as they fish from suitable perches near the hides.

The Scrape is ideal for gaining close views of breeding terns, avocets and other waders. Since it was made, forty-six species of wader have been recorded here. From April to mid-September there is good birdwatching here, but it is in late summer and early autumn when there is a mixture of plumages — summer, winter, adult, juvenile or a combination of any of these — that the fun of identification can really be enjoyed to its fullest.

Plants The large heathland is largely ling and bell heather with patches of gorse and bracken. A natural succession of Scots pine and birch with some oak and hawthorn is spreading into the heath. The woodland originates from 19th century game coverts and is mixed with oak and Scots pine dominant and sweet chestnut, sycamore, hazel, birch and beech are very noticeable.

There is a small area of pasture with a marvellous array of plants such as ragged robin, bog cotton, yellow rattle, marsh stitchwort, lousewort, various clovers, marsh orchids, interesting grasses, sedges, and rushes. In the surrounding ditches grow water violet and pondweeds. While common reed dominates the reedbeds there are odd patches of bulrush with a sprinkling of willow, oak and hawthorn and a large amount of marsh sowthistle.

Invertebrates The variety of habitats provides a good number of insect species. So far identified are over 300 species of moth, twenty-four butterflies and sixty-six species of beetle.

Mammals Coypu are often seen on the meres and another, more unwelcome, escapee from fur farms has been recorded here, the American mink. Otters are present in winter and sometimes breed. Also in the marshes are the abundant water voles, prey of the marsh harrier. Harvest mice nest in the reeds and feed in autumn on the nuts of alders. Three species of shrew are present. Red deer are rarely seen because they hide in the woods during the day, but they come to the reedbed to feed at night. Brown hares can be seen feeding on the new saltmarsh vegetation on the Scrape.

Morecambe Bay, Lancashire

SD467666   *6,200 acres*
SSSI, NCR1*. Intertidal mudflats and saltmarsh supporting the largest population of wintering waders in Britain. To the west of the estuaries of the Rivers Kent and Keer.

Sandflats These cover about two-thirds of the reserve. The rivers bring freshwater and silt to mingle with the tide and create ideal living conditions in which crustaceans, molluscs and worms

Kingfisher

can thrive. By late summer thousands of curlews and oystercatchers arrive to feast on this abundance. For birds on passage Morecambe is a staging post and this is the time to see and hear whimbrel and grey plover. Although there are small numbers of non-breeding bar-tailed godwits and the occasional knot present throughout the summer, the really large numbers are found in winter when northern birds move in. Dunlin from Iceland and Greenland stop on passage to Africa, but the northern European and Russian birds stay for the winter. In most years there is a rush of sanderlings in late May, with smaller numbers on the return journey in autumn.

As the tide retreats shallow pools are left and here wildfowl are seen in winter. Small flocks of wigeon, mallard and pintail, joined by the occasional teal and shoveler, feed along the channel of the Keer. Shelduck are present throughout most of the year and in summer their ducklings scuttle over the sands in crèches behind anxious 'aunts'.

As these feeding-grounds are covered at high tide, the birds must roost until they are uncovered again. One of the roosting places is Hest Bank at the southern extremity of the reserve. On this sandbank ten to fifteen thousand birds regularly gather on the high spring tides and when the spring migration of knot is at its peak, numbers may exceed this. The first arrivals at this roost are oystercatchers from the Heysham mussel-beds, which are soon joined by curlews and bar-tailed godwits. The smaller waders, redshank, dunlin and knot, continue to feed along the rising tideline, eventually coming to rest close inshore, where they are joined by ringed plovers and turnstones from the beaches of Morecambe and Bare.

Parties of wigeon float up on the tide and redbreasted mergansers, goldeneye and great crested grebes may be seen in quite large numbers when the sea is calm. Sometimes the rapid, powerful flight of a hunting peregrine creates a spectacular, swirling panic of waders and as the saltmarsh channels fill there may be a blue flash of kingfisher.

Saltmarsh A belt of saltmarsh of varying widths on which waders also roost runs between the sands and the shore. These sea-meadows, flooded at the highest spring tides, are grazed by sheep throughout the year and in some places the resulting fine turf is removed to be sold. Few plants can withstand such conditions but the marsh turns pink in June with thrift and sea milkwort. Coarser grasses and rushes offer nest-sites to redshanks, lapwings and the occasional dunlin and oystercatchers nest in the shorter turf. In spring and summer the air is alive with the song of skylarks and the parachuting display of meadow pipits is a common sight. Black-headed gulls with a few lesser black- backed gulls and the occasional greater black-back nest. All of these birds are at the mercy of the tides and sometimes their breeding success is low.

As the river channels constantly alter their courses, the saltmarsh may be rapidly eroded. Since the late 1970s much of the marsh at Silverdale has disappeared in this way. As the Kent moves out again the sand will build up and the pioneer grass, sea pea, will restart the growth of saltmarsh.

The Shore The saltmarsh backs on to shingle beaches, bright in summer with the flowers of yellow horned poppy. The hawthorn thickets, sea walls, railway embankment and, at Silverdale, cliffs of carboniferous limestone form a natural rock-garden, brilliant with horseshoe vetch, bird's foot trefoil, rock-rose, sea campion, thyme, hawkweeds, harebell, rue-leaved saxifrage, bloody cranesbill and dog-rose. Cotoneasters and wallflowers give an exotic appearance, but the yews, junipers and whitebeams clinging to the cliff-face are all native. Grayling and brown argus butterflies occur here and sun-bathing wall browns are common.

Mull of Galloway, Dumfries and Galloway

NX148303   *40 acres*
SSSI, NCR1. This section of cliffs has a variety of interest with moderate-sized colonies of guillemot, razorbill, shag, cormorant and fulmar. Considerable botanical interest with a range of uncommon species. The cliffs are at the extreme south-west tip of Scotland, south of the Port of Stranraer.

Although small by comparison with many other Scottish colonies, the seabirds of the Mull of Galloway are quite varied, including razorbill, guillemot, black guillemot, shag, cormorant, kittiwake and fulmar. Despite the height of the cliffs, over 200 feet in places, the nature of the rock is such that there are few ledges suitable for nesting.

The cliffs are, however, of great interest for their plant communities. Spring squill and purple milk vetch are abundant in cliff-top turf (though unknown on the coast of north-west England) and species such as golden samphire, rock samphire and rock spurrey reach their northern British limit here. At the same time, Scots lovage and roseroot have their southernmost colonies.

Rowan

Nagshead, Gloucestershire

SO606080   378 *acres*
*SSSI, NCR1. Mature, broad-leaved woodland
(mainly oak) planted in 1814 and supporting a
range of typically western woodland birds,
including pied flycatcher and wood warbler. Near
Parkend in the Forest of Dean.*

The main habitat on the reserve is the pendunculate oak woodland which was planted in 1814. This oak area is divided into two sections. The first, which is grazed by the flocks of wandering forest sheep, is characterised by an open shrub layer with scattered rowans, yew and odd clumps of holly with a field layer consisting mainly of bracken. The ungrazed section has a much more varied shrub layer with sweet chestnut, downy birch and sycamore, and in some areas holly, being dominant. The field layer is also varied but over most of the area bramble is abundant. Running from the Cannop Ponds through part of the oak woodland is a fast-flowing stream with numerous alders growing alongside. The one other type of deciduous woodland is found along the Sausage Ride, an area of mature beech planted in about 1920. The other habitats on the reserve consist of a mixture of different conifer plantations in various stages of development, and the species present include Norway spruce, Scots pine, larch, Douglas fir and Corsican pine. The last major habitat on the reserve is the now disused Point Quarry and its associated birch and bramble undergrowth.

Management   As the reserve is owned by the Forestry Commission the conifer plantations are managed in accordance with standard forestry practices. The mature oak woodland, however, is being managed to ensure that it is perpetuated with an opening up of the canopy and removal of shrubs to encourage regeneration of the oaks.

Birds   In the oak area nestboxes have been provided for hole-nesting species, the boxes being occupied by blue, great and coal tits, nuthatches, the occasional redstart and also the pied flycatcher. A special study of these attractive flycatchers has been carried out on the reserve since 1942. The population has unfortunately declined from a peak of 100 pairs in 1951 to between 35 and 40 pairs in recent years. Other characteristic oak woodland species are to be found with a good selection of breeding warblers, including wood warbler, three species of woodpecker, woodcock and hawfinch. Along the stream grey wagtails and dippers are to be found and in the open young conifer plantations tree pipits and whinchats are to be seen. Overhead sparrowhawk, buzzard and the occasional raven can be seen on sunny days. Since 1974 just over 100 species have been recorded.

Flowers   Although the only plant of special interest on the reserve is the ivy-leaved bellflower, as it is the only known site in the county, there is a rich community of typical plants throughout the oak woodland. In the spring the ground is covered in bluebells and later the conspicuous and attractive foxglove is abundant. Along the ride edges an increased variety of plant species is to be found, both beneath the oak and also in the young plantations.

Other Animals   Associated with the diversity of plant species is a good selection of butterflies, the most interesting being the white admiral and silver-washed fritillary. Of the larger mammals fallow deer are resident, but in small numbers, and there is also an active badger sett.

North Hill, Papa Westray, Orkney

HY496537   510 *acres*
SSSI, NCR1. The reserve is situated at the
northern end of the island of Papa Westray. The
entrance is at the grid reference given above while
a warden is in residence during the summer at the
cottage of Gowrie, 100 metres east of the gate.*

Papa Westray was one of the last sites where the great auk could be found, one being killed at Fowl Craig in 1813.

Not actually on the reserve, but close by, is the Knap of Howar, one of the oldest known settlements in Western Europe, while offshore, on the Holm of Papa Westray, is a superbly preserved chambered cairn, some 5,000 years old.

Almost the entire reserve is dominated by the plant community known as maritime heath, a community confined to Orkney and the north Scottish mainland. The North Hill is, in fact, the largest continuous area of such habitat left in Britain. The east coast of the reserve has a line of low cliffs which peter out northwards to become rather dangerous sloping flags.

Management   The reserve is held under an agreement with the people of Papa Westray who themselves have the right to graze stock on the North Hill. These rights are only exercised to a

Black guillemot

*Silver-washed
fritillary*

small extent in summer but, in autumn, considerable numbers of cattle utilise the reserve.

Birds The North Hill holds the largest colony of arctic terns in Britain, a 1980 survey putting the number of breeding pairs at 6,610. This huge assemblage of birds, present on the reserve from mid-May to mid-July, is an extremely impressive sight. Almost ninety pairs of arctic skuas also breed and the continual interaction between skuas and terns may be watched for hours. Oystercatchers are the commonest wader with some sixty pairs but ringed plover, lapwing, dunlin, curlew and snipe also breed. The cliffs of Fowl Craig hold fulmars, kittiwakes (almost 1,500 pairs in 1980), guillemots, razorbills and shags while numerous black guillemots nest beneath boulders and loose flagstones.

Passage migrants are often drifted to the island by easterly winds while an added attraction in recent years has been a resident drake Steller's eider.

Mammals Both grey seals and common seals are regularly seen offshore.

Plants The maritime heath community is of great interest in itself but of the individual species to be found, alpine meadow rue, awl-leaved pearlwort, alpine bistort, Scottish primrose, slender bedstraw, frog orchid and few-flowered spike-rush are worthy of note.

Grey heron

Northward Hill, Kent

TQ784761   *134 acres*
SSSI, NNR, NCR2. Oak woodland, containing a large rookery and the largest heronry in Britain. Situated off Northwood Avenue, High Halstow.

Following the ravages of Dutch elm disease in the early 1970s, much of the reserve's mature woodland disappeared. Elm now appears as two interesting habitats: stands of dead, rotting trees, now mostly devoid of branches, and blocks of vigorous young scrub. The roots of the elm are not killed by the disease and can produce new shoots, only a small proportion of which have so far been re-infected. Fortunately, there are also oakwoods on the northern slope and these now house the heronry which was formerly in elms. Almost all of the rest of the reserve (and most of the area open to the public) is covered with dense scrub, mostly hawthorn. Much of this has grown up on abandoned farmland and is dense, gloomy and poor for birds. Younger areas, and areas which have been managed by the Society, contain smaller bushes and a variety of other scrub species. It is here the greatest variety of small birds, flowers and butterflies is found.

Management Much of the work on this reserve is aimed at 'reviving' areas of old hawthorn. Here the canopy is so dense that little light penetrates, there are few low branches and the ground is bare. Working in small blocks of an acre or less, all but a few well-formed or very large bushes are felled. The huge quantities of brushwood which result are not burnt, but cut up and stacked to provide nesting habitat for small birds and support for climbing bramble and honeysuckle. The cut stumps sprout rapidly (though some may require protection against rabbits), and after a few years produce healthy scrub with room for bramble and flowering plants. Different areas are cut in successive years and a varied habitat, ranging from clearings to well-grown scrub with scattered mature bushes, results. After a number of years re-cutting is necessary and so the process is continuous.

Birds Northward Hill is best known as Britain's largest heronry: 215 pairs bred in 1982. These breed in the oaks on the north face of the wood from February to August. They are absent in winter. The heronry is closed to visitors, but the birds can be viewed from a distance from several points. Many birds breed in the scrub areas; outstanding are nightingale and turtle dove. Long-eared owls breed and roost in impenetrable scrub and there is little chance of the visitor seeing one. All three woodpeckers and several pairs of little owls breed; hawfinches are sometimes seen in spring. The best time to visit the reserve is April to June — nightingales are at their best in May.

Plants   This reserve lies on clay, and so lacks the exciting flora of some other Kentish reserves on chalk. The visitor in early spring may be rewarded with a spectacular display of bluebells and red campion; three species of violet grow beside the trails.

Insects   Butterflies are abundant along the trails on hot summer days, amongst the common species such as speckled woods and gatekeepers may be found the scarce white letter hairstreak; this should be looked for on bramble flowers in elm areas.

Mammals   A wide variety of mammals have been recorded, including a healthy population of badgers. Prints may be seen in the mud on the trails, and claw-marks on fallen elm trunks. The animals themselves may sometimes be seen on the trails at night.

North Warren, Suffolk

TM455587   *237 acres*
SSI. Remnant heath, with dry reedbed, scrub and birch woodland supporting a variety of bird species. North of Aldeburgh, inland from the village of Thorpeness.

North Warren was one of the first reserves acquired by the RSPB. It is a remnant of the Suffolk 'sandling' heaths and originally had a covering of heather, but much of the area has since been cultivated and the vegetation is now very different. Gorse and bracken are common, but the ploughed fields, although fallow for a number of years, still have very short and sparse plant cover. The soil, being almost pure sand, dries out very quickly and this is an area of exceptionally low rainfall, so most of the surviving plants are adapted to a short season of growth and many are annuals. There is a large rabbit population (as might be expected from the reserve's name) which helps to keep the vegetation short and maintain open areas of sand.

In complete contrast to the heath is the adjoining 50-acre reedbed known as the Fen. This area at one time had nesting marsh harrier, Montagu's harrier and bittern, but the reedbed is gradually drying out and has lost much of its bird interest. The Society hopes to carry out large-scale management of this area which will, with luck, restore the value of the reedbed for wildlife.

North Warren also has some areas of scrub and woodland, alder and willow in the low-lying fen and birch and a variety of shrub species on the higher sandy heath.

Birds   The bird life of the reserve is of less interest than when it was first acquired. Not only have the reedbed specialities disappeared, but two heathland rarities, for which the reserve was first established, have also gone. These were the stone curlew and red-backed shrike, both of which have declined dramatically in this country, largely due to natural changes such as the recent tendency towards cooler, wetter summers. However, some interesting species do remain, with teal, reed bunting, reed warbler, sedge warbler, grasshopper warbler, coot, moorhen and snipe in the fen; skylark, yellowhammer, linnet and nightingale on the heath and in its associated scrub; and many typical birds such as turtle dove, five species of tits and willow warbler in the woodland.

Other Animals   Butterflies recorded on the reserve are mostly common species, but include grayling, Essex skipper, green hairstreak and common blue. Mammals seen include coypu, harvest mouse, water shrew and, in 1980, otter.

Plants   The plant life of North Warren is as varied as might be expected. In addition to the typical species of fen, woodland and heath, there are recent records of royal fern, mossy tillaea, southern marsh orchid and the now almost extinct corn cockle, which was at one time a common cornfield weed.

Noup Cliffs, Westray, Orkney

HY393499   *35 acres*
SSI, NCR1*. The cliffs are in the north-western corner of the island of Westray. They lie about 3 miles west of the village of Pierowall and are reached by a minor road as far as Noup Farm and thence by a rough track to the Noup Head lighthouse.

The major habitat is almost two miles of sandstone cliff up to 70 metres in height. The horizontal strata forming the cliffs provide ideal nesting ledges for seabirds. A narrow strip of cliff-top sward is also included in the reserve. No management of habitat has been attempted.

The Noup Cliffs hold an astonishing number of seabirds. A 1978 census revealed totals of 40,348 individual guillemots and 24,855 apparently occupied kittiwake nests. In addition, 1,248 razorbills and 1,011 fulmars were counted, together with small numbers of shags, herring gulls, puffins and black guillemots. Only a narrow zone of cliff-top sward comes within the reserve boundary but skylarks, meadow pipits, rock pipits and wheatears all breed. Despite its north-westerly location within Orkney, Noup Head does attract migrants, especially in spring, and species such as wryneck and black redstart have been seen on occasion.

Dog violet

Mammals Both grey and common seals may be seen offshore as can various species of Cetaceans, the latter especially in late summer and early autumn.

Plants Floristically the cliff-top sward is now poor, the maritime heath community having become very patchy as a result of previous grazing and fertilising practices. However, thrift puts on a spectacular showing in late spring.

Ouse Washes, Cambridgeshire

TL471861   *2,100 acres*
SSSI, NCR1*. The largest area of regularly flooded freshwater grazing marshland left in Britain. Of national importance for its breeding birds and of international importance for its wintering Bewick's swans and other wildfowl. To the north-west of Ely in the Cambridgeshire Fens.

Although basically a single habitat reserve, the area can be divided into three — the washes or flood meadow fields, the ditch and river systems including the flood waters and thirdly the osier beds and willow holts.

Management The Washes provide an excellent example of farming practices being used for conservation management. The aim of this management is to provide a variety of lengths of sward by control of the grazing by cattle, horses and sheep. The reserve wardens shepherd about 2,000 head of stock daily in summer, moving them from field to field as necessary.

The provision of numerous pools of different types has been one of the most significant factors in increasing the success of breeding waders and ducks. Some are mechanically excavated, others are simply flooded field bottoms and some have been created by using a highly selective herbicide on dense monocultures to produce shallow, mud-based lagoons.

Research and survey work has shown how valuable regular ditch maintenance can be to water plant communities. Each year, therefore, on a rotational basis, several miles of ditch are cleared by machine to improve plant diversity. By digging new ditches parallel to existing ones, 20-yard-wide islands with shallow-shelving margins are created: these provide safe nesting cover for ducks such as gadwall, pochard and tufted duck, as well as creating extensive 'nursery' ditches in which the ducklings can feed.

The osier beds are cut in rotation to provide willows of a variety of ages with a consequent variety of nest-sites for birds. Young crack willows are pollarded at six to eight feet. Doing this provides nest-sites in the crown for such diverse species as mallard and barn owl and

Black-tailed godwit

prolongs the life of the tree. New crack willows are planted to ensure regeneration, interspersed with alders, which are a source of food for birds and whose roots withstand flood water.

Birds Black-tailed godwits chose the Ouse Washes as a site when they returned to breed in Britain in 1952. Since then it has remained the godwits' national stronghold with an annual total of forty to sixty pairs. Ruff became a breeding species in the mid-sixties, and although their numbers are less stable than the godwits' their leks (breeding displays) can be watched for a brief period each spring. The grass tussocks and damp ground of the Washes are nesting and feeding areas for other waders, snipe, lapwing and redshank all breeding in large numbers. Nine species of duck also breed here — starting with the most numerous they are mallard, shoveler, gadwall, tufted duck, shelduck, teal, garganey, pochard and pintail.

The insects associated with grazing stock attract yellow wagtails and several hundred pairs breed. Black terns have bred sporadically and in 1975 a pair of little gulls attempted breeding. Spotted crakes, heard at night, but rarely, probably breed.

The more mature osiers have nest sites for turtle doves and low branches near the water are used by nesting coots and moorhens. Redpolls and goldfinches nest high in the three- to six-year-old willows while reed warblers sling their nests between the slender shoots of the one- to three-year-old trees. The crack willows have many cavities in which birds such as stock doves and little owls can nest. In the tops of the willows along the railway bank there is a heronry.

In winter the Bewick's swans, which come in increasing numbers each year, make the Washes internationally extremely important. The peak winter population has risen in a dozen years from a few hundred to about 3,000 birds. The Washes is the most important British inland site for wintering wigeon and 30,000 are regularly present with peaks of over 40,000. The large number of other ducks, together with the Bewick's swans and wigeon, make this the country's most important inland site for wildfowl.

The deep waters of the river and high flood conditions attract diving duck such as pochard and tufted and a few sawbills — goosander, red-breasted merganser and smew are recorded. Great crested grebes linger over the winter into early spring before pairing and moving to the surrounding pits to nest. Little grebes stay to breed, but kingfishers, unable to find suitable steep banks along the straight cuts, are usually only winter visitors. The floodwaters provide safe roosts for huge numbers of gulls and assemblies of 30,000 gulls, chiefly black-headed, are not uncommon.

Plants For over 300 years, a regime of summer grazing and winter flooding with a varied sward of sedges and grasses has given fast-growing feed for stock and an abundance of nest-sites for birds. Reed sweet-grass, reed canary-grass and tufted hair-grass are among the commonest grasses, but rarer plants such as sulphur water dropwort, slender spike-rush and mousetail have a refuge from harmful sprays on the reserve. Species such as meadow rue, great yellow-cress and great water-dock, which are becoming scarcer nationally, remain undisturbed on the Washes.

The ditches and rivers hold 44 per cent of aquatic species in the British flora, including at least nine rare species, such as whorled water-milfoil, tasteless water-pepper and fringed water-lily.

Several types of bracket-fungus, some spectacularly large, grow on the crack-willows. Common meadow-rue, creeping yellowcress and bittersweet grow in the bottom of the osier beds.

Mammals Foxes, rabbits, stoats and weasels are frequently seen on the Washes. Bank and short-tailed voles along the banks are the common prey of kestrels and short-eared owls. Along the river banks the many holes are evidence of the activity of water voles. Harvest mice nest in the young osiers. Otters have been sighted infrequently and have used the cavities in crack-willows as holts. Mink are occasional and unwelcome visitors.

Priest Island, Highland

NB925020   *300 acres*
One of the Summer Isles, lying north-west of Loch Broom.

This is the most westerly of the Summer Isles, which lie off the north-west of Scotland near Ullapool. It also stands apart from the twenty or so other islands in terms of geology and flora and fauna. The variety of topography has resulted in a variety of habitats in the space of 300 acres.

Birds In addition to the nesting shags, fulmars and black guillemots also found on the other islands, Priest Island has a few razorbills and kittiwakes. At one time there was an extensive cormorant colony on part of the cliff, but sadly this species is thought no longer to be breeding on the island.

On rocky platforms around the coast are extensive gulleries with predominantly herring gulls and a few pairs of both lesser and greater black-backed gulls. A very few pairs of common gull breed by one of the eight lochans.

Greylag geese breed and are joined in winter by barnacles. Eiders are present in small numbers.

Most conspicuous of the passerines are the wheatears, but twite is a common breeding species as are meadow pipits, rock pipits and skylarks whose songs merge overhead in summer. Snipe can be heard drumming or stonechats scolding occasionally.

The most important species on the island is storm petrel. The colony is huge and difficult to count but it is thought to approach or even exceed 10,000 pairs. They are not confined to any particular habitat and nest all over the island in holes in the peat, crevices in the cliffs, boulder beaches and in the ruins of an old building. This species probably also nests on others of the Summer Isles but nowhere is it as abundant as here. On each summer night, as darkness gathers, the reserve is lulled to sleep by the continuous and comforting churring of its hidden chorus.

Plants The cliff has a variety of maritime plants including roseroot, sea pink, sea plantain, buck's-horn plantain, sea campion and scurvy-grass.

Although fairly oligotrophic, the shores of the lochans are the site of profuse growths of royal fern and yellow flags.

Areas of wet flash are interspersed with dry, healthy hummocks. Dense carpets of bog cotton move in the wind over many areas of flash, although in some places a herb-rich community exists with plants such as lesser butterfly orchid, ragged robin, bog asphodel, sundew and butterwort.

A heather-dominated community characterises the hummocks, but there are some extensive areas of alpine bearberry and a certain amount of juniper in the rocky areas where the muirburn has not penetrated. Other plants here include the profuse bird's-foot trefoil as well as devil's-bit scabious, golden rod, eyebright, lousewort, heath spotted orchid and mountain everlasting.

Even the most optimistic of ecologists would use the word 'vestigial' to describe the woodland, which consists of a few scattered birches, rowans, aspens and holly. There are signs of regeneration, which is probably prevented by the grazing of sheep in winter.

A small patch of saltmarsh holds a few more plant species and there is a small reedbed at the head of one lochan.

Storm petrel

Wigeon grazing

Radipole Lake, Dorset

SY676796   *192 acres*
SSSI. Reedbed, open water and rough grazing
supporting a variety of birds during the breeding
season and of importance during migration.
Situated in the centre of Weymouth.

From a distance, Radipole Lake appears to have just two habitats — reedswamp and open water. Closer examination, however, shows that there is more to the lake. The open water is generally very shallow, but the channel running parallel to the road on the eastern shore is very deep. Colonisation by reed has been recent, since the last war and, therefore, there has been little invasion by scrub.

Through the reedbeds in the southern part of the lake some paths and tracks have been laid using the rubble from Weymouth houses bombed during the last war. With the rubble came the roots and seeds of many garden plants and these paths are now bordered by a dense corridor of scrub consisting mainly of buddleia and bramble. A closer examination of the largest block of 'reedbed' will show that there are three large areas of old saltmarsh. These were the original islands in the days when, prior to 1924, the lake formed the estuary of the River Wey and was then known as the Backwater. Saltwater used to flow in twice daily as far as Radipole village until the building, in 1924, of Westham Bridge with its sluices, prevented the tideflow and the area slowly became a freshwater lake. The only other habitat to be found on the reserve is an area of water meadows at the northern end of the reserve in the valley of the River Wey. These meadows are flanked on the west by dense scrub and to the east by housing development.

Management The long-term management aim is to achieve a balance between areas of open water for breeding and winter wildfowl, and good quality reedbeds for the nationally important breeding populations of birds. It is also planned to develop the fringe habitats to improve the diversity of more common breeding species and to increase public awareness of the value of the reserve by encouraging recreational and educational use of the lake.

Birds Winter visitors to the lake will delight in a wealth of wildfowl dominated by pochard, tufted duck and teal. Pintail are far less frequent, but good numbers of shovelers are seldom absent, mallard now breed well and are numerous in winter, whilst scaup, goldeneye and gadwall are regular features. Snipe can often be seen, and water rails are frequently heard squealing from the cover of the reeds, whilst overnight, several

Razorbill

hundred pied wagtails roost in the reeds together with starlings several thousand strong.

In the spring and summer the reedbeds come alive with the chattering song of reed and sedge warblers, grasshopper warblers reel through the night and reed buntings, extrovert as ever, can easily be seen. One of the specialities of the reedbeds are the bearded tits, which first colonised the lake in 1964 and now breed in small numbers. Twelve years later another of the specialities arrived, the Cetti's warbler. This is now well established as a breeding species with chiffchaff, willow warbler, common and lesser whitethroats and the occasional nightingale. Huge numbers of swallows, martins and swifts are often to be seen feeding over the lake from April until late August.

A very spectacular time on the reserve is late summer and early autumn when large numbers of sedge warblers use the reedbeds on their southward migration, fattening themselves up on the tiny plum reed aphids. A roost of sometimes up to 3,000 yellow wagtails develops in the reedbed, and they are joined by tens of thousands of swallows, martins and starlings. Around the muddy margins of the lake a good variety of waders can be found including greenshank, redshank, spotted redshank, common, green, wood and curlew sandpipers, ruff, godwits, dunlin and plovers. Kingfishers become more obvious and the patient observer may be rewarded with the sight of a spotted crake.

By the autumn of 1981, a total of 236 species had been recorded for the area, including several American species such as pied-billed grebe, Bonaparte's, Franklin's, laughing and ring-billed gulls. Other unusual species recorded in recent years have included corncrake, woodchat shrike, little auk and Dartford warbler.

Insects The entomology of the area has only been closely studied since the establishment of the reserve and already over 400 species of moths, including several scarce migrant species, have been recorded. With the abundance of buddleia and nettles on the reserve, butterflies can be found in large numbers and interesting species include marbled whites and clouded yellows.

Plants The flora contains a mixture of both freshwater and estuarine plants, two species of interest being the summer snowflake and the southern marsh orchid.

For Visitors. There is an information centre, designed and equipped with particular attention to the needs of disabled visitors. The paths around the reserve are suitable for wheelchairs and there are tap rails and listening posts for the disabled.

Rathlin Island — North Cliffs, Co Antrim

D120530   *124 acres*
Breathtakingly dramatic, the North Cliffs stretch for about 3 miles, for most of which they are sheer and reaching 400 feet. Situated 2 miles off the north coast of Co Antrim.

Birds The inaccessibility of the cliffs and their plentiful ledges attract large numbers of cliff-nesting seabirds. Guillemots breed in tens of thousands of pairs and razorbills, puffins, kittiwakes and herring gulls in their thousands. The fulmar also breeds here. Northward, towards the Scottish island of Islay, gannets and Manx shearwaters can be seen skimming the tops of the waves. In addition to seabirds, rock pipits, ravens and buzzards breed on the cliffs. The plentiful supply of rabbits on the cliff-tops are a source of food for the buzzards.

The spectacle of tens of thousands of seabirds is best seen from a boat, because access to the cliff top is restricted because of the danger of the sheer cliffs. The best time is June, because most of these birds only come ashore to breed.

Visiting If a boat trip around the island is impossible, good views of the birds are to be had from the Kebble Nature Reserve, owned by the Department of the Environment and managed by the RSPB.

On this area of heather and grassland at the western end of the island, meadow pipits, skylarks and wheatears can readily be seen. For botanists there is the very rare limestone bugle here. There is also a marsh where bogbean, marsh cinquefoil and dense stands of reed grow that attract sedge warblers and reed buntings. A freshwater lough is used for bathing by gulls and is a breeding area for coot, tufted duck and little grebes. Mountain hares may be seen on the way to the West Lighthouse from whence there are spectacular views of a guillemot-crowded sea-stack and an adjacent cliff-face where nesting kittiwakes, fulmars and razorbills may be seen with their chicks.

Rye House Marsh, Hertfordshire

TL386100   *18 acres*
Beside the old Rye House, built in 1443 by one of the ancient crossing points of the Lee and its marshes, and later famous for the Rye House plot. By the River Lee down Rye Road, Hoddesdon.

The reserve is mainly reed sweet grass marsh crisscrossed by drainage dykes, but also includes shallow pools and scrapes, areas of common reed, wet meadow, mixed fen and bordering willow scrub. Some of the hides overlook extensive water areas in the adjacent sewage works.

Management Aimed at conserving the different types of marshland habitats and providing facilities for the 20,000 visitors each year from the public at weekends and education groups on weekdays.

One highly successful project has been the construction of nesting rafts for common terns on the sewage works lagoons. Over eighty young terns are reared each year by some of the most productive terns in the country.

Birds The south end of the reserve is carefully designed and managed to provide the best possible opportunities to observe marshland wildlife. Here, shallow pools with muddy edges grade into reeds and tall herbs, and are enclosed by a ring of willow and alder scrub.

In winter, teal, snipe and kingfisher are present daily and often water rail, jack snipe and water pipit can be seen. In the summer, nesting birds include common waterfowl, reed and sedge warblers, reed buntings, cuckoos and several finches. On passage the pools are used by yellow wagtails, green and common sandpipers and little ringed plover, and the scrub teems with warblers.

The reserve is also part of a larger area which regularly holds Cetti's warbler and in winter, bearded tits and bitterns.

Other Interesting Species Marshland wild flowers in abundance include ragged robin, marsh marigold and water forget-me-not. There are good populations of cray-fish, grass snakes and harvest mice, and at least five species of bat feed over the reserve.

St Bee's Head, Cumbria

NX962118   *55 acres*
SSSI. An important cliff seabird colony with guillemot, razorbill, black guillemot and kittiwake. 5 miles south of Whitehaven.

Birds The cliffs here are of sandstone. Along the top a few areas of gorse provide cover and nesting habitat for the reserve's few breeding landbirds. The main breeding seabirds are the auks, with guillemot, razorbill and puffin all breeding and the reserve's speciality, black guillemot, for which St Bee's is the only English colony. Other breeding seabirds are kittiwakes and fulmars, with kestrel, little owl, stonechat, rock pipit, grey wagtail, wren, whitethroat, willow warbler and raven the regular breeding landbirds.

Many other species are recorded every year, and include red-throated diver, Manx and sooty shearwaters, Sandwich, common and arctic terns,

Bloody cranesbill

gannets and both great and arctic skua. Passage migrants include wheatear, redstart, whinchat and chiffchaff.

Butterflies   Most noticeable of the other animals on the reserve, apart from the rabbits, are butterflies with fifteen species recorded.

Shanes Castle, Co Antrim

J111881   *80 acres*
Entrance via the park gate 1 mile outside Antrim on the Randalstown Road. There is an admission charge at the gate during the summer months, winter visits can be arranged with prior notice.

The reserve itself is enclosed by a large tract of park and farmland owned by The Lord O'Neill, and lies on the shores of the United Kingdom's largest freshwater lake, Lough Neagh. Visitors to the reserve can use the nature trail and two hides, which overlook Antrim Bay. An information centre is also provided which helps give the casual visitor an insight into what he can expect to see. Various other facilities are provided by the estate such as a steam railway, a fun fair and a café. The two-mile nature trail starts at the castle, some parts of which date back to 1607. Unfortunately, the castle itself is now completely ruined, destroyed by fire caused by a jackdaw's nest in the chimney!

The lough once lapped the wall (look for the old mooring rings). It has, in fact, been lowered twice this century for various drainage and drinking water schemes, the old shorelines are clearly visible when you walk along the first mile of the nature trail. The changes in water level have a dramatic effect on the woodland that makes up the bulk of the reserve, with the oldest trees, mainly beech, lime, sycamore and exotic pines, and nearest the shore growing in semi-marsh, a dense belt of alder and willow carr.

Management   Has been mainly experimental, opening up areas of the marsh adjoining the shore by removing the cover of alders and removing some of the ancient tangles of rhododendrons which dominate the understorey of the wood.

Birds   The summer visitor to the reserve will be able to see all the commoner woodland birds found in the Province. Of particular interest is the unusually high density of blackcaps.

Antrim Bay comes into its own in the winter months, when in excess of 10,000 duck can be seen from the castle under the right weather conditions. Pochard and tufted duck are the two main species, but goldeneye are also quite plentiful. Mallard, teal and wigeon are all present in smaller numbers. Greylag geese and both whooper and Bewick's swans also frequent the reserve, often

roosting in Hide Bay. The diligent observer may also be lucky enough to find the odd rare duck among the large rafts; smew, goosander, black duck and American wigeon have all been recorded in recent years.

Flora   The flora is also very typical, the highlights being a carpet of common spotted orchids growing on the Castle Meadow with a profusion of yellow rattle. The woods themselves hold a few interesting species, such as giant bellflower, broad-leaved helleborine and a confusing array of garlics.

Butterflies   The visitor may also be lucky enough to glimpse some of the thirteen species of butterfly recorded, including the diminutive wood white and the very attractive silver-washed fritillary.

Skinflats, Lothian

NS930835   *1,020 acres*
SSSI, NCR1. Part of a very important wintering site for waders and wildfowl. An extensive area of mudflats on the south side of the Inner Forth Estuary between Grangemouth and the Kincardine Bridge.*

Birds   The chief importance of the site is as a feeding ground for large flocks of wintering wildfowl and waders. The 10,000 knot and 1,200 redshank are typical peak numbers of international importance, while the 1,000 shelduck, 5,000 dunlin and 2,000 golden plover are all of national significance. With the adjacent mudflats, this site forms one of the best estuaries for wintering birds in the whole of Great Britain.

Unfortunately, the reserve is located close to the industrial complex at Grangemouth, and there is a serious risk of large-scale reclamation for the expansion of industry in the area. Now that Skinflats has become a nature reserve, it is hoped that these threats can be successfully averted in the future.

Snettisham, Norfolk

TF648333   *3,250 acres*
SSSI, NCR1. Part of the ecologically important North Norfolk Coast, with a large area of intertidal flats, saltmarsh, brackish lagoons and shingle beach. The reserve is on the east shores of the Wash, near the village of Snettisham.*

Management   Intensive wardening, the erection of hides, fences and screening banks, together with the construction of islands, have changed the southernmost two pits from a public playground to a sanctuary which regularly accommodates 15,000 birds on spring tides.

Birds   The 2,880 acres of sand and mudflats con-

Puffin

tain a rich source of invertebrate life that is food for waders and wildfowl. Some 70,000 waders roost on the mudflats off the beach through winter high tides. Peak numbers have included 35,000 knot, 1,000 grey plover, 4,000 bar-tailed godwit, 12,000 oystercatchers, 10,000 dunlin, 3,500 red-shank, 1,500 curlew, 1,000 turnstone, 800 sanderling and 250 ringed plover.

Among the 10,000 wildfowl to use the mudflats at various times are 5,000 pink-footed geese, 2,000 shelduck, 1,000 mallard and 1,000 brent geese. On the pits can be seen goldeneye, red-breasted mergansers and other diving ducks, dabbling ducks and grebes. The islands on the pits are graced during the summer months by up to 150 pairs of common terns, as well as many gulls. Waders and passerines breed on the shingle and among the bushes. Dozens of redshank, skylarks, meadow pipits and reed buntings breed on the 300 acres of saltmarsh and some 450 pairs of breeding waterfowl use the 50 acres of brackish water-filled shingle pits.

Flowers   The beach has some good examples of shingle flora, including yellow-horned poppy, seaside curled dock, sticky groundsel, hound's tongue, sea sandwort, rocket, beet and a small quantity of sea kale. Elsewhere are good stations of hoary mullein, shrubby seablite and a little hen-bane. Rabbits dominate the flora, leaving only the unpalatable plants to grow, but watching them is a favourite pastime from the hides.

South Stack Cliffs, Anglesey

SH205823   *780 acres*
SSSI, NCR1. The cliffs display a classic example of folded pre-Cambrian rocks of the Mona Complex and hold an important seabird colony. High botanical interest, with several rare species. Located on the western coast of Holy Island.

Although South Stack is famed for its magnificent cliffs and coastal scenery, the reserve also includes two separate areas of maritime heathland which are of great botanical interest. In the north there are the rocky, heather-clad slopes of Holyhead Mountain; to the south is a low, damper plateau known as Penrhos Feilw Common.

Birds   The cliffs rise up to 120 m in Gogarth Bay, where they are rent by deep chasms and dark caves. The land drops away in height to the south, but the cliffs are no less rugged. From April to July the ledges between Ellin's Tower and the Light-house steps are crowded with over 1,500 nesting guillemots, with several hundred razorbills and puffins. Since nesting auks are very susceptible to human disturbance, the RSPB has negotiated a voluntary ban on rock-climbing, canoeing and

helicopter exercises near the main colonies during the nesting season.

There is a rapidly growing kittiwake colony on Penlas Rock, about half a mile south of the light-house, and other breeding seabirds include shag and fulmar.

Choughs, which nest in some of the inaccessible sea-caves, can often be seen searching for insects in the cliff-top sward around Ellin's Tower. Several pairs of ravens also nest on the cliffs and sometimes make egg-stealing raids on the auk colonies.

The mountain, at first sight, seems a very barren area, apparently devoid of birdlife. However, its slopes hold a strong population of stonechats and form an important feeding ground for the choughs. The pockets of gorse provide nesting cover for whitethroats and shelter for resting migrants.

Adders and lizards bask amongst the rocks and often fall prey to kestrels and little owls.

Penrhos Feilw Common, to the south, has a much richer flora and fauna. The heather and furze here form a gently undulating, wave-like plain, of a type that once covered much of Britain's south-west coast.

Lapwing and redshank nest on Penrhos Feilw Common; other waders, including whimbrel, greenshank and dotterel, regularly pause here on migration. Harriers, merlin and short-eared owls sometimes hunt over the common on passage.

Plants   Early spring brings a rich variety of colourful blooms to the cliff-top — spring squill, thrift, sea campion, bloody cranesbill, kidney vetch and many others, including the rare and unusual spathulate fleawort.

In June the mountain is dotted with hundreds of heath-spotted orchids and the reserve's rarest plant, the spotted rock rose, grows in a few small colonies near the old coastguard shelter.

There are a number of scarce and interesting plants, including pale heath violets, devil's-bit scabious and four species of orchids on the common.

The heathland is dominated by four plants — ling, bell heather, cross-leaved heath and dwarf furze. In warm weather the vegetation rapidly becomes tinder dry, so much of the management work is aimed at preventing serious fire damage.

In past years, the Common was used as an artillery range and an unofficial rubbish tip — so much effort was put into clearing the area up when the reserve was established.

Butterflies   Warm, calm days bring out dozens of silver-studded blue butterflies, plus small pearl-bordered fritillaries, graylings, gatekeepers and the occasional marsh fritillary.

Yellow horned poppy

Stour Wood and Copperas Bay, Essex

TM190313   *333 acres*
SSSI, NCR1. Approximately 15 miles east of Colchester on the south shore of the Stour Estuary close to Wrabness.

The countryside here is well-known from the paintings of John Constable. On the reserve are two main habitats — deciduous woodland of which there is 134 acres, and intertidal flats of which there is 185 acres, together with small areas of bramble scrub and estuarine reedbeds.

Management Diversity of structure within a sweet chestnut wood comes about through coppicing — areas of the wood being cropped on an approximately fifteen-year rotation. In this way different parts of the wood are always at various stages in their growth. Some are newly cut, others due for cutting as fairly substantial trees, and others are left completely uncut as standards.

It is this varied age structure, coupled with a diversity of tree species, that provides habitat for a wide range of flora and fauna. Following coppicing the dormant seeds of many flowers are able to germinate thanks to the increase in light and warmth reaching the woodland floor. This is followed by several years of lush growth which gradually recedes as the canopy closes over again.

Thus, the maintenance of an active coppicing programme will be a major feature of the management of this reserve — the wood will be further enhanced by plantings of selected tree species and the creation of new pools. Glades and clearings will be opened up and maintained, especially with butterflies in mind.

Birds Stour Wood supports a varied population of small birds, including all three species of woodpeckers, several species of warblers and nightingales. Due to a cessation in coppicing for some years before the Woodland Trust acquired this property, populations of birds are currently small, but active coppicing should soon bring numbers of breeding birds up to levels comparable with already coppiced woods nearby. The estuarine scrub and reedbeds hold many warblers, including both common and lesser whitethroats and reed warblers, as well as nightingales.

Without a doubt it is the bird populations of the estuary that visitors will remember most. From late summer to late spring a wide range of waders feed on the exposed flats of the bay. Most important amongst these are black-tailed godwits with the estuary holding up to 1,000 birds at times. Internationally important populations of redshank, grey plover and dunlin also occur, along with many other species of waders. Ducks and geese feature strongly during the passage and wintering periods with many brent geese, pintail and shelduck — again in significant numbers, whether nationally or internationally. Other ducks include wigeon and mallard, and a large herd of mute swans is a feature of the upper reaches of the estuary. Many shelduck breed as do smaller numbers of mallard.

Flora Although Stour Wood is essentially an ancient 'coppice with standards' sweet chestnut wood, a wide variety of other tree species occur, including pedunculate and sessile oaks, silver birch, hawthorn and wild service tree. The shrub layer consists mainly of hazel, elder, blackthorn and dogwood.

In early spring, much of the woodland floor is covered by wood anemones. Bluebells dominate the scene a little later. A wide variety of flowers occur especially around the edges of the wood, by damp rides or in clearings. Common amongst these are red campion, moschatel, yellow archangel, celandine, several species of violet and pendulous sedge. Bramble and honeysuckle are found throughout the wood, the latter often forming dense patches around trees.

Mammals Grey squirrels are abundant in Stour Wood, which also supports badgers, rabbits and dormice. Foxes occur both in the wood and out on the estuary mud.

Insects Although insects are largely unrecorded, Stour Wood is one of Essex's most important sites for lepidoptera. Many species of butterflies occur, including the white admiral and as a moth site it is regarded as unrivalled in north Essex. Many of the species that occur are very local.

Strumpshaw Fen, Norfolk

TG342063   *600 acres*
SSSI, NCR1*. An area of open mixed fen communities, very rich in both plant and animal species. 6 miles to the east of Norwich on the north bank of the River Yare.

The complete range of Broadland habitats are found here — the open water of river and broad, reed-fen, sallow and alder carrs, grazing fen and many miles of assorted ditches. Because of nutrient enrichment from sewage works and to a lesser extent from farming run-off, the river and connecting waterways are no longer the lovely, weedy, clear waters of thirty years ago. Instead they are murky and impoverished of wildlife. Many are silted and will soon be lost. On the

Wild service tree

other hand many ditches on the reserve and Strumpshaw Broad itself are isolated from the river's influence and here we have clear water, many weeds and much more wildlife.

The reed-fens too have suffered. In some areas reed and the rich assortment of fen species are no longer dominant and have given way to great hairy willow-herb and nettles. As sallow bushes and alders seed into the fen and gradually shade out the reed and other plants, carr is formed. Large areas of carr have grown up in recent years and, while some of it is important for the scarce Cetti's warblers, it is one of the main aims of management to prevent further encroachment. Eventually the carr is dominated by mature alder.

The grazing marshes originated from the draining and grazing of the reed-fen after it had been protected from river flooding. As a result, fen plants are present, but in a suppressed form, and other species, such as marsh orchids, marsh helleborine and grass of Parnassus, invade to form a distinctive and rare community of plants. With severe grazing, mowing, fertilising, liming, weedkilling and re-seeding, these marshes become excellent grassland for stock. Downriver from Strumpshaw at Buckenham, the rich pasture attracts a locally unique wintering flock of bean geese.

Management At Strumpshaw, management is intensive — every habitat is subject to some form of rotational manipulation such as ditching, mud-pumping, coppicing, grazing and mowing.

However, the most important work is to prevent the river from flooding, particularly since it has become heavily polluted. Thus, embankments have been built over the years and are maintained and improved. Fortunately for visitors, these make ideal trails above the surrounding land. Within these banks management can go on unhindered by water levels. Miles of ditches are being re-excavated from a derelict condition to improve them for aquatic plants, invertebrates, amphibians, wildfowl and, we hope, the bittern. The Broad is undergoing steady mud-pumping and re-excavation to extend it and deepen it now that silting up is no longer a problem. The fringes of the Broad, along with other much poorer areas of willow-herb fen, are mowed and sprayed to turn them into wader feeding areas.

New water areas or small Broads can be very worthwhile shooting-free wildfowl refuges. Two have been dug recently and these are being monitored at present for recolonising plants and animals.

Sallows are being cleared from the few areas of fens with plants like marsh pea, greater spearwort and lesser tussock sedge, but they are not being totally eradicated, because it is important for birds to have a few in which to sing and feed. Reed-cutting has almost been stopped, except where it helps in other management tasks.

Areas of dense sallow carr are allowed to remain, but any spread is controlled. They are maintained and diversified by random coppicing of small blocks every year. Similar management happens (though on a much longer time-scale) in the alder carrs with the timber being sold. Here, too, ditching, ride maintenance and tree planting are main jobs.

Finally, the grazing marshes too are intensively managed. They are grazed every year and later mown after the end of the breeding season or when some of the distinctive plants have set seed. No fertilising, liming or weedkilling is allowed here on what is now a very scarce habitat in the Broads. Again, miles of ditches are maintained and we try to maintain wet flooded areas at times for breeding waders and so on.

Birds The reserve can show visitors most of the characteristic Broadland birds. All the typical breeding species are represented except the bittern at the moment. Waterside birds are increasing through management, — shoveler, gadwall, pochard, tufted duck, dabchick, water rail, and kingfisher. The reed-fens are rich, much richer since reedcutting was very reduced, in reed, sedge and grasshopper warblers and reed buntings. Marsh harriers began breeding for the first time this century in 1980, and Savi's warbler and bearded tits are recently established breeders.

In the sallow carr, always next to a waterway, breed Cetti's warblers, a scarce breeder in Britain, but common now in the Yare valley with about thirty male territories.

The woodlands have all the species of woodpecker, nuthatch, treecreeper and all the warblers found locally, spotted flycatchers and goldcrests. Sparrowhawks are likely breeders too these days.

The grazing marshes are a springtime place — yellow wagtail, lapwing, snipe and redshank breeding in one of the very few Broadland meadow sites left. Masses of hirundines and swifts feed over the area.

In winter, too, the reserve is improving for birds. It is now a regular roosting site for good numbers of hen harriers; bearded tits and water rails are much commoner, and great grey shrike is a regular. There are good roosts of winter thrushes and waxwings are fairly regular. Siskins are found in the alders in good numbers. Downriver on the Buckenham marshes, November to mid-February is the time to visit the hide to watch the flocks of bean geese and up to 5,000 wigeon.

Spotted rock-rose

Other Animals The area is very rich in all forms of wildlife and it is difficult to pick on particular species or groups for a mention. Good examples of typical Broadland species are the swallowtail butterfly, the Norfolk aeshna dragonfly and some species of pondweed.

However, among the invertebrates the dragonflies are worth a closer look and the area is very rich in butterflies, moths, mayflies, caddisflies and other aquatic fauna.

Amphibians are increasing, and it is no longer unusual to find a frog, toad or newt. Grass snakes and lizards are a regular sight sunning themselves, and the naturalised European terrapin can be seen on logs in the waterways.

Most of the common mammal species are here, but of particular interest to the visitor are coypu, otter, mink and Chinese water deer, any of which might be glimpsed.

Sutton Fen, Bedfordshire

TL205475   *94 acres*
Situated between Sandy and Sutton.

Sutton Fen is basically a mixture of young pine plantation and dense birch scrub, with several small areas of old oak woodland. A maturing poplar plantation lies in the south-west corner of the reserve, and the boundary is marked by ancient oaks and willows. The pine areas form about 60 per cent of the reserve and are typically poor in bird life. These plantations grow on the sands of the same Greensand ridge on which The Lodge is situated. The birch scrub grows in the old peat of the fen to the south of the ridge and is also rather poor in bird life, with few other tree species providing any diversity of habitat. The oak areas are rather too small to support good populations of birds, but the poplar plantation has a very good scrub layer and has perhaps the best diversity of bird life on the reserve.

Management Is directed primarily at developing the birch scrub into a more attractive habitat for birds, with the creation of clearings, a coppiced area and the establishment of wide rides along the network of ditches that cross the woodland. Planting of oaks in the thinned birch areas should increase the potential for typical woodland birds and stimulate an increase in populations. The pine plantations are being commercially thinned and eventually these will be replaced by a mixed woodland of oak, beech, birch and pine. The poplar plantation is also to be thinned and an area of oak woodland with dense scrub layer will be established, creating a very attractive piece of woodland.

Little tern at nest

Birds Sutton Fen is most attractive during the summer and supports relatively good populations of willow warbler, chiffchaff, blackcap, garden warbler and turtle dove. Cuckoos also occur, while tawny and little owls are both regular breeders. Woodcock have recently begun to breed, and roding is commonly seen on spring evenings. There are reasonably good populations of the commoner woodland species, such as wren, robin, great and lesser spotted woodpecker and treecreeper, while marsh and willow tit also occur, but do not breed regularly. In winter the birch areas attract flocks of finches and redpolls, and siskins are common. In some years, brambling and crossbill are frequent.

Other Animals and Plants In many ways, Sutton Fen is more important for its insect life than it is for birds, and the reserve has an impressive list of moths and other insects, many of which are rather local or rare. There is a large colony of common helleborine associated with the poplars and several other species of orchid occur. The reserve is quiet enough for some of the larger mammals to breed, with fox and badger both having done so.

Swan Island, Co Antrim

J424996   *¼ acre*
Can be viewed from the Larne–Whitehead road; no access.

The RSPB's smallest reserve, but by no means the least important as it holds around thirty pairs of roseate terns in most years; these are heavily outnumbered by 250 pairs of common terns and a controlled black-headed gull population of around 200 pairs. Sandwich terns, once an irregular breeder on the island, have in the last two years increased to forty pairs, other breeders are less regular and include herring and great black-backed gulls, red-breasted merganser, mute swan and ringed plover.

The recent increase in tern numbers must, at least in part, be due to the recent programme of spraying the vegetation in the spring with herbicides, providing more nest sites for the various species.

The island is also one of the more important high tide roost sites in Larne Lough; in the spring and autumn it is thronged with curlew, redshank and other waders as well as providing a shelter for rafts of duck, mainly mallard, but also a few eider and mergansers.

Curlew

Tetney Marshes, Lincolnshire

TA355035   *3,111 acres*
A mixture of saltmarsh, sand-dunes and intertidal sandflats, this reserve is most important for its colony of little terns. On the coast of Lincolnshire south of Cleethorpes, near the villages of Tetney and North Coates.

Birds Several species of shore-nesting birds breed here, including oystercatchers, redshank, ringed plovers and, most important, little terns. Unfortunately, the terns are largely unsuccessful in their attempts to breed, because they normally breed on sand and shingle banks that are submerged by the highest tide each month. Each year the warden makes strenuous efforts to save as many eggs and chicks as possible by raising them on tideline debris during the spring-tide period. Although many of the parents seem to accept this disruption, the overall losses are still high, and a better long-term solution may well be the construction of a bank of chalk rubble, shingle and sand on the saltmarsh, where it would be well above the level of the highest tide.

Flowers A good variety of flowering plants exists here. Many of them are characteristic of saltmarsh (sea wormwood, annual sea-blite, sea lavender and sea purslane) or sand-dunes (sea beet, sea rocket and bird's-foot trefoil). There is little shrubby growth on the reserve, but hawthorn, blackthorn and other hedgerow species do occur.

Other Animals The butterfly population is not very varied with common residents joined by migrant red admirals and painted ladies from across the North Sea. Mammals include wood mouse, brown hare, stoat, weasel and red fox, which unfortunately is a predator on ground-nesting birds, particularly the colonial little terns.

Titchwell Marsh, Norfolk

TF750436   *423 acres*
SSSI, NCR1*. Part of the ecologically important North Norfolk coast, its freshwater lagoons forming a haven for wintering and passage wildfowl and waders. The shingle beach has a colony of little and common terns. North of the A149, 6 miles east of Hunstanton.

Saltmarsh forms the most extensive habitat on the reserve, but thirty years ago it did not exist at all. The land produced potatoes and beef until January 1953 when the sea-defences were breached, and since then an average of twenty-five tides a month have ebbed and flowed over the hitherto well-drained farmland. Natural vegetation colonised and eventually developed into 'aster marsh' — vegetation dominated by sea-aster, but including glasswort, common sea-blite and sea-purslane.

Banks of sand and shingle were formed on both sides of the 1953 breach, and one has gradually increased in area and height above sea-level. Sea sandwort, sea couch grass and prickly saltwort grow on the higher areas and are responsible for the formation of dunes by trapping wind-blown sand.

On the southern edge of the saltmarsh there is an extensive bed of reed. Like the saltmarsh, it is subject to tidal flooding so this, and the resulting paucity of insects and amphibians, restricts the bird life there.

The following three areas were once part of the tidal regime as well, but the completion of a sea-wall across the reserve in 1979 changed their habitats and considerably improved them for breeding and non-breeding birds.

The brackish marsh, originally aster-marsh, is an area of vegetation-free mud and shallow water which accommodates large quantities of food, ragworms, fly larvae, small fish etc, for birds such as diving ducks, grebes and waders.

The freshwater marsh, also originally aster-marsh, is an expanse of open mud covered with 50 centimetres of water in winter, spring and summer, but only a few centimetres in autumn. Deep channels, originally tidal creeks, dissect the area and several islands provide nest sites and nesting areas. These conditions are ideal for a wide range of insects and other invertebrates.

The freshwater reed-bed, originally tidal reed-bed, has reed growing in standing water and so also has good numbers of insects as well as sticklebacks, toads and eels.

Management Unless certain habitats are managed, they will gradually change and become less suitable for birds.

The tendency for the large shingle bank to become sand-dunes is prevented by bulldozing away any accumulated sand, thereby retaining a habitat of bare sand and shingle for nesting little terns.

Vegetation will attempt to recolonise the brackish marsh, so occasional deep flooding with saltwater will be necessary to maintain the areas of open mud and shallow water.

Colonisation by aquatic plants will eventually occur on the freshwater marsh, but such vegetation often provides food for ducks and so may not need removing. Reed, on the other hand, is advancing over the freshwater marsh at the rate of one to two metres a year and will eventually need containing. This can be achieved by excavating a deep channel between the two habitats which will restrict the spread of reed rhizomes.

Bittern

Willows, elder and brambles will attempt to colonise the freshwater reeds and so will need to be removed to prevent the reed-bed drying out. However, the plants can be moved to a section of already dry reeds in order to encourage a fen-scrub habitat.

So by maintaining different habitats in their most productive states, the wildlife on the reserve will be as diverse, and therefore as interesting, as possible.

Birds The main bird species are generally ducks, waders, gulls and terns with a few others which are dependent on reed-beds.

The saltmarsh has no nesting birds because of the tides, but in winter it holds a few hundred teal and mallard and often several hundred twite.

The main shingle area is noted for its colony of little terns (usually thirty to fifty pairs), common terns, oystercatchers and ringed plovers. Up to 40,000 knot and godwits roost there when the Wash is flooded with equinox tides, but during the winter the only birds there may be a few snow buntings and twites.

Several hundred pairs of black-headed gulls nest on the brackish marsh. Dunlin, curlew sandpiper, greenshank and other waders feed there in autumn, and goldeneye, mergansers, little grebes and sometimes brent geese occur there in winter.

Gulls, coots, little grebes, shoveler, tufted duck and gadwall nest on or around the freshwater marsh. Over twenty species of waders feed there in autumn, the main ones being snipe, dunlin and ruff, and thousands of swallows, martins and swifts catch insects over the water. Wigeon, teal, mallard, gadwall and shoveler occur in winter, often totalling 800 or more birds.

The rare marsh harrier and bittern nest in the reed-bed, together with bearded tits, reed warblers and reed buntings. In September the reeds may hold vast numbers of roosting swallows.

Other Animals and Plants Apart from a dwindling patch of matted sea-lavender, there are no specialities of other fauna and flora.

Vane Farm, Tayside

NT145987   *229 acres*
SSSI. Adjacent to Loch Leven, which is a NCR1* site, and of chief importance as a wintering site for greylag and pink-footed geese. Either side of the B9097 which links the M90 with Glenrothes.
Vane Farm has been a reserve since 1967. The hill, the Vane, rises to 824 feet and commands a panoramic view north and west over the old county of Kinross-shire and east over Fife and the Firth of Forth. Dominating the view is the 4,000

acre Loch Leven, a National Nature Reserve and wildfowl haven. The Nature Centre building was restored from an old sheep steading with a cobbled courtyard and pantiled roof and is now a listed building. It opened in 1971 as an educational focus for the area with its access to a range of habitats, and a commanding view over the Loch. It was the first of its kind in Britain.

The reserve stretches from the loch shore to the top of the Vane and includes marsh, rough grazing land, arable fields, birch woodland and heather moor.

Birds The drier parts of the marshes on the edge of the loch support gorse which provides nesting cover for reed buntings and chaffinches, and a long-term management aim is the encouragement of the gorse for thicker and more protected nest-sites. There are a number of small springs which keep part of the loch-edge damp and small pools have been dug to allow birds secluded drinking and bathing.

A lagoon and scrape have been excavated to cover half of the rough grazing in order to attract water birds to roost, feed and nest near the Nature Centre. Among the birds regularly seen are tufted duck, teal, grey heron, and passage waders such as greenshank and ruff.

Although, apart from a few pairs of breeding partridges and a good collection of cornfield plants, the arable fields appear to be relatively poor for wildlife, from autumn to early spring they are the feeding ground for many thousands of geese, a spectacle that draws birdwatchers from all over Scotland. The geese are mainly pinkfeet, with smaller numbers of greylags, but there is always a chance of seeing a wandering barnacle or brent gose among them.

The woodland is nearly all birch, but there is a long-term planting programme which adds rowan, gean and oaks, which have to be planted in 'exclosures' to prevent rabbit damage. Here, willow warblers are the commonest breeding birds, but there are also redpolls, tits, tree pipits, spotted flycatchers and the occasional pair of redstarts.

Much of the moorland is grazed and is relatively poor for birds. Meadow pipit and skylark dominate, red grouse, curlew and wheatears breed. Cuckoos can be seen searching for meadow pipits' nests and visitors may see a fulmar from the strange colony on the crags just beyond the reserve boundary, some 22 miles from the sea.

For the enthusiast the real treat at Vane Farm must be the wildfowl. An autumn day with two or three thousand grey geese wheeling above the fields, ten or more species of duck on the loch and lagoons and large flocks of fieldfares and redwings

Little grebe

feeding on the rowan berries is a day to remember. **Plants** Four species of orchid, common butterwort and grass of Parnassus highlight the rich and varied flora of the loch-edge marshes. While the rough grazing is botanically poor, sundew grows on the wet banks of the lagoon and water mint and marsh marigold provide splashes of colour.

Bracken and other ferns form the field layer of the wood, whose open character is ideal for the wealth of fungi that springs up in late summer and autumn. In spring, wood sorrel, primroses and wood anemones grow in profusion. Although dominated by ling, the moorland has a few wet flushes and a limestone outcrop where the less common flowers include yellow mountain pansy, rock-rose and butterwort.

West Sedgemoor, Somerset

ST365255 *500 acres*

SSSI, NCR2. Part of the once extensive Somerset Levels meadow system. Some fields are botanically rich and the area is nationally important for numbers of breeding waders. Lies approximately 6 miles east of Taunton.

The main reserve lies in the middle of West Sedgemoor, which is a 2,500-acre area of flat, low-lying wet grassland. The moor consists of numerous rectangular fields, each surrounded by a water-filled ditch which acts as a cattle fence. In winter the land is waterlogged and heavy rain can bring floods, whilst in summer the surface dries out sufficiently to allow haymaking and cattle grazing.

From the southern edge of the moor there rises a steep ridge, whose deciduous woodland provides a contrast to the wide flat expanse of the moor.

Birds The whole area is well-known for its large numbers of wintering birds, particularly waders and wildfowl. Lapwings occur in huge numbers and other species include snipe, dunlin and golden plover. Parties of Bewick's swans may be found at various places in the Levels.

Extensive drainage has reduced the value of the Levels as a habitat for breeding waders and wildfowl, but West Sedgemoor still remains damp enough to provide breeding conditions for snipe, redshank, curlew, lapwing and a small population of black-tailed godwits. Other interesting breeding species include whinchats and yellow wagtails. For a few weeks each spring, the Levels are used by whimbrels on passage and up to 300 are sometimes present on West Sedgemoor.

The adjacent woodland has breeding buzzards and nightingales. It also contains a heronry; with about sixty pairs it is the largest in Somerset.

Plants Many of the meadows on the reserve remain 'unimproved' agriculturally, and can consequently contain a wide variety of attractive flowers, giving a colourful display in spring. Of particular interest is a slightly raised field, full of cowslips and green-winged orchids, which is very different in character from the surrounding fields.

Other Animals Mammals are well represented with good numbers of hares, foxes, badgers and roe deer, but seeing any of them is a matter of good luck and care. Butterflies and dragonflies occur in high numbers on the reserve. So far, twenty-four butterfly species and twelve dragonflies have been identified on or near the reserve.

Wolves Wood, Suffolk

TM054440 *92 acres*

SSSI, NCR1. Mainly ancient woodland of a variety of types, supporting typical plants and animals. No rare species of bird is present, but there are good populations of woodland species. Immediately to the north of the A1071, 2 miles east of Hadleigh and 8 miles west of Ipswich.

One of Suffolk's few remaining ancient woodlands, containing standards of ash, oak, field maple, hornbeam, cherry, both downy and silver birches, elm and one example of wild service tree. Compartments are divided by footpaths and corridor rides. The understorey consists chiefly of hazel and hawthorn, with a dominant shrub layer of bramble. Within the woods there are forty-three ponds, although the majority are dry in summer. An area of approximately 15 acres in the south-west of the reserve has an area of short-term (fourteen-year at present) coppice rotation, with aspen and birch as the dominant species, forming a large scrub habitat.

Management In the areas of coppice rotation, management is directed at providing the best conditions for breeding nightingales, warblers and finches. Rides and ponds are being opened up to encourage bird, plant and butterfly species. An extension to the present coppice plots is planned as are further plots elsewhere in the wood.

Birds The avifauna of the woodland is diverse, including species of woodland edge, scrub clearings, waterside and marsh. Important breeding species include ten pairs of nightingales, two pairs of woodcock and a pair of hawfinches. Several species of warblers, six species of tits, two of woodpeckers and nuthatch are also regular. The scrub areas are particularly important in winter for roosting finches and thrushes.

Flowers Among the woodland plants growing here are five species of orchid, including violet

Hawfinch

helleborine and bird's-nest, and herb Paris. Spurge laurel and orpine also grow here.

Insects The roadside verge is important for a colony of Essex skippers and both white-letter and purple hairstreaks occur in reasonable numbers. Approximately twenty-two species of butterfly are recorded annually.

Yell Sound Islands, Shetland

HU370390   *400 acres*

There are over eighty small uninhabited islands in Shetland, forming a valuable part of the habitat available to birds and animals. In Yell Sound, the sea area which separates the island of Yell from the north Mainland of Shetland, about a dozen islands and holms are scattered, most of them lying in the path of the strong tidal streams, and help to create eddies, whirlpools and fierce 'tide-rips'.

The sea approaches to the new oil terminal of Sullom Voe are also through Yell Sound, and the presence of the small islands and reefs do nothing to make navigation safer for the large oil-tankers and other ships entering and leaving the port.

The islands vary in character and in the number and species of birds and, while one or two may not be considered of high importance, collectively they contain examples of nearly every type of small island habitat found in Shetland.

The Islands Starting from the North, Gruney is a cliff-bound island of about 20 acres adjacent to the Ramna Stacks Reserve, and like them is inaccessible except in the calmest weather. Even then there is no safe landing place, and the only regular visitors come in by helicopter to service the small lighthouse which was built to help guide the ships in to Sullom Voe.

The cliffs on the north side of Gruney hold good numbers of breeding seabirds including about 2,500 guillemot, about 2,000 puffin and over 600 kittiwake, while the top of the island is taken over by a large colony of great black-backed gulls and some cormorants. Recently Leach's petrels have been found in small numbers.

In the autumn a colony of grey seals clamber up on to the island, and usually over fifty pups are born, while in the winter there are flocks of rock dove, snow bunting, twite and sometimes a party of barnacle geese.

Muckle Holm is about the same size as Gruney, but the cliffs are not high enough to attract seabirds other than fulmar, a few shags and tystie's and some gulls, but it has other breeding birds such as eider, oystercatcher, hooded crow and small colonies of puffin and arctic tern.

Common seals breed round the shore and,

although breeding has not been proved, Muckle Holm is regularly visited by otters.

Two islands which can be considered together are Uynarey and Fish Holm as they are rather similar in character. Uynarey, the larger of the two, has some 60 acres of rough grass. Fish Holm is only half as big and has a more uniform pasture of good grass.

The breeding bird list contains small numbers of shag, eider, oystercatcher, great black-backed and herring gulls, tystie, puffin and the odd pair of hooded crow, rock pipit and wren. A boggy patch on Uynarey usually has a pair each of bonxie and dunlin.

At 200 acres Samphrey is the largest of the islands, and it also has the best variety of breeding birds, with about twenty-two species.

The shores are low and for the most part rocky, but there are a few shingle beaches and caves in which rock doves roost and probably breed.

The breeding bird list contains all those on the previous two islands, but in greater numbers, and in addition a few pairs of snipe, arctic skua and skylark frequent the middle of the island.

There is evidence of former human occupation in a few ruined crofts and stone walls, and these are tenanted by storm petrels, tysties and starlings; the once cultivated small fields now hold a colony of arctic terns which sometimes numbers over a thousand pairs.

There is a small brackish loch near the shore on which the tysties display in spring, and a patch of yellow iris on the shore provides concealment for nesting eider.

In the winter the loch is attractive to duck, and flocks of over seventy wigeon have been recorded, with smaller numbers of goldeneye, long-tailed duck and merganser. Common seals breed in the summer, and there are several otter holts in the earthy banks from which one can have the pleasure of watching an otter bring her cubs down to the shore to catch crabs and small fish.

Sheep are kept on all the islands, the grazing being rented by crofters from Yell and Mainland and, except for specific studies there are no arrangements for visitors at present.

Grey seal

Tonbridge filmy fern

Ynys-hir, Dyfed

SN683963   *630 acres*
SSSI, part NCR1. A mixture of habitats, including estuarine flats, salt-marsh, farmland and woodland. The Dyfi estuary is an important roost for wintering wildfowl, among which is a flock of Greenland white-fronted geese. On both sides of A487, 6 miles south-west of Machynlleth.

For a panorama of Ynys-hir you can follow a trail that soon reaches a high viewpoint looking northwards across the rest of the reserve. The habitats to be seen are wooded ridges, tangled thickets, marshes, farmland, a leafy stream, saltings and tidal mudflats — all against a background of Snowdonia's foothills at the head of the Dyfi, a river famous for salmon and sea trout.

Management   The oakwoods are a precious relic of former days. Most of the region's tree cover vanished in the 17th and 18th centuries to be used as charcoal in the local iron and lead smelting industries. Since then, Ynys-hir has been fortunate in having owners who have been careful to restore the woodlands. Since the RSPB bought the reserve in 1968, through an appeal, woods which had been open to grazing have been enclosed with the result that a dense spread of undergrowth has developed, and blackcaps, garden warblers and other bush-nesters have increased.

The wetland that once spread along the south side of the estuary has long been drained, and only survives in isolated patches. Several pools have been excavated to encourage waterfowl and aquatic plants.

Birds   At Foel Fawr, the viewpoint hill, wheatears, stonechats, whinchats, tree pipits and yellowhammers nest among the rocks and bracken, and nightjars churr in the summer dusk.

Spring is the best time to visit the woodlands, when birds are heard singing and calling all round. Tits, finches, warblers, thrushes, nuthatch, treecreeper, redstart, jay and all three woodpeckers breed. Buzzards circle overhead and at night tawny owls fill the woods with their calls. Of the small birds, the most popular is the pied flycatcher which nests in many of the nestboxes provided. From a pylon hide among the trees, even the shyest birds can sometimes be watched at close quarters.

The farmlands, chiefly sheep and cattle pastures, are of most value to wildlife when they are at their winter wettest, and are then good feeding grounds for lapwings, curlews, gulls, starlings and thrushes.

The Einion stream, which comes splashing down a wooded gorge below Foel Fawr, past the much-photographed Furnace Mill and under the main road to flow more sedately to the Dyfi, is the home of dippers, grey wagtails, common sandpipers and red-breasted mergansers.

Hundreds, sometimes thousands, of wigeon, as well as other ducks and a flock of Greenland whitefronts, make the estuary their winter home. There are also usually plenty of curlews, oystercatchers, redshanks and dunlins. Sightings of peregrines, sparrowhawks and hen harriers are frequent, and red kites and merlins are seen occasionally. In spring, the breeding mergansers and shelduck appear, and there is a heronry high in the trees above the river. There is an impressive list of waders recorded on spring and autumn passage. Kingfishers move down to the estuary in late summer and may be seen here often from July until the end of the year. It is the morning high tides which come every second week that provide the best birdwatching, because many birds move up the estuary and can be seen closely from the hides.

Plants   Ynys-hir has plenty of interest for botanists. In the damp hollows on Foel Fawr are butterwort, bog pimpernel, lesser skullcap and bog St John's wort. Lower down at sea level the remaining bogs are a last refuge for sundews, several species of orchid, asphodel, myrtle, rosemary and other increasingly scarce plants. They are also the scene of a constant battle against invasive rhododendron, which would, if given a chance, engulf the wetlands and much of the woodlands. The Einion's banks are worth a second glance, because they support an interesting community of flowering plants and ferns.

Insects   There is an impressive butterfly list which includes green hairstreak, grayling and five kinds of fritillary. There has been considerable work on moths here, and among the more spectacular to be recorded are emperor, fox, northern eggar, beautiful yellow underwing and small elephant hawk.

Mammals   The mammals here are mostly nocturnal. Polecats, dormice and otters have all been recorded, but are seldom seen in daylight. Otters occasionally pass along the Einion on their way to and from the estuary and their spraints can be seen beneath the bridges.

Great skua

Rocky Islets and Stacks
Offshore islands and stacks, often grass topped and predominated by seabirds.

Rocky Coasts, Cliffs and Cliff-tops
Cliffs and rocky coasts on mainland Britain and the larger islands. Cliff-top is defined as area between cliff and hinterland, sometimes fenced from farmland and often covered with dense scrub.

Sand Dunes/Shingle/Low Offshore Islands
Includes dune and shingle formations above high water mark of medium tides together with associated low profile islands regardless of soil or rock type.

Mud/Sand Flats/Saltmarsh
Intertidal mud and/or sand up to high water mark of medium spring tides, together with associated saltmarsh formations and associated shallow sea water.

Brackish Water/Mud
Water areas close to the sea, brackish, associated with seasonal mud areas. Includes 'scrapes'.

Coastal Grazing Marsh
Rough grazing above spring tides, often behind a sea wall, usually with a dyke system which can be brackish and can include remnant fleets. Often reclaimed saltmarsh.

Lowland River Systems/Flood Meadows
River systems of typically eutrophic lowland rivers, generally slow running and bounded by wide alluvial flood plain.

Reed Swamps
Phragmites beds with associated open water areas.

Lowland Lakes/Reservoirs
Generally eutrophic, reed, sedge or grass fringed, gently shelving profile, mostly below 500 ft above sea level, and generally excluding water areas with large *Phragmites* beds.

Gravel Pits
Flooded gravel pits, in all stages of succession from bare sand/shingle to dense willow scrub.

Upland River System
Fast running upland rivers and streams, regardless of height above sea level, characteristically on a rocky substrate, can often rise and fall in level very quickly, includes bird community of adjoining areas where these are strongly influenced by the presence of the river.

Northern Marshes
Confined to Scotland, covers all wetland areas excluding mainly open water and upland bogs, but includes acid and alkaline wetland as well as machair marsh.

Upland Pools and Lochs
Confined to Scotland, ranging from small lochans to lochs generally in open hilly or mountainous country and mainly over 500 ft above sea level.

Dry Moorland/Bog
Calluna moorland/grass moorland above the natural/artificial tree line and below the Arctic/ Alpine zone, together with associated 'flows' and blanket bog or more localised *Sphagnum/ Eriophorum* bogs.

High Montane
Arctic/Alpine zone of mountainous highlands, including 'bare stony tops'.

Heaths
Lowland acidic heaths, occurring only in southern Britain, usually *Calluna* covered with associated *Erica* species and often with pine or birch trees and scrub.

Mixed Upland Broadleaf
Typically hanging oakwood or birchwood, but includes many other species including rowan, ash and alder. Includes associated scrub.

Mixed Lowland Broadleaf
Typically confined to English lowlands and often dominated by pendunculate oak. Very varied mixture of species, typically high canopy with thicker shrub layer and less acid soil conditions than upland broadleaf, often with old coppice. Includes associated scrub.

Native Pine Forest
Probably confined to the Caledonian forest relicts in the Scottish highlands, open pine woods intermixed with birch and rowan.

Open Canopy Broadleaf
Typically over-mature parkland or woodland, scattered trees often with a bracken field layer, dominated by trees but not sufficiently so to be normally categorised as woodland.

Index